Creative and
Mental Growth

A Textbook on Art Education

Viktor Lowenfeld
PROFESSOR OF ART EDUCATION
THE PENNSYLVANIA STATE COLLEGE

The Macmillan Company • New York • 1947

Copyright, 1947, by The Macmillan Company

Printed in the United States of America

Preface

THIS BOOK IS WRITTEN FOR ART TEACHERS—TEACHERS WHO TEACH ART, teachers and kindergarten teachers, and all who want not only to appreciate the creative production of children merely from an aesthetic viewpoint but would like to look behind the doors to see the sources from which their creative activity springs. It is written for those who want to understand the mental and emotional development of children. The idealistic concept of the child as an innate artist who has simply to get material and nothing else in order to create has done as much harm to art education as the neglect of the child's creative impulse. Books that are written from an idealistic view discourage teachers who are unable to produce the same easy and "beautiful" responses described by the writers of such books. Much of the literature in art education deals with results achieved under ideal conditions rather than with the outcomes which may be reasonably expected in the average classroom. These books are usually written by successful intuitive educators, who have the power to bring out what is in the child. They are apt to create a feeling of inferiority in teachers who do not possess this special gift and who therefore feel discouraged by the discrepancy between the results achieved in their own classroom and what is reported in these books.

Some subjects require an individual approach in teaching. The aversion shown by some educators for suggesting *any* teaching method in such fields has brought progressive art education to a point where it relies almost completely upon the mere intuitive approach, which the teacher either has or has not. Most books on art education today deal with ideal classroom situations and do not face the reality of schools with large classes and limited use of materials. The effect of such books is to provide an excuse for not using art at all rather than to use it with "insufficient" means.

It also seems to me of little use to emphasize—as has been frequently done—that the working process is of greater importance than the final outcome, without analyzing the reasons behind this opinion. Strangely enough, we see the same educators who stress this important viewpoint showing illustrations that are selected from the mere aesthetic viewpoint, thereby laying stress on the effect of the final product. "What should we do if the child does not draw large, with big motions in his uninhibited straightforwardness, as we have read the child is supposed to do?" "My children, even if I give them a large sheet of paper, draw only small." Such questions and many similar ones were asked by discouraged teachers who had read books on art education that neither presented methods nor gave an insight into the connection between the child's creative activity and his general development.

In this book an attempt has been made to show how the child's general growth is tied up with his creative development and vice versa. Creative expression is as differentiated as are individuals. This is as clearly evident in the minds of artists as it is in the minds of educators and psychologists. However, the child's creative expression during specific stages in his mental and emotional growth can only be understood and appreciated if the general causal interdependence between creation and growth is understood.

Since such an investigation necessarily cannot deal only with the analysis of individual expressions but must also be concerned with general findings, much of the discussion on the quality of the single child's work has been sacrificed to questions of general importance. Only through the understanding of these basic questions will the teacher arrive at the proper stimulation of the child during the different developmental stages. This book is an outcome of the study of many thousands of creative works over a period of more than twenty years. It tries to introduce methods which are results of the child's needs, and are therefore flexible. It attempts to give any teacher, not only art teachers, an understanding of the psychology necessary for the understanding of the child's creative production.

It is the conviction of the author that all teachers who desire to learn and understand the child's needs, thinking, and emotions should use creative expression as one of the richest sources of teaching method. In the same way that the kindergarten teacher should see the connection between the achievement of motor coordination in the child's creative work and motor coordination that is necessary for proper eating, the high-school teacher should know of the changing imaginative activity of a pre-adolescent child and an adolescent youth, an activity that commences as an unconscious approach and evolves into controlled critical awareness. For the art teacher, in particular, this book tries, by avoiding any rigid statements or methods, to present the psychological background and understanding necessary for a correct art stimulation suited for the different age levels. An attempt has been made to apply this psychological background to the practical teaching situation. Thus the connection between technique, topic, and material has been stressed and analyzed in both its emotional and mental aspects.

On the elementary-education levels, the meaning of the final product is treated in a subordinated way according to its nature. The discussion of methods of approach and the general effect of art education upon the mental growth of the child is primarily the problem during this important initial period. The reason why so many children lose their creative abilities when they approach adolescence has been discussed and analyzed. The kind of stimulation is shown that may prevent the child from stopping his creativity. During adolescence, skills become increasingly important, and the creative approach changes from an unconscious creation to one done with critical awareness. That is why it has been found necessary to include a discussion of the various techniques and their functions, as well as an analysis of the meaning of line, shape, form, color, and unity.

An analysis of extreme cases usually results in a greater clarification of our common problems. For this purpose a chapter on "The Art of the Handicapped" has been included. In this chapter an attempt has been made to show the close interdependence between creative activity and mental status in extreme cases. Also the adjustive effect of art has been demonstrated by means of case histories.

In this book an attempt has been made to show methods of approach in art education based upon psychological relationships between creation and creator on the different age levels. Since these relationships cannot be bound by strict rules, the methods must necessarily be flexible. It is, however, the author's belief that as long as art is taught merely intuitively, art education is either the special province of a few privileged educators or a source of failure for the general classroom teacher.

The author owes his indebtedness to Mr. Victor E. D'Amico, director of The Educational Project of The Museum of Modern Art, New York, for providing him with a wealth of illustrative material. He is especially grateful to Miss Dorothy Knowles, secretary of the Educational Project and art educator in her own realm, for her assistance in explaining the sources and data of the illustrative material placed at the author's disposal by Mr. D'Amico. Acknowledgments are due to Dr. Marion R. Trabue, dean of the School of Education, the Pennsylvania State College, for his continued interest in the book and his encouragement, and to Dr. Willis E. Pratt, head of the Department of Education, who kindly helped to select the title of this book. Most especially is he grateful to Dr. A. Eason Monroe, director of the Reading Clinic of the Pennsylvania State College, who kindly undertook the task of putting the content into more readable English.

Viktor Lowenfeld

Table of Contents

Creative and
Mental Growth

CHAPTER 1   # The Meaning of Creative Activity in Elementary Education

INTRODUCTION

IF CHILDREN DEVELOPED WITHOUT ANY INTERFERENCE FROM THE OUT-side world, no special stimulation for their creative work would be necessary. Every child would use his deeply rooted creative impulse without inhibition, confident in his own kind of expression. We find this creative confidence clearly demonstrated by those people who live in the remote sections of our country and who have not been inhibited by the influences of advertisements, funny books, and "education." Among these folk are found the most beautiful, natural, and clearest examples of children's art. What civilization has buried we must try to regain by recreating the natural base necessary for such free creation. Whenever we hear children say, "I can't draw that," we can be sure that some kind of interference has occurred in their lives. No Eskimo child would express such lack of confidence. These interferences might come from anywhere. To provide children with the kinds of stimulation necessary for their creative growth, it is important to examine some of the interferences that thwart such growth.

For the child, art is not the same as it is for the adult. Art for the child is merely a means of expression. Since the child's thinking is different from that of the adult's, his expression must also be different. Out of this discrepancy between the adult's "taste" and the way in which a child expresses himself arise most of the difficulties and interferences in art teaching. I have seen and heard educators, intrigued by the beauty of children's drawings and paintings, asking for the "right" proportions and "good" color schemes. The child sees the world differently from the way he draws it. Precisely from our analysis of this discrepancy between the representation and the thing represented do we gain insight into the child's real experience. Therefore it is easy to understand that *any* correction by the teacher which refers to reality and not to the child's experience interferes greatly with the child's own expression. This interference starts perhaps when children scribble and eager parents expect to see something that fits their own adult conception. How ridiculous to overpower these little children's souls!

The seriousness of the problem of providing the appropriate stimulation every child needs for his work is illustrated by two typical case histories which follow:

The first is an example of the youngster who says, "I can't draw." The boy was completely incapable of (or better, inhibited from) producing any kind of picture. He did not want to draw a line. Under no circumstances could he be brought to use visual percepts. The child made a very nervous and unfree impression. His mother told me that he usually came home from school without speaking or telling anything of his experiences. He was very inhibited in his bodily movements. He had no friends at all.

Since nothing else availed, it occurred to me to try to distract his attention altogether from visual impressions, and I asked him to control his images by bodily feelings, which I emphasized by the choice of the topics. The stress was laid upon what the boy was doing and what he felt while doing it. The boy began to draw, and the more he drew, the more he drew out of proportion. He emphasized his experiences in proportions of value rather than in proportions of actual physical objects. At the same time, his mother reported that the boy had changed considerably, that he had begun to speak freely, that he was no longer shut in, that his nervousness had diminished, and that even his body movements were freer.

I investigated this case more closely and found that this child, the child of a teacher, had been influenced repeatedly to copy nature, to draw "beautifully" in correct proportions. Such an influence, which came in this case from the father, who wanted to see "good" and "nice" pictures and not the drawings of a child, had stifled the imagination of the child and diverted it into personal, rather than visual experiences. As the child learned that he could not draw as his father required (mothers usually have more instinct), he lost confidence in his creations and stopped his work. This loss of self-confidence inhibited the child as a whole. Encouraged to return to his own individual way of expression through the stimulation of his bodily feelings, the child found again his confidence in his own creations and his whole personality. What can we learn from this case? Don't impose your own images on a child! All modes of expression but the child's own are foreign to him. We should neither influence nor stimulate the child's imagination in any direction which is not appropriate to his thinking and perception. The child has his own world of experiences and expression.

The second case illustrates another way in which family influences upon art education may be unfortunate—the case of a brother and sister. The girl was very gifted; the boy just average. The girl, who was a very bright child, was always the favorite in the family; the boy was neglected. The girl drew very well. The boy, who could not draw as well as his sister, began to imitate her by taking over the same kind of representation his sister uséd in her drawings. He hoped this could be a way of getting the attention of his parents, as his sister got it with the same means. The boy became more and more bound up with a kind of representation that was not at all in accord with his own experience. It was as though he tried to speak a language that he was not able to understand. Whereas his sister was happy in creating new forms and thoughts, his anxiety to copy his sister prevented him from living his own life. So the child grew more and more sick mentally as well as emotionally. When he came home, he would throw himself on his bed and cry. His mother could not discover the reason. The child became extremely introverted. In this stage his mother brought the child to me. With my help, the boy returned to his former kind of expression and found again his own manner of representation, which I appreciated in the same way as I did that of his sister. Having found self-confidence in his own creations, the child grew happier, lost all the signs of disturbance, and was quite changed. The parents, very happy about this result (which required seven months to achieve) learned the correct way of showing their appreciation for both children.

What can we learn from this case? We see that through the efforts this boy made to compensate for his feelings of inferiority, he grew more and more fixed on a kind of representation that was not the expression of his own experiences. This fixation on strange expressions finally stopped the whole mental development of the child! Therefore, never prefer one child's creative work over that of another! Never give the work of one child as an example to another! Never let a child copy anything! This case exposes also the very devastating effect of the numerous color books which our children still get in school for the sake of "developing a sense of color," but which in reality inhibit their free creative development.

After this short introduction, the double function of art in the elementary-school classroom as self-expression and as a means of self-adjustment appears evident.

Self-Expression

The term "self-expression" has been misunderstood so often that I feel it necessary to clarify this term before using it. It would be wrong to think that self-expression means the expression of thoughts and ideas in general terms of content. This is the greatest mistake made in the use of this word. Thoughts and ideas can also be expressed imitatively. If one finds himself truly and originally occupied in any kind of medium, the outcome of this occupation and the mode of its expression are of decisive importance. What matters then is the mode of expression, not the content; not the "what" but the "how." That is why "scribbling" or, in another field of expression, "babbling," can be a means of self-expression as well as a potential high form of art creation. It can even happen that scribbling or babbling is a truer means of self-expression than a higher form of art, when the work of art moves from the sincere mode of expression to a form which is based upon the dependency on others, on imitation. In this connection it seems important to point out that the more primitive the stage of creative activity, the weaker the effect of such formal influences or interferences. The explanation of this fact seemingly lies in the nature of the more complex expression of art. Rarely can there be found a scribbling or babbling that is not a direct expression of an adequate mental and emotional state. However, more complex forms of art expression can be influenced easily by stronger personalities. This influence often grows to such an extent that complex forms of art, even in spite of technical perfection, lack completely the inner spirit or the adequate mental and emotional state of the "creator." They are, then, facades without substance, masks without life, condemned to die. However, this condemnation holds not only for the single art work, but also for the "creator," who cannot live because he cannot breathe with strange lungs. In the same way that a babbling child is unable to pronounce words correctly, even if urged to do so, a scribbling child if forced to draw "reality" can neither understand nor conceive what he is supposed to draw. Both would express themselves by strange means, which would not only inhibit them but would block their further development. This applies to all stages and all levels of creative activity. Such an education toward truth is one of the highest and deepest meanings of self-expression. This development toward freedom of expression, this great experience of individuals in finding themselves rests upon the knowledge of what truth is in art education. This knowledge cannot be achieved without a thorough study of what we can expect in modes of expression in the different age groups and on the different mental levels.

Self-Adjustment

Any work that is forced upon a person creates tension and dissatisfaction. When the individual feels unable to perform a task, he becomes conscious of his own insufficiencies and develops lack of confidence, or even feelings of inferiority. All this, as we have seen in the Introduction, can happen if art education is applied improperly and if children are urged to do something not appropriate to their development, or even if their work is criticized in a way that is not adjusted to the level of the child's ability to understand.

For instance, when a scribbling child, whose control of body movements is not developed to the extent that he can correlate them with his visual experiences, is forced to represent something "real," he not only would be unable to perform a task which depends upon ability to achieve such correlation, but the child may also lose confidence in his own means of expression (scribbling). The child might even become aware of the fact that he does not represent anything real. A child who expresses the importance of an object by overemphasizing it—like the Egyptians who drew the king larger than the servants—would become confused by criticism based on our visual sense of proportion. The child not having another means to determine the importance of the object, would first become aware of the inadequacy of his expression, would then lose confidence in his own experiences, and would finally start to measure proportions rigidly until blocked in his further development. Inhibited by such a stimulation, the child would then stop expressing himself altogether. "I can't draw it" would be the known indication for such a discouragement.

However, if the child expresses himself adequately and freely by repeating his motions during scribbling with ever greater certainty, by expressing importance with his own adequate means, by feeling and expressing his space experience (contradicting that of adults), the satisfaction from such creative work documents itself in the profound feelings of a great achievement. And we all know how achievements create confidence. Since it is an established fact that nearly every emotional or mental disturbance is connected with a lack of self-confidence, it is easily understood that the proper stimulation of the child's creative abilities will be a safeguard against such disturbances.

Besides this natural adjustive effect, there is another way of using creative activity as a type of therapy. A special chapter deals with this approach for the abnormal individual. Here I would like to point out the principles in the use of creative ability as a therapy for merely retarded or maladjusted children, who can be found everywhere. Three points will be of especial interest. (1) How can such deficiencies be recognized? (2) What is their nature? (3) What means for adjustment can be used?

Two characteristics in particular make it possible to recognize deficiencies from children's drawings:

(1) If there is an abnormal discrepancy between chronological age and the development stage, which average periods of duration are given in our discussion, the existence of a mental retardation can be accepted as a certainty. For instance, if a child of seven years still scribbles, we can say that he is still concerned with the primitive experiences of uncontrolled kinesthetic feelings when he should feel the desire to represent something. The lower the mentality, the greater these discrepancies, and the greater will be the differences between chronological and mental age. Creative developmental stages, however, are always characterized by wide ranges in chronological age and in variety of forms of expression. Therefore, it is important to be flexible in the evaluation of creative products.

(2) If a child is emotionally blocked, his rigid repetitions demonstrate his inability to express experiences. In both cases, I have found that the stimulation of body experiences leads to an adjustment of these deficiencies in a rather short time, if the deficiencies are not too deeply rooted. As an example, I would like to discuss a case of an exceedingly shy girl who could approach her playmates only with great difficulty and who showed in her representations a great deal of such rigid repetitions. I asked this girl to catch a ball which I had thrown high into the air, and I said, "Who can catch it sooner, you or I?" This competitive stimulus aroused in her a greater insight into what she was doing. Then I asked her to draw this event. With repeated individual stimulation, she found such enjoyment in the newly gained correlation between her actions and her representations that she started to introduce all kinds of experiences as her own contribution. Thus, she gained, through this constant correlation between herself and her draw-

ings, a more conscious and free relationship to the world around her, which finally helped her completely to overcome her shyness. Although this analysis does not pretend to be scientific (such an analysis would require a more specific treatment of this special question beyond the limits of this textbook) the success which results from using this method of therapy makes it worth mentioning even in this very concise way. In the last chapter of this book questions of this kind are treated in more detail. In summary, it seems important to point out the contrasting effects upon the child's development of creative activity as a means of self-expression and as a means of mere imitation.

Self-expression we have defined as the appropriate mode of expression according to the age level of the child. Imitation, however, is expression according to adult, or at least foreign, levels. If the child expresses himself according to his own level, he becomes encouraged in his own independent thinking by expressing his own thoughts and ideas by *his own* means. The child who imitates becomes dependent in his thinking, since he relies for his thoughts and expressions upon others. The independent, thinking child will not only express whatever comes into his mind but will tackle any problem, emotional or mental, that he encounters in life. Thus his expression serves also as an emotional outlet.

Dependent thinking, however, restricts the child in his choice of subject matter as well as in his mode of expression. Since the imitative child cannot give expression to his own thoughts and emotions, his dependency leads directly to feelings of frustration. The child who uses creative activity as an emotional outlet will gain freedom and flexibility as a result of the release of unnecessary tensions. However, the child who feels frustrated develops inhibitions and, as a result, will feel restricted in his personality. The child who has developed freedom and flexibility in his expression will be able to face new situations without difficulties. Through his flexible approaches toward the expression of his own ideas, he will not only face new situations properly but will adjust himself to them easily. The inhibited and restricted child, accustomed to imitating rather than expressing himself creatively, will prefer to go along set patterns in life. He will not be able to adjust to new situations quickly but will rather try to lean upon others as the easiest way out. Since it is generally accepted that progress, success, and happiness in life depend greatly upon the ability to adjust to new situations, the importance of art education for personality growth and development can easily be recognized.

The following diagram depicts clearly what has been said in the foregoing summary:

Self-Expression	contrasted with	Imitation
Expression according to child's own level	———————	Expression according to strange level
Independent thinking	———————	Dependent thinking
Emotional outlet	———————	Frustration
Freedom and Flexibility	———————	Inhibitions and restrictions
Easy adjustment to new situations	———————	Going along set patterns
Progress, success, happiness	———————	Leaning toward others, dependency, stiffness

THE TEACHER'S NEED FOR KNOWING DEVELOPMENTAL STAGES

As has been pointed out, the need for properly stimulating the child derives from the basic psychological connection between the child's emotional experience, his mental level, and his creative expression. It is this psychological connection which we have to study. Since subject matter in creative activity has such a different meaning from that in other fields, a thorough clarification of the relationships between developmental stages and subject matter is necessary. In arithmetic, for instance, only a gradual increase in the difficulty and amount of subject matter will allow the child to grasp it properly. According to the child's mental development, the amount and difficulty of subject matter is thoroughly balanced. The child starts by learning the single symbols for numbers. Then he learns to count, to add, to subtract, to multiply, and so forth.

How does subject matter relate to creative expression and how is subject matter in creative activity related to the mental stages of the child? Before answering these important questions, it is necessary to clarify the meaning of subject matter in creative activity.

Whereas subject matter in other fields is almost exclusively related to content, in creative expression it is quite different. The content, the "what" we represent, are trees, houses, plants, flowers, men, and so forth. In creative activity there is no changing subject matter which must be taught, because the same subject matter is used in all the various age levels. There is no orderly sequence of subject matter, as in arithmetic or other fields. A man can be drawn by a five-year-old child or by a sixteen-year-old youth. What then can be expected to be the difference in teaching a five-year-old child or a sixteen-year-old youth? The difference in teaching of arithmetic is evident. There, the child may first learn to distinguish between one and two, and later he will study the higher forms of mathematics. Subject matter in creative art, as stated above, does not change during the different age levels. It is determined by "man and environment" throughout elementary-school levels and beyond. "Man and environment" do not change. *What changes is our subjective relationship with man and environment.* It is this subjective relationship between the world and ourselves that has to be studied in order to know how to stimulate a child properly according to his age level. A "man" to a five-year-old child means mainly the self, the ego, which needs a head for thinking and eating and two legs for running (head-feet representation). For a ten-year-old child, a "man" still means mainly a projection of the self. However, consciously aware of the variety of man's actions, movements, and body parts, the ten-year-old represents "man" accordingly. A sixteen-year-old youth, however, has already discovered that man is a part of environment and he represents "man" with conscious consideration of size and proportions in comparison to what surrounds him. So changes a tree—for a five-year-old child the tree is something undifferentiated, a trunk and something indefinite on top; for a ten-year-old, the tree is a trunk with branches to climb on; and for a sixteen-year-old youngster, a tree is a part of the environment, with which he is acquainted in detail. The subjective relationship of these young people to the tree has changed entirely, though it is still the same tree—the same subject matter. This makes it clear that it would be entirely wrong to teach how to draw a tree or a man. Moreover it would be beyond the comprehension of a five-year-old child to perceive or understand a tree in all its details as a part of environment. He would not even be able to take in an explanation of the realistic meaning of a tree. Accordingly a "perfect" drawing of a tree with all its details would be entirely out of place. "Perfect" is a relative value judgment, and in creative activity it means "perfect" in relationship to the child's experience. "Perfect" for a five-year-old child is a representative symbol for tree. It would be unnatural if the child drew it realistically with all details. Hence, it is clear that "subject matter" must be more confined to the "how" than to the "what." In creative activity subject matter is based upon *the subjective experience of man and environment according to the various age levels.* A proper application of subject matter in creative activity requires the study of the change of the subjective relationship of the child to man and environment throughout the age levels. There is no subject matter "tree," only the different ways a tree is experienced in the various years of life. However, since there are so many possible ways of drawing a tree in each school grade and since there are besides trees, an almost unlimited number of things in the environment, it will be necessary to investigate the common base of children's experiences. This investigation will lead to the understanding of all the various forms of expression used in their representations.

The answer to the question, "What makes the child express one and the same thing differently at different age levels?" will be of essential importance for the understanding of the child's creative work. It also will be significant for the nature of stimulation on the part of the teacher. What makes a child of four or five years express a man by drawing only a head and two legs? Does this really represent the child's knowledge of a human being? Certainly, every four- or five-year-old child knows that we have a body, two arms, hands, and even fingers. He even knows that we have fingernails if his attention is directed towards them. But no child of this age would ever draw such details. *What the child draws is his subjective experience of what is important to him during the act of drawing.* Therefore, the child only draws what is *actively* in his mind. Thus in such a drawing of a "man" we get only a report of the *active knowledge* the child has of a man while he was drawing. *In other words, the drawing gives us an excellent record of the things which are of especial mental or emotional importance to the child.*

Still another factor has to be taken into consideration as an important means for the proper stimulation of a child's creative activity. The change of the child's *relationship* to environment involves *emotional* as well as *mental* growth. This is one of the most important facts in the child's emotional and social adjustment. The child, depending upon the help and care of others (at the beginning on the parents), does not feel the necessity of cooperating or collaborating with others. His most important experience is the experience of the self. That is why his spatial correlations are very indefinite in the beginning. The growing interdependence between the child and his environment is expressed in his drawings. If, in this emotional experience, the experience of perceiving environment sensually (bodily, kinesthetically, or visually) is included, the investigation of the child's relationship to what surrounds him is placed on a broader base. This investigation still lacks an important part if size, dimensions, distance, and relative proportions of the self to environment are not also included. The differences in the concept of size and distance of children and adults point clearly to the psychological importance of these questions. Distances and sizes which appeared large in childhood appear different to the adult. But since these psychological questions of the child's relationship to outside experiences can scarcely come under the heading "environment," all these experiences are put together under "space"—experiences in space or of space. To simplify matters, *all experiences that refer to things outside of our body will be regarded as experiences of space.*

As a result of this discussion, it can be understood why no proper stimulation of the child's creative activity can be given without a thorough knowledge of what changes may be expected, at the various developmental stages, in the child's subjective relationship to man and environment.

The First Stages of
Self-Expression

Scribbling Stages (2 to 4 years)

THE MEANING OF SCRIBBLING

IN ORDER TO UNDERSTAND THE MEANING OF SCRIBBLING, IT IS NECESSARY
to know the importance of kinesthetic experiences in early infancy. It is
known to everyone how definitely the baby is affected when the mother
rocks it in the cradle or in her arms. Such *passive* kinesthetic experiences,
in which the baby only experiences the effect of rocking, have a definite
calming influence. *Actively* the baby, lying on his back, moves his arms
and legs in an uncontrolled fashion. Also it has been observed by psychologists how great the satisfaction is which results from these activities.
At some point, usually at about two years of age, the child, when given
a crayon, will start to make marks on the paper.* These motions will
be uncontrolled in the beginning, and their outcome are lines, which
indicate these undirected movements. The first stage of scribbling thus is a
disorderly scribbling, bold or dainty in its lines, depending on the personality of the child. The conclusion to be drawn from such scribbling is that
at this age level the child has no control over motor activity. Parents and

* Gesell, Arnold, *How a Baby Grows.* New York: Harper and Bros., 1945. Bayley, Nancy,
"The Development of Motor Abilities During the First Three Years." *Child Development,*
Monograph 1, 1935.

teachers should therefore regard disorderly scribbling as an indication that the child is not yet able to perform tasks that require proper motor coordination such as eating, dressing, sweeping the floor, and so forth. How often we hear complaints about children who cannot learn to eat properly! A glance at the child's scribbling would be very revealing. As long as the child has not reached a stage of scribbling in which he has established control over his motions, it is both senseless and harmful to teach activities requiring proper motor coordination. Such attempts would be similar to trying to teach a babbling baby to pronounce words correctly or even to use them in sentences. As clear and understandable as this fact appears in the realm of speech development, it is entirely neglected in the field of creative activity. Not only are there parents who have not yet discovered the causal interdependence of uncontrolled scribbling and the inability to perform controlled motor activities, but frequently even teachers encourage scribbling children to draw something "real" to satisfy their own adult imagination. Such imposition of ideas that are far beyond the abilities of the developmental stage of the child can be disastrous to his further development. *No child must ever be interrupted in his scribbling.*

DEVELOPMENT OF SCRIBBLING

Without differentiation (Fig. 1)

After the child has for a considerable time practiced scribbling (approximately six months after scribbling has started), he will at some point discover that there is a connection between his motions and the marks on the paper. Exceptions, however, with regard to the period over which scribbling is extended are quite frequent.

Longitudinal, or controlled, scribbling (Fig. 2)

As soon as the child repeats his motions again and again, we may be sure that the child has discovered visual control over them. From this time on, the child draws his lines consciously up and down or left and right, frequently still mixing his now controlled lines with uncontrolled motions. Gaining control over his motions is a vital experience for the child. Not only does he gain confidence from this feeling of mastery, but also for the first time he experiences visually what he has done kinesthetically. This fact is highly significant for the guidance of the child on this age level, for it is at this point that the adult will succeed in requesting of the child the proper execution of activities requiring motor coordination. The child will understand and enjoy the practice of the newly won experience.

Fig. 1. Disordered scribbling of a two-and-a-half-year-old child showing no control of motions.

Since motor coordination is one of the child's most important achievements during this period of age, we will readily understand that any discouragements in this activity would cause inhibitions. It also should be known that the child at this stage has usually no other creative intentions but to move his crayon on the paper. All his enjoyment is drawn from this kinesthetic sensation and its mastery.

Fig. 2. Longitudinal scribbling of a three-year-old child showing repeated motions and thus established control of motor activity.

Circular scribbling (Fig. 3)

Enjoyment of this new discovery stimulates the child to vary his motions. After having assured himself through constant repetitions, he now tries different, more complex types of motions. As an outcome of these motions, the child develops circular lines as an expression of the movement now usually executed with his whole arm.

Naming of scribbling (Fig. 4)

One day the child will start to *tell stories* while going through his motions of scribbling. He may say, "This is a train, This is the smoke," or "This is mother going shopping," although neither train nor mother can be recognized. This "naming of scribbling," however, is of highest significance for the further development of the child, being an indication that the child's thinking has completely changed. Until now the child was perfectly satisfied with the motions themselves, but henceforth the child

Fig. 3. Circular scribbling of a three-year-old child showing simply the urge for variation.

connects with his motions imaginative experiences. *He has changed from a kinesthetic thinking* in terms of motions, *to an imaginative thinking* in terms of pictures. This decisive change can only be appreciated, if one considers that most thinking during a life span is concerned with thinking in terms of pictures. Mention of every noun, action, association of past experiences is usually connected with imaginative thinking. Surely, when such great steps occur in the mental growth of the child, we expect teachers to give confidence and encouragement in this new kind of thinking.

THE MEANING OF COLOR

From the previous discussion, it is quite obvious that the experience during scribbling is mainly connected with motor activity. In the *beginning,* the important experience was derived from the satisfaction of *motor activity, later* from the attained *mastery* and *visual control* of the lines. Color, therefore, plays a decidedly subordinate role in scribbling. It goes

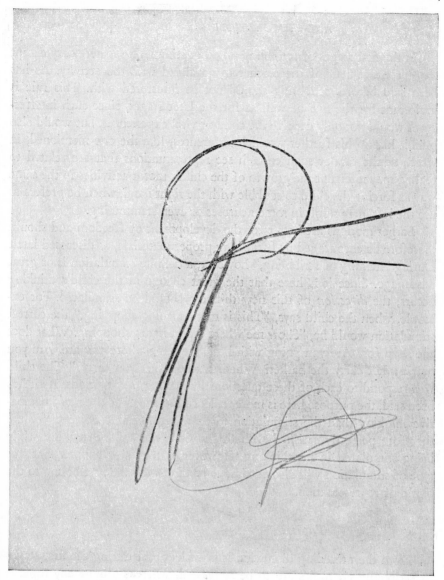

Fig. 4. "Mother Goes Shopping" (four year old). Indicates naming of scribbling. Notice the different kinds of motions.

without saying that the child during this stage enjoys the use of color; however, it is likely, as we shall see in the next chapter, that the use of colors will divert the child in the important experience of establishing motor coordination. The child too much attracted by color frequently interrupts his scribbling.

ART STIMULATION

In the first stages of scribbling no other stimulation is necessary except the encouragement of the teacher to go ahead with the activity. As has been said before, scribbling should not be interfered with. This rule is important for the first as well as for the later stages, since such interferences would not only deprive the child of vital experiences, but would also inhibit him in his further work. Interferences, like the one mentioned, in which adults cannot soon enough see representations that are related to reality, may interrupt the growth of the child's motor activities in the same way as forcing the child to scribble with the right hand, when he prefers to use the left, may result in some neuroses or even stammering.

Larger motions are better for the development of freedom and should therefore be encouraged by furnishing proper materials, as discussed later. During "naming of scribbling," however, a definite stimulation is of great advantage. Since it is here that the great change in the child's thinking occurs, the *direction* of this new thinking should be stimulated. For example, when the child says, "This is mother going shopping," the correct stimulation would be, "Show me where mother goes shopping. What does she shop for? Are you going with her? Show me where *you* are. Are you helping her carry the basket? Where is the basket you carry?" The child will respond to each of these questions by making new motions. As it has been said, the purpose here is more the encouragement of the new imaginative thinking than the stimulation to draw recognizable objects. We are therefore perfectly satisfied with the motions the child is making while being stimulated in his thinking. However, it may also happen that this type of stimulation will also encourage readiness to relate scribbling to the world of representation.

Topics

From the preceding discussion it is evident that during the first stages of scribbling no topics are to be suggested, whereas almost any topic is suitable to encourage the imaginative activity during the last stage of scribbling.

Techniques

Any technique used with children must fit their needs. Since during scribbling the child needs to practice and experience kinesthetic sensations, the technique used should encourage free expression without intruding technical difficulties. Water color, for instance, is a very poor medium because these colors tend to run, giving an indistinguishable blurred mass that renders the child's motions as such indistinguishable. The child is unable to follow or gain control over his own motions and is discouraged by such a technique. Pencils are also unsuitable for this purpose because their sharp points prevent the proper gliding along the paper, apart from the fact that the points break easily. In many progressive kindergartens, finger painting is being used. The advantages of this medium are by no means great enough to justify its use in such *early* stages. During certain stages in early infancy the child likes to play with dirt or even with his own excrements. One of the great differences between men and animals is that men use tools and animals do not. The desire to use tools can be seen even in early infancy, and should be encouraged. In fact, children using finger paints during these early stages are frequently again encouraged to play with dirt, because the two materials are associated by similar physical consistency. Instead of progressing in control over their muscular activity, children become so involved in the enjoyment of the paste-like consistency that the activity for which finger painting was planned becomes subordinated. Finger painting might be a useful stimulant for maladjusted children, whose emotions need strong means of stimulation, but for the normal child, the best material in the early stages of scribbling will be big black wax crayons and smooth, large sheets of paper, or blackboard and chalk. The use of such materials permit the child best to follow his motions, because they give the clearest and most unblurred reproduction of the child's kinesthetic experiences. It might even be pointed out that, in the very beginning, the use of a variety of colors should be avoided because of their distracting effect. The child would frequently interrupt his motions to search for new colors, and such interruptions certainly would restrict flowing arm motion.

However, when the child begins to name his scribbling, the use of different colors may be stimulating, since the child frequently uses different colors to express different objects while scribbling.

During this age level three-dimensional techniques, such as clay or, better, plasticine (because of its less sticky consistency), are helpful. Experience in handling material for the production of three-dimensional objects is of significance because it gives the child an opportunity to use his fingers and muscles in a different way.

Beating and pounding the clay without any visible purpose is the parallel stage to the scribbling, called "disordered." As the child gets acquainted with the material and feels the need to control his activity, he starts to *break the clay,* sometimes without order, at other times watching

SUMMARY   SCRIBBLING STAGE—TWO TO FOUR YEARS

Stage	Characteristics	Human Figure	Space	Color	Design	Stimulation Topics	Technique
Scribbling: (1) Disordered.	Kinesthetic experience. No control of motions.	None.	None.	No conscious approach. Use of color for mere enjoyment without any intentions.	None.	Through encouragement. Do not interrupt or discourage or divert child from scribbling.	Large black crayon. Smooth paper. Finger paint only for maladjusted children.
(2) Longitudinal.	Repeated motions, establishment of coordination between visual and motor activity. Control of motions.	None.	None, or only kinesthetically.	Same as above.	None.	Same as above.	Same as above.
(3) Circular.	Self-assurance of control through deviations of type of motions.	None.	Kinesthetically.	Same as above.	None.	Same as above.	Same as above.
(4) Naming of scribbling	Change from kinesthetic to imaginative thinking. Mixing of motions with frequent interruption.	Only imaginatively by the act of naming.	Purely imaginatively.	Color used to distinguish different meanings of scribbling.	None.	In the direction of the child's thinking by continuing the child's story.	Colored crayons. (four colors) Plasticine throughout scribbling stage.

the similarity of the pieces he breaks; or he may start to form shapes (coils or balls). This first conscious approach of shaping the clay without purpose or meaning can easily be compared with the second stage of scribbling, which is consciously controlled. At some point the child picks up one lump of clay and perhaps with accompanying noises, *calls it* an airplane or says, "This is a train." Psychologically, this is exactly the same change in the process of thinking as discussed in the "Naming of Scribbling." Whereas the activity of shaping or breaking was in the foreground in the previous stages, now the imaginative activity which is connected with the symbol (lump of clay) is predominant. Also here, the child has changed his kinesthetic thinking to an imaginative thinking. With this change he shows a readiness to establish a relationship between his representations and the things he wants to represent.

EXERCISES

(1) Follow up the case history of a child by means of his scribbling.
   (a) Collect all scribblings of a child.
   (b) Write name and age on the back of the scribbling.
   (c) Attach to the drawing any remarks the child makes during scribbling.
   (d) Keep a notebook in which observations are recorded. Observations pertain to:
      1. Type of motion and technique.
      2. Concentrated or easily diverted.
      3. Physical execution (with joint of hand only, with lower arm and elbow joint, with whole arm from the shoulder).
      4. Emotions.
   (e) Observe the child's motor coordination in life situations: when dressing, eating, walking, lacing the shoes, and so forth.
   (f) Notice changes in scribbling.
   (g) Draw conclusions from your notes and scribbling of the child with regard to the child's growth.
(2) Collect many scribblings and classify them according to motions: disordered, longitudinal, circular, and naming.
(3) When child names his scribbling, try to observe whether he introduces certain lines or motions for certain things.
(4) Observe first relationship between drawing and reality.
(5) Find out the effectiveness of your stimulation during the period of naming by comparing one scribbling where you left the child completely alone and another where you stimulated the child in the direction of his thinking.

(6) Follow up a case history of a child by means of his modeling. Follow the same procedure as indicated for the scribbling of a child.

LABORATORY WORK

Prepare finger paint consisting of:

$$1 \text{ part paint pigment}$$
$$5 \text{ parts starch}$$

Do some finger paintings yourself.

CHAPTER III

First Representational

Attempts

Preschematic Stage (4 to 6 years)

THE MEANING OF THE PRESCHEMATIC STAGE

For the psychology of the child

FROM THE DISCUSSION OF THE LAST STAGE OF SCRIBBLING, IT BECAME evident a discrepancy existed between the child's intention and his execution. The child intended to depict something, yet his representation did not reveal anything of this intention. But as we have seen, it was important for the child to become accustomed to and to be encouraged in his new type of thinking. Thus it will be obvious that the establishment of a slightest relationship to the thing intended to be represented will create a great feeling of satisfaction. In the beginning, therefore, the mere fact that *a relationship with reality has been achieved* will be of greater significance than the quality of the depicted objects. A circular motion for "head" and longitudinal motions for "arms" or "legs," brought in to functional relationship will give resemblance enough to a "man" of living quality.* The mere fact that the child was able to relate his representation is exciting enough to fill his mind and emotion with a profound feeling of satisfaction. It may, however, be of interest that in many cases it is the round form of the head and the longitudinal form of arms and legs that are the first inspiration to real-

---

* Mott, S. M., "The Development of Concepts. A Study of Children's Drawings." *Child Development,* Monograph 7, 1936.

Fig. 5. First representational attempt in clay modeling: "Snakes." (Courtesy Educational Project, Museum of Modern Art, N.Y.)

istic attempts. Henceforth, as the child establishes his relationship to the outside world in his representations, he feels the need to enrich this newly won discovery. It is extraordinarily interesting to observe how the child begins to abstract a line from the previous scribbling. Whereas circular scribbles become indicative of the head, longitudinal scribblings symbolize the extension of the body. This is how we must understand the meaning, both of the vanishing scribbling and of the beginning desire for representation. Scribbling loses more and more the causal relation between bodily movements and its result on the paper to make way for representation, which is related to the object. A different mode of drawing begins: the conscious creation of form. In this newly discovered relationship the child is constantly searching for new concepts, for which he will soon establish his own individual pattern, his *schema*. Before he reaches this stage— that is, during the preschematic stage, however, this search is clearly characterized in his drawings by a constant change of form symbols. The child will represent a man today differently from the way he will draw a man tomorrow. As yet, he has not established a fixed aspect, and we see at this stage in particular the greatest variety of form symbols representing one and the same object. Therefore, it will be easy for the educator to determine, for means of evaluation, whether the child is still in the preschematic stage or has moved beyond it (Fig. 7 a, b, c).

For the enrichment of the child's active knowledge

For the understanding of this chapter, it will be necessary to clarify what we mean by active knowledge. The child sees the world differently from the way he draws it. Even a very young child knows that a man is more than a head with legs and arms attached to it; he knows that a man has features, fingers, and even finger nails; but in his representations the child expresses only what is actively important to him during the process of creating. *In his drawings, thus, only the active knowledge, or what actively motivated the child, can be seen.* This is of decisive significance, because it permits the educator to record how far the child has proceeded in the grasp of himself and of the surrounding world. A knowledge of what actively motivates the child further reveals to the educator the emotional significance which the represented objects have for the child. *The passive knowledge,* however, is the knowledge which the child has, but does not use. Education, not only with regard to creative activity, consists to a great extent in activating the knowledge not used. Many people understand and enjoy reading the great works of Shakespeare, yet in their everyday language they use a limited number of words. Our passive vocabulary thus is large enough to understand the wealth of words which Shakespeare offers; actively, however, we are restricted to a rather limited vocabulary, depending a great deal upon the education received. Certainly a good teacher should be able to stimulate the individual to use words actively which hitherto were not used.*

* McCloy, W., *Passive Creative Imagination*. Psychological Monographs, LI, No. 5, 1939.

Fig. 6. "I am on the Street" (five and a half years). No spatial correlations are perceived. Proportions are drawn according to significance. Head-feet representation. Pre-schematic stage.

During the preschematic stage the child is most ready to build up new concepts of form, to enrich his form symbols. As we shall see in the paragraph on "stimulation" in this chapter, it is most important during this age level, that is, as long as the child still is most flexible, to activate his passive knowledge through individual *experiences.*

DEVELOPMENT TO REPRESENTATIVE SYMBOLS

Although the discovery of an established relationship between representation and the thing represented satisfies and fascinates the child in the beginning of the preschematic stage, we shall see that later this fascination loses importance and an eager search for the establishment of a definite concept of man and environment begins.

However, it is of great importance for the teacher to notice that all lines, although they are supposed to represent reality, are not in direct representational relationship to the object. The child establishes substitutes, lines which lose their meaning when separated from the whole. An oval

Fig. 7a. "I am Running for My Ball" (five-year-old boy). (Courtesy Educational Project, Museum of Modern Art, N.Y.)

might mean a body within the whole representation of a man, but when separated from the whole, the oval *loses* its meaning as "body." Such lines we call *geometric* since they refer to geometry, which is abstract. If such lines are used to represent something, they are "representative symbols." *Thus, a representative symbol consists of geometric lines which, when isolated from the whole, lose their meaning.* An important and extensive study has been made by Herbert Read * of the significance of these lines in relationship to the emotions and character of the creator. Since the development of the representative symbol frequently has its origin in scribbling, we can readily understand that in it are reflected some of the personal and even body characteristics of the child. Thus, the representative symbol of the human figure developed by a crippled child was distorted on the side which conformed with its own defect. The individuality of the schema has its roots not only in the body; in many cases it expresses the psychological constitution of the child. For instance, in the representative symbol of a man drawn by a timid child of delicate sensibilities, I could trace anxiety in the round, unclosed, uncertain lines just as much as I could find the charac-

* Read, Herbert, *Education Through Art*, p. 320. London: Faber and Faber, 1943.

Fig. 7b. "Mother is Looking for Me" (drawing of the same five-year-old boy). See frequent change of symbols. (Courtesy Educational Project, Museum of Modern Art, N.Y.)

teristic resoluteness of another child in its rectangular representation of the body. Both representations are characteristic of the child's total personality structure. These facts show clearly *that even the earliest representational attempts are closely bound up with the individual self.*

Human figure

Out of the scribbling motions, circular for the head and longitudinal for the legs, the child develops his first representation of a man. These head-feet representations are common for a five-year-old child. With this representation, as has been said before, the child has merely satisfied a desire to *establish a relationship between his drawing and reality.* To what extent the child will enrich this concept of a man depends on the child's mental growth and the proper stimulation by the teacher. The teacher has to use to the fullest extent this period in which the child is searching for his concept. Since the child is most flexible during this period, the teacher's task will be made easy by the use of the type of stimulation described later.

Fig. 7c. "I and My Dog." Drawing of the same five-year-old child. Notice change of representative symbols, proportions of value, use of geometric lines. (Courtesy Educational Project, Museum of Modern Art, N.Y.)

Space

For reasons of simplification *we call space everything outside of the body*. Therefore, all experiences that we have with or in environment are spatial experiences. In the same way that the child is fascinated by the newly discovered relationship between a man and his drawing, he is satisfied with the establishment of mere relationships between objects and their representation. He is perfectly satisfied with the representation *itself* without relating the objects to each other. *In the earliest drawings of children the interrelations of things in space are not subject to any law.* The child thinks, "There am I. There is an ambulance. There are airplanes. There is the sky" (Fig. 6). No relationship between the objects has been established. The child did not think, "I am standing on the street. The ambulance comes along the street. Above there is the sky. The airplanes fly in the air." The child has not yet achieved an experience of space which is of general validity. He has not yet experienced himself as a part of environment.

Fig. 8. "I and My Sister in the Snow" (six years old). Space relations with sister have been perceived because of emotional significance. He is leading her through the storm; therefore "legs" are unimportant, and have been omitted. (Courtesy of Educational Project, Museum of Modern Art, N.Y.)

Since the experience of the self as a part of environment is one of the most important assumptions for cooperation and visual coordination, the child's inability to correlate things properly in space is a clear indication that he is neither ready to cooperate socially, nor has he the desire to co-ordinate letters or to learn to read. The teacher in the kindergarten will therefore use the child's drawing expression as a diagnosis of the child's ability to participate in tasks which require cooperation. Forcing coopera-tion upon the child too early might rather create undesirable reactions, than be of use for the group. First spatial relationships are usually experienced emotionally. Therefore experiences which refer to subjective relationships will be stimulating, as "Do you like your doll?" "Draw yourself with your doll." In such drawings we might find no relationships among the objects outside of the child, whereas the emotional relationship of the child and the doll are clearly represented (Fig. 8). Such reactions show that space relations in this early stage are to a high degree conditioned by value judgments.

Fig. 9. "Girl Picking Flowers" (five and a half years). Proportion of value. The girl is outlined in blue color.

THE SIGNIFICANCE OF COLOR

Also, in color no relationship between the object represented and its actual color has been perceived. A man might be red, blue, green, or yellow, depending on how the different colors appeal to the child (Fig. 9). Surely there are deeper psychological meanings in the choice of color, but these meanings are so highly individualized and dependent upon subjective interpretations that such discussions fall outside of the framework of this book. Likewise, *first relationships of color are determined by emotional qualities.* Perhaps the only thing of objective color relationship in Fig. 6 is the red cross on the ambulance, which might be of emotional significance.

ART STIMULATION

Since all contact or communication with environment is established through the self, it is of greatest importance to stimulate the consciousness of the self. For the enrichment of the active knowledge of the self, it is necessary to stimulate the child's concept of *his body parts.* This is best done through the stimulation of the function of the parts by means *of individual experiences.* Once, during a visit in a first grade I saw children drawing just a line as a symbol for "mouth." Purposely I had a bag of candy in my pocket. After rattling the bag, I asked the children, "What do I have in my pocket?" "Candy," was the answer. "Do you think it is hard or chewy?" From the rattling the children deduced that it was hard candy. "Do you like candy?" was my question. "Yes," was the unanimous answer. Placing some candy on each child's desk, I asked them not to put it in their mouths until a given signal. "Now you may crush the candy, in order to find out how hard it is." And all the children bit the candy into pieces. After we had gone through this experience, I asked the children to draw "eating the candy." Every child in the classroom included the *"teeth"* in his representation. This *individual experience activated their passive knowledge.* This account should serve as only one example and should not be interpreted as meaning that such actual experiences are always necessary. It depends on whether the teacher is able to replace an actual experience by an intensive classroom discussion.

It is, however, of great value for the teacher to know *what outcome* she expects from her stimulation. It will prove to her whether or not she was successful in activating the passive knowledge of her children. This can easily be controlled by *comparing former drawings with those drawn after the stimulation.* If an enrichment of the form concept has taken place, the teacher was successful. Usually in classroom discussions it is preferable to create *first the general atmosphere* of the environment in which the action takes place and then gradually concentrate on the special topic. The following classroom stimulation will serve as an example. The topic: "Brushing My teeth." As the outcome, an enrichment of the form concept of the "mouth" and a closer coordination between mouth and arm may be expected. Originality and individuality in expression are taken for granted. The general atmosphere is characterized by the *"where and when."* "Where do you sleep? What do you do when you get up in the morning? When do you get up in the morning? Where is your bathroom located? What do you see in your bathroom? What do you do to clean your teeth and protect them properly?"

The "what" (brushing the teeth) should always follow the general atmosphere. After the "what" has been discussed, *every stimulation should culminate* in a thorough discussion of the *"how."* "How do you brush your teeth? Do you brush them horizontally or up and down? How is your tooth brush? How do you hold your tooth brush? Show me how you brush your teeth." A short demonstration by one child would contribute to a more effective stimulation. "Now let us draw 'Brushing my teeth in the morning in my bathroom.' " It is important at the end of the stimulation to include in the topic the formerly discussed environment, "where and when." In onclusion, every stimulation should contain first the *"where and when,"* second the *"what,"* and third the *"how."*

Topics

The following topics are suggested with the understanding that it is better to adjust a topic to a classroom situation than to choose it without regard for the class. The topics chosen during this age level are signified by the words *"I"* and *"my."*

I and Mother (sizes).
I and *My* House (size).
Brushing *My* Teeth (teeth).
Drinking *My* Milk (mouth).
Blowing My Nose (nose).
Eating My Breakfast (mouth).
Searching for a Coin *I* Lost (hand, eyes).
Playing Ball (arms, hands).
Hurting *My* Knee (knee).
Playing Tag (arms, legs).
I, Sitting on the Swing (body).
I Am at the Dentist (teeth).
Listening to the Radio (ears).
Reaching for an Apple (hand).
Picking Flowers (hand, arms).
Eating with Spoon and Fork (mouth).
I Am Swimming (legs, arms).
I Am Getting a Ring (fingers).
My Birthday Present (emotional relationship).
My Doll (emotional relationship).
My Party (emotional relationship).
I Am Tired (yawning, mouth).
I Am Led by a Policeman Across the Street (emotional relationship).

Techniques

For developing greater freedom, a *bristle brush, poster paint* (thickly prepared) on a somewhat *absorbent, large sheet* of paper are the best materials for this age level. Absorbent paper is recommended because it prevents the paint from running. The desk, or if the desk is too small, the floor or easels, can successfully be used. If, however, large classes do not permit

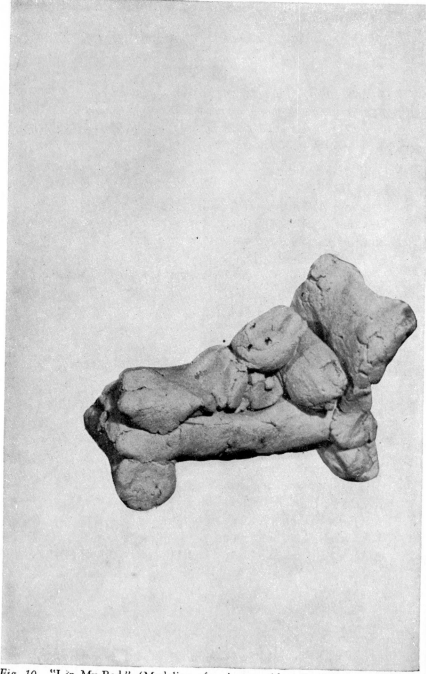

Fig. 10. "I in My Bed." (Modeling of a six-year-old girl). Emotional relationship establishes proper spatial correlations. (Courtesy Educational Project, Museum of Modern Art, N.Y.)

Characteristics	Human Figure	Space	Color	Design	Stimulation Topics	Technique
(1) Discovery of *relationship* between drawing, thinking, and reality.	Circular motion for head. Longitudinal for legs and arms. Head-feet representations develop to more complex form concept. Symbols depending on active knowledge during the act of drawing.	No orderly space relations except emotionally. "There is a table; there is a door; there is a window; a chair." "This is *my* doll" (emotional relationship).	No relationship to reality. Color according to emotional appeal.	No conscious approach.	Activating of passive knowledge related mainly to self (body parts).	Crayons, clay, powder paints, (thick) large bristle brushes, large sheets of paper (absorbent). Also, unprinted newspaper.
(2) Search for concept.						
(3) Change of form symbols because of constant search for them.						

the use of these materials, colored crayons and smaller sheets are excellen
The quality of the crayon can be determined by the surplus wax that ca
easily be scratched off the paper. The more surplus there is, the poorer th
quality of crayon.

In *clay work* (clay is now preferable to plasticine), the preschemat
stage is also characterized by the search for a definite concept of form. Als
here this search is seen in a *constant change of modes of representation*
and representations themselves. *Pulling* out from the lump of clay a
things that stand out, like noses, arms, and legs, implies a *lesser consciou
ness* of the form than holding the form (nose, arm, leg) in the hand, forn
ing it, and *adding it* to the body (Fig. 10). Purposely, no decorative tecl
niques are yet suggested, since on this level no child feels the consciou
need for decoration. As long as the desire for the search of a concept c
form and space is predominant, the desire *for decoration does not develo*
(Fig. 5).

EXERCISES

(1) Collect several drawings of one child and describe the changing qualit
of his representative symbols.
(2) Show the different use of geometric lines in the drawings of this perioc
(3) Analyze a child's drawing with regard to:
    (a) Changing quality of representative symbols.
    (b) Active knowledge of the child.
    (c) Spatial relationship of objects: ability or inability to establish rela
        tionship; is relationship established on account of emotional connec
        tions?
    (d) Color relationship.
(4) Find out how many different symbols for "mouth," "nose," and "eyes"
you can find in one classroom. Can you relate them to personalities?
(5) Give similar topics, once without stimulation and then with the bes
stimulation you can provide. Did you accomplish a change in the child'
active knowledge? Describe the amount and quality of the change.
(6) Analyze a child's clay work as indicated in step 3.

LABORATORY WORK

(1) Prepare "thick" paint by mixing pigments with water.
(2) Draw a "door," or the "entrance of the school" first without looking a
it, and then after having looked at it. Has your active knowledge im
proved? To what extent?
(3) Paint other objects before and after individual observation. Control the
growth of your active knowledge.
(4) Do the same in clay. Find also here the increase of your active knowledge

The Achievement of
a Form Concept

Schematic Stages (7 to 9 years)

THE SCHEMA IN DRAWINGS BY CHILDREN

THE MEANING OF THE SCHEMA CAN ONLY BE FULLY REALIZED WHEN we understand the child's longing, after a long search, for a definite concept of man and environment. This concept is, as has been said before, highly individualized. There are scarcely two schemata alike. The wealth of the concept of form, the schema, depends on personality and on the degree to which the teacher was able to activate the child's passive knowledge. Thus, a child can enter the schematic stage with a rich concept of man and environment, but he can also arrive at the conclusion of a concept with a rather meager schema. I use the term "pure schematic representation" in cases where there appears to be no further representational intention beyond that which is represented. Where such a further intention is present, one can no longer speak of a pure schema. Thus, *a pure schematic representation is a representation with no intentional experiences represented.* We shall find a pure schema in a child's drawing, whenever the child's representation confines itself to the object, "That is a tree; that is a man." When he says, "This man is big and this one is small," the differences with which the child expresses larger or smaller allow us to draw certain conclusions. Conversely, a study of the kind of modification undergone by the schema allows us to understand the intention underlying the representation. This method is of especial importance to the teacher, who ought, by this means of comparison between the schematic and subjective drawing, to study the effects of his teaching. *The schema refers in the same way to space and objects as it refers to figures.* The schema of an object is the concept at which the child has finally arrived, which represents the child's *active knowledge of the object.* Also here, the deviations from the schema he usually uses to represent the object express the experience which was of importance in this particular drawing. For example, a child might draw a house with roof and windows only. For a particular experience, however, the door might be of special significance. He will then change his schema and add the door. *Through this deviation from his schema the child has manifested his particular experience.*

Human schema

The term *human schema* is used to describe the form concept of the human figure at which the child has arrived after long struggles of searching during the preschematic stage. The child's schema of a man is the incorporation of all the knowledge that he, emotionally, connects with the thought "man." Every achievement becomes an achievement when it grows out of the unconscious realm into the realm of consciousness. We do not believe in our achievements unless, *through repetitions,* we convince ourselves of our mastery. The child too, assures himself through repetition that he has arrived at a definite concept of the representation of a man. *Thus, the human schema is the form concept of a man at which the child has arrived and which he repeats again and again whenever no intentional experiences influence him to change his concept.* The schemata of the human figure consist of the most different and *highly individualized* form symbols.* As has been investigated in my work *The Nature of Creative Activity,* schemata are not arbitrary signs but are *intimately related to both the bodily and the mental constitution.* That is why we will find in a classroom as many different schemata of human figures as there are individuals.

Space schema

What we have said about the human figure is very largely true of the schematic representation of objects as well as of space. The great discovery, however, of the child during this age level is that there is a *definite*

* For a variety of schemata see Goodenough, Florence L., "Children's Drawings," *Handbook of Child Psychology.* Worcester: Clark University Press, 1931.

order in spatial relationships. The child no more thinks "there is a tree," "there is a man," "there is a car," without relating them to one another as he has done during the preschematic stage. The child now thinks, "I am on the ground," "the car is on the ground," "the grass grows on the ground," "Bob is on the ground," *"we are all on the ground."* This first *mass consciousness of discovering that the child is a part of environment is expressed* by a symbol which we shall call *"base line."* From now on this consciousness, which includes all in a common space relationship, is expressed by putting everything, objects and figures, on this important space schema, the base line. This has, however, great psychological implications for the education of the child. *Consciously being a part of environment is the most important assumption for cooperation.* It is therefore highly significant to recognize that the introduction of this fundamental experience of the base line is a clear indication that the child is now ready to cooperate intentionally. It is also a sign of the child's ability to correlate objects properly with one another. This again has its psychological implications. For instance, in reading, this very same correlation is necessary in relating letters to one another in order to form a word symbol. Thus, whenever the base line is introduced by a child, it is an indication that the child has grown out of the ego into a world of *which he feels a part.* We can speak of schemata, however, only when the representation of an object or space *through repetition has become stereotyped.* The schema in space or objects can originate in visual or nonvisual experiences. In other words, the impression the child gets in *looking* at things might determine his schematic representation just as much as the *importance* or the *emotional significance* the child attaches to it. Very often, as we shall see, *kinesthetic experiences* or touch impressions also influence the concept of the scheme. It is, however, important to keep in mind that we speak of *a space schema when space is represented by some signs or others which, through repetition, assume a constant meaning in the drawings of a child.* Because the child has not yet discovered in his drawings the three-dimensional quality of space, he is frequently forced to introduce lines, which are merely individual symbols. These lines are supposed to substitute for the third dimension. Consequently, the space schema is almost entirely abstract and has only an indirect connection with reality.

DEVIATIONS FROM THE SCHEMA

Highly interesting is that if we accept the schema as the concept of man and environment at which the child has arrived, every deviation

Fig. 11. Schematic representation of "A Man." In schematic representations n
conscious experiences are represented.

from it will have to be investigated according to its origin and its mear
ing. From this understanding of origin and meaning of the deviations i
their various forms, we can draw conclusions about the child's experience
Three principal forms of deviations can be noticed in children's drawings
(1) *exaggeration of important parts,* (2) *neglect or omission of unim
portant parts, and* (3) *change of symbols of emotionally significant parts*
It should be understood that exaggeration and neglect refer *to size only*
whereas the change of symbols refers to *their shapes.*

The origin of such deviations lies either in autoplastic experiences—
that is, *feelings of the bodily self,* in the *importance of value judgment*
with regard to certain parts, or in the *emotional significance* which thi
part has for the child (Fig. 15).

A particularly interesting piece of work which displays all types o
deviations in a single drawing is shown in Fig. 12 titled "Searching fo
the Lost Pencil." * Fig. 11 shows the schematic representation of a mar

* Discussed by the author in his *The Nature of Creative Activity.* See list of reference.
at the end of this book.

ig. 12. "Searching for the Lost Pencil." The schema has been modified according to the experience. Emphasis on meaningful parts. Neglect of unimportant parts. Several sequences are expressed in one drawing. (Schematic stage). Use of geometric lines.

hat the child has drawn when simply asked to "draw a man." Thus, in his drawing no intentional experiences are represented; rather is it the form concept of a man, at which the child has arrived and which he repeats again and again whenever asked to draw a man. In comparing this schema with the subjective drawing, "Searching for the Lost Pencil," we shall clearly see the deviations and the experiences that these deviations express. In this picture the arms and hands are the vehicles of expression, and by means of them four phases of the theme are symbolized. The intense experience of searching and of groping about after the pencil is expressed, on the one hand, by the different emphasis and exaggeration of the arm, and on the other hand, by changes in the shape of the symbol for "hand." The enormously lengthened, groping arm shows how the representation of the hand has been modified by the experience of clutching. "With this hand he has just found the pencil," the child says, pointing to the other hand holding the pencil. The arm still shows a double line (compare with schema) indicating its special functional importance. The hand, however is now less emphasized because the experience of clutching is no longer the dominant one. Notice particularly the enormously exaggerated pencil showing the emotional importance it had for the child when he found it "With *this* hand he puts it in his pocket," the child says, and points to one of the arms of the second figure which, in fact, represents the same figure as the first one.

In other words, the child has represented four temporal phases by means of two figures. He might just as well have given one figure four arms; but this would have contradicted his experience. The arm which is putting the pencil into the pocket is now far less emphasized and is represented by a single line only while the second arm of the figure having no longer a function, has shrivelled to a mere stump. Bending down and standing upright are represented by means of differences in the length of the legs. It would be difficult to find a drawing that more clearly shows in a single picture, the origin and meaning of the different deviations from the schema.

We can illustrate still another experience originating in bodily sensations. According to the child the left figure is supposed to be bent forward, and this is expressed by means of shorter legs and a lowered head. The other figure on the right is standing upright while putting the pencil in his pocket, and this is expressed by longer legs and an upright head. But when the head is bent forward, blood accumulates in it, and we become more intensely aware of it. This is expressed in the drawing by an exaggeration of the size of the bent head.

This example has shown clearly that the child does not fall prey to an inflexible schema, but by using his own individual experience, he creatively transforms the schema in the act of creation. Furthermore, it shows that "disproportions" nearly always result from some definite intention or, better, experience, though this does not mean that the experience is necessarily conscious. *We therefore no longer have the right to speak of "false proportions,"* since such a judgment is determined by our visual attitude, the attitude of "objective experience of the environment." On the contrary, as we have seen, it is only when we understand the reasons for these apparent disproportions that we are able to penetrate into the true roots of creativeness. *Naturalistic tendencies and conceptions therefore, are totally unsuitable means for the understanding of children's drawings.* The child is intimately bound up with the experience of the self, and experiences his world subjectively.

REPRESENTATION OF THE HUMAN FIGURE—
GEOMETRIC LINES

We have seen that the schema is merely the form concept, the basis
or the creative experience. The richer this concept, the more possibilities
re at hand for its expression. If the representation of a "man," the schema
t which the child has arrived, consists only of head, body, legs, and arms,
ne creative possibilities are very restricted. The child, then, has only the
ossibility of using these four form symbols for the expression of his ex-
eriences. Soon he will be condemned to a certain rigidity, which educators
lways see as an outcome of poor schemata. *Therefore the child should
e kept flexible as long as possible until he has built up a rich source
f active knowledge, which is the basis for a sound creative develop-
ient.*

As has been said before, the type of representation to which a child
omes depends largely upon personality development, body constitution,
nd, to a great extent, upon the stimulation the child has received. If for
child the symmetry of the body—the *two* arms, the *two* legs, the *two* eyes,
he *two* ears—is of importance, the child's schema will be the front view.
f, however, the experience that the nose is protruding was of greater
ignificance, the child's schema will show the profile. The opinion that the
rofile represents a more advanced stage in the child's creative concept is
ncorrect. I have seen numerous children starting out with a profile concept
of a man. If the two eyes and arms and the protruding nose are all of
ignificance for the child, he derives from this experience the concept of
nixing front view and profile, and often includes both eyes and the nose
(Fig. 12).

From this discussion it seems evident that such a concept has not only
the right to exist, but represents a high form of active knowledge and
should by no means be "corrected." It shows again that the child's concept
of the world, during this age level, is derived from visual experiences to
a limited degree, if at all. This point is also revealed by the fact that the
schema still consists of geometric lines, lines which, when separated from
the whole, lose their meaning. Although I have seen some children include
"dresses" or "clothes" in their schemata, it is not done generally. Usually,
schemata of the human figure consist only of symbols for body parts.
There is, however, no limit in the variety of such form symbols. I have
seen ovals, triangles, squares, circles, rectangles, irregular shapes, thick
or thin lines used as schemata for "body," and all kinds of shapes for legs,
arms, and so forth.

SPACE

Psychological aspects

The most important and basic experience of the child's spatial development is the discovery of an orderly and related space concept. The child now includes himself into his concept in the same way that he includes the tree, the house, the whole environment. This first common experience of space—"I am on the street, John is on the street"—*is sometimes a most deciding factor in the psychological development of the child.* His attitude now changes from a completely *egocentric* attitude to a *cooperative* attitude. The difference between these two stages can easily be seen in watching children of a kindergarten and comparing their behavior reactions with those of the elementary-school level. Kindergarten children play and work together or cooperate only when urged to do so. In freedom they will generally follow their own directions. Thus we see one child going in one direction, imitating a train, another child sitting on the slide, self-concerned, whereas a third child plays in the sand, scarcely noticing the others. The only collision occurs when one child wants the toy another happens to have. This is clearly indicated, as we have seen, in the spatial concept of children during this age period. *Whenever the first common experience of space has occurred, the child relates himself to others, sees himself as a part of the environment.* The child then starts to cooperate with understanding. He has discovered for the first time a definite order in space.

Introduction of the base line

As an indication of the child's conscious relationship between himself and environment, he places everything on one line, the base line. All things standing on the ground are now related to this important symbol.

The line upon which trees as well as human beings are standing represents, therefore, not only the base line on which the represented objects stand, but the street itself. We cannot, of course, assume that the child knew nothing about the width or other characteristics of the street, since every child of this age level has crossed streets on numerous occasions. This experience seemingly has not yet reached the active level of knowledge. I do not refer here to the three-dimensional concept and the "inability" to represent it. I refer rather to the lack of desire to represent both sides of the street with the space between. The child, however,

Fig. 13. "Street Scene." Base-line representation expressing first spatial order.

expressed the street merely with one line, the base line. The line is merely a symbol for everything connected with "street."

In this picture (Fig. 13) we see both sides of the street. In order to understand that the space between the two base lines does not represent the surface of the street, refer to Fig. 14, which is also a picture with two base lines, representing an orchard. The two base lines are purely conceptual formulations, and the drawing is nothing more than the representation of *one* orchard, regardless of whether it has two rows of trees or not. The represented phases are the ones of main significance, "Picking the apples" on the lower base line, and "carrying them home" on the upper base line. That the space between has no meaning (or the meaning "air") will immediately be realized when we notice that every base line has its own sky. In other words, this picture has "two skies." We can only understand this concept if we consider the two base lines not as boundaries, but only as *base lines.* "We stand on the ground and above is the sky." Since every ground has its sky wherever I may stand, every base line is related to a sky. That is why we never see children draw anything between base lines. Exceptions can only be seen *on an emotional base*—that is, when the child through a *special emotional experience* comes to the realization that the space between *is* meaningful. However, before we continue our

Fig. 14. "Fruit Harvest." "I am Picking Apples" (seven-year-old gifted child).
Picture is divided in two sections.

discussion on the meaning of this important space symbol, it seems proper
to discuss the origin of the base line.

Origin of the base line

It is quite obvious that in reality neither objects nor persons standing
on the ground are standing on a line. That is why we can clearly state that
the base line can not have its origin in visual experiences. The investigation of primitive stages in the development of mankind has frequently
been of great help for the understanding of the single individual. In creative products of primitive stages we often see the use of the base line as
a means of indicating motion. I have seen in an early Indian drawing an
Indian fleeing along a line, presumably indicating by means of this line
the direction of flight. The use of the base line to indicate motion
appears in the same way in Australian drawings made on the bark of trees,
or in drawings of Arctic tribes. Many other such examples could be stated,
and from them we conclude that *the first origin of the base line is the
kinesthetic experience of moving along a line.* From the play of our early

Fig. 15. "I am Throwing Something into the Trash Basket" (seven-year-old girl). The hands are of significance, therefore exaggerated. (Courtesy Educational Project, Museum of Modern Art, N. Y.)

childhood we know, too, that we frequently connect with the experience of moving the thought of going along a line.

The base line and the characterization of terrain

When the child represents his space concept, the base line, he uses this line to symbolize at one time *the base* on which things stand, and at another time, to characterize *the surface* of the landscape. In Fig. 16, one base line symbolizes *the plain,* another base line represents *the mountain.* In other words, the child wishes to indicate that this base line is elevated over the plain and represents the *surface character* of the landscape. How much this "mountain" is still a "bent" base line can be seen from the fact that the trees stand *perpendicularly* to the "mountain." The growing upward of the trees is bound to a base line. We can realize this experience most clearly if we would consider the base line to be a line of wire, a straight wire with trees attached to it. If we bend the wire according to the kinesthetic experience of going up and down, the trees attached to the wire stand out

Fig. 16. "I am Climbing a Hill" (seven years). Base-line "goes up and down symbolizing terrain.

perpendicularly as we see them in the child's drawings. Clearly, it is n the "shape" of the mountain which is of significance, but the line itsel This is very characteristically expressed in Fig. 16, in which the house drawn perpendicularly to the mountain. We can understand this only whe we realize that the line representing the mountain becomes the base lin for the house. Upon this base line the house is drawn vertically.

If, however, as in Fig. 18,* the line indicating a mountain is not in tended to be a base line (the shading indicates that the mountain "as whole" had meaning), a new base line is introduced for houses and tree After making a trip to the hilltop, the child wished to indicate a shelter o the top of a hill. Seemingly, the top of the hill, with all the excitement o climbing to it, made such a vivid impression on the child, that he did no want to sacrifice the peak for the house, which would cover the peak. Th conflict of having the house standing on the peak brought the child to thi creative concept. He first drew the hill, using the lower edge as base line

* Because of its interest, this example is taken from the author's *The Nature of Creatu Activity.*

Fig. 17. "Playing Checkers" (seven-year-old boy). The checker board is "folded over" because of its significance.

Although the child usually does not shade, in this drawing he did shade the hill, thereby showing that in this case he did not intend to give a special meaning to the outline. Thus the child emphasized the space inside the lines that represented the hill. He had created a distinct representative symbol for "hill." After he had drawn the hill, he drew a base line for the house and trees which just touched the peak of the hill. In this way he wished to indicate that the house stood on the top.

The child's conception, determined by his emotional experience, may be analyzed as follows. In a plain (the lower edge of the paper also represents the plain in the form of a base line) there is a hill, the hill which he has climbed (representative symbol for "hill" is the shaded triangle). On the top of the hill stands a shelter and trees. But, since every house stands on a base, and there is as yet no such base present (the outline for the representative symbol for "hill" does not here function as a base line because the child did not want to sacrifice the peak), he had to create one. The house must stand on the hill, therefore, its base must be on the hill. Consequently, the base line of the house is drawn in such a way that

Fig. 18. "A Shelter on Top of a Hill." Symbol for mountain. Symbolic association of the house with hilltop.

it touches the top of the hill, and thereby indicates the relation between the two. *This drawing shows clearly that the base line is not a rigid symbol* and that the child departs from the base line whenever an emotional experience interferes with it. How the child uses the "base-line experience" in still greater variety will be described in the following paragraphs.

Subjective space representations

We call subjective space representations all representations in which an emotional experience forces the child to deviate from his space schema. There are basically two different types of deviations. One type is that in which the base line still functions as the vehicle within the spatial concept of the child. Then base lines as such are still used in the child's representation, but in modified forms. In the other type of deviation the emotional experience overpowers so much the child's feeling of being a part of environment, that he drops his "base-line experiences" altogether and introduces a space relationship which is founded purely upon his emotional feelings. The frequently used process of "folding over" belongs to one of the typical deviations. *Under "folding over" we understand the often-used process of creating a space concept by drawing the objects perpendicularly to the base line,* even when the objects appear to be drawn "upside down."

Fig. 19 is a typical painting of a child which shows the process of folding over. In this drawing the child depicts himself as waving to the ferry. After the child had drawn himself waving his handkerchief, standing on one side of the creek, he felt the need to draw the boat. He fulfilled this need by turning the paper around (or better, going around the paper which was lying on the floor) and painting the boat seemingly upside down. *This concept can best be understood if we fold the paper along the base line.* We then get the perfect experience of the child standing upright and facing the boat. Since the other shore line is also standing upright, as the boat does, it is drawn accordingly. Also here the correct understanding can only be perceived in folding the paper along the base line, which represents the other shore line. We then receive a perfect model of the scene and we suddenly realize the interesting concept of the "two skies," one on the bottom and the other on the top of the paper. Under the condition of "folding over," both skies are on top above the houses. Basically, the subjective experience of the child was of being in the center of the scene, seeing one shore to the left and the other to the right. This experience shows very clearly that it is of *great advantage to have children work on the floor or on desks, on which the drawing can be approached from all directions.*

The other type of deviation is characterized by the fact that a child who usually uses base lines in his space schema drops the lines altogether. As has been said before, the emotional experience can be so strong that it overpowers the feeling of being connected with the ground. Fig. 20, "On the Seesaw," is a typical example of such a drawing in which the child's

Fig. 19. "Norfolk Ferry" (eight years old). Space is expressed by "folding over" one shore line. Both sides of the creek are related to the middle.

Fig. 20. "On the Seesaw" (nine-year-old boy). Subjective expression of the experience of going up and down.

feeling of being a part of environment was overpowered by the emotional feeling of swinging up and down. The sensation of this kinesthetic experience determined the spatial concept. The boy artist shows himself way up near the sky and sun. His emotions are visibly expressed by the exaggerated size of his body as well as by his facial expression: the mouth is wide open. "My older sister lifted me up so high," he said. With this he indicated that his "older" sister was at least heavy enough to lift him up high. Through the exaggeration of himself (a result of his own subjective experience) the size of his sister seems so small that she could not possibly lift him. Since the sister was sitting opposite, the boy painted her seemingly upside down. In reality, this is *his* subjective view and can be understood only if we fold the pictures of him and her along the little base line on which they are sitting (the ends of the seesaw). We then again realize what a marvelous space concept the child has created through the power of his subjective feelings.

If the principle of "folding over" is used frequently, we shall understand from what has been said before, that such children are depending upon their subjective, emotional tie-ups. It can be concluded *that children who often use this principle of space representation are usually egocentric.* They regard themselves as the center of the world and relate everything to themselves.

Another important means of subjective space experiences results in drawings with *the mixture of plane and elevation.* We can very well understand this experience if we ourselves or our friends draw the following subjects:* "A Chessboard on a Table." Then turn your paper and draw on the other side "A Glass of Water on a Table." Since the chessboard demands the top view, usually the table is also drawn in top view. The glass of water, however, can better be seen in side view and thus will determine the changed view of the table. This experiment only works with persons who are subjectively minded. For visually minded persons, the table will not change whether there is a glass of water or a chessboard on it. The child, however, who develops an emotional relationship to his drawing, will become bound up with the chessboard (Fig. 17) and surely draws it from the top view. The table, however, would not be a table if it did not have legs too. The child then draws a table with legs and when necessary, folds over the top of the table to show its significance, thus mixing plane and elevation in one drawing.

Another drawing of great interest, which shows the same type of experience, is the drawing in Fig. 21, "An Amusement Island." The child

---

* Of course it is important to stress at the beginning that it makes no difference *how* things are drawn.

Fig. 21. "Amusement Island" (eight-year-old boy). Boats are grouped around the island because of the subjective experience of the boat ride.

visited an island on which were all types of amusement, people playing cards, hot-dog stands, and so forth. There were also boats for rent, and in such a boat the child took a ride around the island. The drawing now shows a top view of the island (that the water surrounds the island is best expressed this way). Everything is standing out of the island; that is why all objects on the island are represented in side view. That the water surrounds the island was most important for the child because of his boat ride. This is clearly expressed in the drawing by grouping the boats around the island. Many other examples of such spatial concepts are discussed in *The Nature of Creative Activity.*

Space and time representations

Space and time representations are of different time sequences in a single space. The child quite naturally uses this type of expression whenever he feels the need. Just as the child has his own way of depicting two-

and three-dimensional objects, sometimes by using plane and elevation at the same time, so he has his own way of depicting events which occur in different time sequences. The child who mingles plane and elevation fuses his space and time concepts. But the psychological origin of space and time is often somewhat different. We can mainly trace two different psychological roots, to each of which there corresponds an adequate formal representation. The knowledge of these two roots seems of importance to educators because it will offer to them a wealth of material for proper stimulation of the child, and especially for integrating art into other subjects.

The child likes both to listen to stories, and to tell them. One manner of space-time representation arises out of this urge for *communication*. That is why we find *different episodes represented by different pictures in one sequence of drawings*. The pictures are separate, like those in comic books, and it is of no significance whether the individual theme really has been divided by a line or whether the division is purely fictitious. It is characteristic of this *"story-telling" representation* that the action as a whole is drawn repeatedly, but usually with different surroundings. Journeys, trips, traveling episodes belong in this type of representation. In such topics, usually the most important events are characterized. *They describe* a complex event by means of separate pictures, whose relation to one another is one of content.

The second psychological root can be seen in the picture in which *temporally distinct actions are represented in one space*. This does not spring from the desire to communicate something; its origin must be sought rather in the emotional tie-up with the representation and in the act of drawing itself. The importance of the action diminishes the child's consciousness of time to such an extent that he is not aware of representing different time phases in one drawing. He is concerned only with expressing within one drawing what he regards as most characteristic about the action, in much the same way as alternations between plane and elevation are used to express what is most characteristic about an object. *In the one case temporally distinct phases, in the other spatially distinct impressions are fused and used for characterization.*

It is important to realize that in this type of expression the picture is confined to a single sequence of actions or movements. Placing the various aspects next to one another in one space is employed merely as a method of characterization. For a typical example of this type of expression, refer to Fig. 12, "Searching for the Lost Pencil," which we have already discussed. Here we are referring only to the content of this drawing, which deals with the expression of different time sequences within one space

"With one hand he is still searching, although with the other hand he already has found the pencil." This means, that in one person the child has represented two temporally different and distinct phases. He was emotionally so much tied up with the content, that the content overpowered his feeling for reality. The representation of one typical phase of the experience would not have served its purpose. The emotional urge—the strong experience he had with all phases of searching, finding, picking up, and pocketing—made him draw all phases. He used the next figure for the expression of putting the pencil into his pocket with one hand, and the other hand was used to signify that the experience was over. In other words, by means of two figures he represented four different temporal phases. He might just as well have given one figure four arms, as we can see it done in medieval manuscripts (Plate 65, *The Nature of Creative Activity*). But this would have contradicted his concept of a man.

In the paragraph on stimulation, we shall see that we can use the knowledge of the two psychological roots of space and time representations to great advantage, in education.

X-ray pictures

In the very same way as plane and elevation are depicted at the same time to show the significant "views" while disregarding the impossibility of such a visual concept, the child still uses another most interesting non-visual way of representation to show different views that could not possibly simultaneously be perceived visually. *He depicts the inside and outside simultaneously whenever the inside is emotionally, for the child, of more significance than the outside.* In other words, while he is drawing he becomes so much bound up with the inside that he completely "forgets" that there is an outside. In this case, he drops the outside altogether. If, however, the outside has also some meaning for the child, inside and outside are frequently mixed up. The picture then shows part of the inside, the part which has emotional importance, and part of the outside, as if it were transparent.*

That the child reacts in his drawings more toward the emotional significance than toward the visual is extremely important for education. It shows very definitely what stands out in the child's thinking. The adult's concept of surface phenomena and views is not the concept of the child. Educationally, in the teaching of art, it should give the teacher a tremendous opportunity to use this concept in integrating his subject matter of other fields into the realm of creative activity.

* Eng, Helga K., *The Psychology of Drawing*. New York: Harcourt, Brace and Co., 1931.

A group of children visited a factory in which was shown the manufacture of a product from the raw material kept in the basement to the finished product on the upper floor. When the children were asked to draw their experience, most of them developed a complete "plan" of the factory. The front wall was eliminated and the "views" into the different floors showed the different important working stages that had been discussed and experienced previously. These working stages, now actively in the minds of the children, had become a part of each child's knowledge and experience and could be readily used.

Another child had just come back from the hospital where she had to undergo an operation. She was first brought to the admission room and then to the X-ray room where an X-ray picture of her injured knee was taken. She was then brought by elevator into the children's ward, which was on the second floor, and from there into the operating room on the top floor. After the operation the child was returned to the ward, where she remained until she left. But before leaving, another X-ray picture was taken. When home, she drew the hospital and all the important events she had experienced. There was no front wall of significance. To her, the emotional experience overpowered all visual concepts, and her picture showed the basement, the floor with the ward in which she was lying, and the top floor with the operating room. All intervening floors had no significance to her, so they were omitted.

Fig. 22, "A Coal Mine," shows a typical X-ray representation in which inside and outside are completely mixed up according to emotional significance. The child from a mining area drew first the "outline" of the mountain as if it were a base line. Then she proceeded to draw the little trees and the house still dealing with the boundary of the mountain as with a base line. This can easily be recognized by the perpendicular way in which she placed trees and house on the base line. After that, she drew the "iron construction" above the "shaft" of the mine. When she drew the "iron construction" she suddenly realized that it is from here that the coal comes out of the ground. Thenceforth she became so absorbed in the interior of the mine that the base line completely lost its significance as an indicator of terrain, and became the "boundary" of the mountain. The emotional experience now shifted from the outside to the inside. She then drew the shaft with the horizontal pit in which the miners are working. (Notice the yellow artificial light.) She further wanted to indicate that coal is produced from this mine, so she divided the space around shaft and mine in sections, indicating her imaginative experience of the consistency of the walls of a coal mine.

In the discussion that follows, we shall see how the phenomena which

Fig. 22. "Coal Mine" (nine years old). Subjective space representation shows also inside of the mountain. X-ray picture. Space-time concept.

were the subject of foregoing pages can be fused into a single experience. Fig. 23 * was done by an almost-blind child. The topic was "Saying Good-bye." The child is saying goodbye to his father at the end of the holidays before returning to the Institute by train. He is concerned therefore with a profound experience. He begins by drawing the coach in outline, to indicate its limits. To characterize it, he adds the axles with their wheels— four wheels, of course, because that corresponds to his *knowledge*. Now he has before him the impression: railway coach.

Leonardo da Vinci said that every picture should somehow look complete in every one of its phases. He meant, I imagine, that every phase of the picture should leave behind it an impression of completeness so as to enable the spectator to relive the experiences underlying the creative process. In a sense other than that intended by Leonardo da Vinci this is particularly true of the education of children. By studying the genesis of a picture we have the possibility of investigating the organic inter-relationship of the things represented and in this way experiencing for ourselves the manner in which thought processes issue in pictorial form.

* *The Nature of Creative Activity.*

Fig. 23. "Saying Good-bye." Different time sequences are expressed in one drawing. X-ray picture shows inside of compartment. Space "is filled" according to importance.

We see, then, that when the child had a complete impression of the coach before him, he considered it necessary first of all to put the railway coach on the rails in order to give it the basis which it had in his thoughts. A coach without rails is, after all, no coach. Next he divided the coach into three compartments in order to create the emotional center for his representation. Thus his attention was concentrated more and more on the true focus of his experience. The part that will ultimately take up his whole attention is treated in more and more detail.

Although the other "compartments" do not interest him, he draws in the left of the picture one seat and luggage rack, then the steps. The inside, of course, is now emotionally of greatest significance. The outside, therefore, is neglected and an X-ray picture is drawn.

If the drawing had been broken off at this stage and we were to consider it as completed, our eyes would already be immediately guided to the focus of the event. Now the child draws himself. He has taken his place, in the preparation of which he has spent enough time. So now we see him sitting there, holding out his hand in greeting. He has put his luggage in order and has drawn it lying in the luggage rack. His father stands next to him in the compartment; therefore his base line has to be drawn. He and his father face each other. This we see from the profiles which are turned towards each other and note that the nose has been accentuated in its importance. "Father already wants to go," the child says, and in order to indicate this, he draws one foot (which he has made shorter than the other) higher. Next the father is outside and waves his hand. The child draws this quite clearly by overemphasizing the waving hand in comparison with the other hand, which has no function in the picture. Then his father remains on the platform. Consequently, the child has to have that important symbol—a base line.

Having now completed the expression of his main experience, the child notices the "empty compartments" and quite automatically lengthens the "luggage rack" and puts in two windows. From this final touch the experience dies down, and we can ourselves feel vividly the emotions he has gone through and which he has portrayed in this picture.

We must ask ourselves whether the feet of the figure representing the father have been neglected "on purpose" while he was supposed to be moving about inside the compartment, whereas while he is standing outside the feet have been carefully drawn in. The child gives us an explanation, "My father puts everything in order in the compartment and then he waits down below until the train goes off." In saying this he indicates that he has represented *all* the most important *phases* of his experience within *one space*. We see again how, in one drawing, *space and time* fuse, the *inside* appears when it is of emotional *significance,* the base line serves as base *or* as rail, and *deviations* from the schema show the real experiences of the child. We further have seen how the tendencies expressed in the drawings of children follow laws of their own that have nothing to do with "naturalistic" tendencies.

THE MEANING OF COLOR

From a mere emotional relationship to color, as expressed during the preschematic stage, the child gradually discovers that there is *a relationship between color and object*. In all spheres of the child's development we see the awakening process of such a consciousness. In the drawing of the human figure the child has arrived at a *definite concept* that has crystallized in the schema. In experiencing space, the child has for the first time experienced that he himself is part of the environment. Also in color the child discovers such a definite relationship. It is no longer his subjective experience, or emotional binding, that determines color. It is a newly won objective relationship to man and environment that makes the child realize that there is a *relationship between color and object.*

We could just as well call this stage in the child's development *the stage of objective color.* In the very same way as we have seen that the ability to repeat a newly won discovery creates confidence and self-assurance in scribbling, in the development of a schema or in life in general, we also see here that repetitions of same colors for same objects have their great significance.. These repetitions do not have the meaning of stiffness or rigidity. On the contrary, they have the meaning of the discovery of a new experience and the enjoyment of *mastery.*

This enjoyment of mastery is one of the most important driving powers in education. It is not "happy accidents" that encourage the child in his work. They can have the very opposite effect when the child discovers the uniqueness of an accident, and his inability to repeat the "achievement," in the very same way as we do not consider accidental happenings in our life as real achievements. The child, having unconsciously the same feeling, gets very much enjoyment out of the mastery of a situation. If this feeling of mastery does not become satisfied, it has missed becoming an important psychological factor in development. The child unconsciously has the correct feeling for mastery, and through repetitions throughout his development satisfies this urge to achieve it.

Once we have understood this important and true meaning of repetition within the psychological development of the child, we will no longer briskly refuse the child's "eternal" questions with answers like "don't ask that again and again." *This self-assurance of an achievement* (here the achievement of an established relationship between color and object) *makes the child repeat the same color for the same object again and again.* This established relationship through repetitions we may call the *color schema* of the child. Thus, in the very same way as the child has come to a definite concept of form (the schema for form) through repetitions, the child also arrives at a definite concept of color (the color schema) through repetitions. Again we would like to emphasize that we are not dealing with single aspects in the development of the child, that we would rather like to see the child as a whole. Only with this in our mind are we continuing the analysis of the *meaning* of the color schema.

The origin of the color schema might be found in a *visual* or *emotional* concept of color. Important for us to know is that whatever experience was of significance at the time when the child *first* discovered the relationship between color and object will determine the color schema. If the child's relationship to "ground" was first established on a muddy ground of the backyard of a shack, the color schema for ground will then be ndicative for the child's basic experience with "ground." *Through repe-titions this basic experience becomes stereotyped* as an experience of gen-eral validity. Thus, all "ground" will be brown, regardless of whether here is grass on it or not.

This established color schema will not change unless a definite emo-tional experience induces a deviation in the color. Therefore, in the same way as we have discussed deviations in the analysis of space and form concepts, the deviations from the schematic representation give us insight into the emotional experiences of the child. It might, however, also be a visual concept which determines the color schema—that is, "the foliage s green." It was green at the time when the child first saw it, when it established the relationship between foliage and color. Now Fall has come and, assuming that the child is still in the schematic stage of development, he will continue to use his established color "green," disregarding the visual experience of the turning colors of the foliage or even the bare trees. Again, however, if the child has had an experience of emotional significance with the turned colors—maybe by making a wreath out of fall leaves and searching for particularly beautiful colors—he would then deviate from a schema of green to a visual concept of fall colors.

From this discussion, it is evident that the color schemata, in the same way as the space and form schemata, of children are *not rigid* expressions. Each child has his own *highly individualized* color relationships based upon very fundamental first experiences. Even within the established color schema we see that deviations are quite frequent whenever special ex-periences of *emotional significance* are dominant.

THE MEANING OF DESIGN

A *conscious* approach in using "fundamentals of design" during this age period, would not only be an artificial adult approach, but could, in the child, under certain circumstances, destroy the spontaneous act of creation. I have not yet seen a child of this age level spontaneously decorating an object with the purpose of beautifying it. All such attempts were forced upon the child, or "stimulated" by adults. It is true that the child is an "innate designer" * in the eyes of the adults, only the child does not know it. Or, as D'Amico says, one "factor responsible for weakening the child's native sense of design is the nature of teaching design, the imposing of fixed formulas on the child, now in general practice."

What is this innate sense for design? From our discussion we have

---

* D'Amico, Victor, *Creative Teaching in Art.* Scranton, Pa.: International Textbook Co., 1941.

realized that the child, by no means, deals with any formal aspects with regard to art. His main inclination is the use of art as a means of self-expression. That is why we expect that no teacher will ever use formal criticisms on products of children of these early ages. Such criticism would be the very death of any free creative teaching. In the very same way as formal aspects on proportions would be detrimental to the free development of the child, because they would interfere with the innate urge for expression, formal elements like "balance" and "rhythm," if used as a "stimulant," miss the purpose. This would serve as satisfaction only for the adult, who likes to see "beautiful drawings," but would be most harmful to the free development of a child.

How does the innate sense for design manifest itself? One of the most important attributes of design is rhythm; one of the simplest characteristics of rhythm is repetition. The innate sense for design thus seemingly has its roots in the very same psychological urge for mastery and self-assurance that manifests itself in repetitions. We shall, therefore, notice that the earliest stages of creativity by no means show this innate sense for design, since the urge for repetition in drawing starts during the schematic stage.

During this age level, however, teachers will have merely to direct the natural urge for repetition into the proper channels in order to stimulate within the child the natural values of design. Fig. 14, "Fruit Harvest," is an excellent example for such a natural tendency for design, grown out of the urge for repetition. The "trees" are by no means intended to be designs: they are the child's form concept, the schema for trees which, through repetition, has become stereotyped. The new experience that has forced the child to deviate his schema was the apples. The apples, therefore, are irregular. This irregularity, however, prevents these trees from becoming monotonous. A real effect of a design has been achieved, without the desire or consciousness of a design approach.*

Another concept, contributing greatly to the unconscious achievement of design, is the way children during this age level deal with space. The quite common division of the drawing space into sections, determined by base lines, also contributes greatly to an achievement of a design. All this is natural to the child as a part of his development. It is his innate *space concept* and his innate desire for repeating *form concept* (schema) that make the child an "innate designer." Surely one can be an innate, an intuitive artist, even without knowing it. The child is such an innate designer, but the difference lies in the fact that the artist may gain through

* For excellent examples, see Cole, Natalie Robinson, *The Arts in the Classroom*. New York: John Day Co., 1940, or Tomlinson, R. R., *Picture-Making by Children*. London: The Studio, 1934.

Fig. 24. Clay modeling. Schematic Stage. (Courtesy Educational Project, Museum of Modern Art, N.Y.)

a more conscious approach and the child can only be disturbed through it, because this consciousness is something strange to him, something which lies beyond his comprehension. One must not teach a child who is still in the babbling stage how to pronounce words correctly, the result would only be frustration. It is the same with design.

MODELING IN CLAY

Modeling is not merely another technique. Since it is three-dimensional in quality, it stimulates another kind of thinking. Modeling gains in significance especially during this age level since it has a very definite function. A technique is used wisely only if it fulfills an original purpose. As long as the same thing can be done in a different technique, adequately, this special technique is not the best one. Thus, nothing should be done in clay that can be painted, and nothing should be painted that can better be done in clay; or nothing should be done in clay that can be better done in wood. Thus, it would be disadvantageous and useless to model in clay a carriage with wheels that cannot be turned: it is a "dead carriage." If, however, the carriage would not be modeled as "carriage" but would merely serve to characterize a man pushing it, it is not the function of the carriage to roll, but to characterize the man.

The real nature of clay is its plasticity. Because of its plasticity it can be used most advantageously during this age level, in which the child has found his concepts on all lines and in which the child should use clay most flexibly. Where lies the definite function of modeling? It lies in the fact that through the plasticity of clay the child has an easier means of deviating from his concept than in any other medium. In building up the figure, the child actually has the opportunity for accompanying it kinetically in some imaginary experiences. I have seen a child who was modeling a picnic scene actually imitating the effect of visitors "coming" and "sitting down" by moving the figures and bending them in the sitting position until the final modeling expression was achieved. Or, I have seen children actually moving up the arm to the position of "eating" when this was the desired representation.

Whereas, the drawing concept demands a simultaneous concept of "one event" (with the exceptions of space-time representations), the process of modeling permits a constant change. Figures can be added or taken away or changed in their position and shape. This is due only to the original meaning of the special material—clay. It is, therefore, important to use this great benefit in our stimulations, which should mainly be confined to "actions." Of course, these actions should be related to the child's experiences. Environment should be avoided because it has the same three-dimensional quality as the material. Distance in external reality would compete with "distance" in clay, the result of which would be small-scale models. Such works can be made, but only when they are meant to be *models* and not self-expression. In the realm of creative production, environment can be included only when it has emotional significance to the child. Thus only the immediate environment will be of significance.

Two different modes of expression can be observed, each of which exists in its own realm—the one of *"pulling out from the whole"* and the other of *"putting single representative symbols together into a whole."* Since both methods reveal different kinds of thinking, it would be disturbing and of greatest disadvantage to a child to be diverted from his own method of thinking. Pulling the clay out from the whole means to have from the beginning a vague form concept of the "whole" from which details will be developed through a continuous analytical process.

This method of pulling out the single details from the whole through analysis is called the *analytic method*. Since this type of thinking is psychologically the same as that applied when observing (seeing) things, we can assume that the thinking underlying this method is a visual.* At this stage, however, thinking is not applied on a conscious level. That is why the creative product still deals with representative symbols, form symbols which lose their significance when detached from the whole.

The other method of expression described as "putting single representative symbols together to a whole" means that the child is *building up a synthesis* out of partial impressions. Because of the fact that the child arrives at a synthesis by putting single details together, we call this method the *synthetic method*. Since this type of thinking does not refer to observation (in observing we do not build up an image by adding single details), we leave it at this point with the statement that this type of thinking derives from nonvisual experiences. These nonvisual experiences can be of many different origins. They can refer to body experiences as well as to the mere activation of passive knowledge. From this discussion it becomes evident that "pulling out" or "putting together" is not a mere superficial technique but, as we shall later see more definitely, is deeply rooted in the child's thinking. Therefore any diversion from one method to another would only block the child's thinking (Fig. 24).

ART STIMULATION

The kind of stimulation the teacher should apply during the different age levels grows out of the need of the child during each particular stage of development. We have seen that, during the schematic stage, the child has formed a definite concept of man, space, color, and objects on all lines of art expression and in his psychological development as a whole. This definite concept has become stereotyped through repetition, has become the schema.

The task of the teacher is to give the child an opportunity to *use* his concepts, not as rigid form symbols, but as living experiences. Thus, our stimulation must create an atmosphere in which the *child's consciousness of being a part of environment* is stimulated in the same way as *the function of the human figure*. The inclusion of actions into an orderly space concept will, therefore, be of the greatest significance. Our stimulation could be characterized by the words *"we"* (stimulating the consciousness of I and somebody else), *"action"* (meaning what we are doing), *and "where"* (referring to the actual description of the place, restricted to the characteristics only and not to depth or distance).

Knowing that it lies in the child's thinking to fuse time and space, it will be educationally and psychologically of advantage to use *time and*

* See page 74.

space stimuli. The stimulation for these time and space representations should be concerned with subjective experiences as hikes, trips, or personal experiences that include different time sequences. Later, there should be added stimulations that refer to objective reports, as the growth from the raw material to the finished product.

In the same chapter with a discussion of stimulation belong the many topics that refer to the representation *of X-ray pictures.* In such stimulations, inside and outside are of the same significance and should be stressed in the same way. Of greatest importance, however, is the need for creating an atmosphere that is strong and tense, and open and flexible to any suggestions from the child. Rigidity is the death of any creative method.

Topics

The following topics are presented only as a means of showing directions our thinking should take when stimulating children at this age level. By no means are the topics to replace a close stimulation. The stimulation cannot be detailed enough. The more emotionally interested the child becomes in an experience, the better will the experience be for his work and his further development. The topics which follow are divided into groups under different headings which point out the type of stimulation to which the topic refers.

Action (to make form concept-functional)
Racing with My Friend on the Grounds ("we" (I and my friend) "action" (are racing) "where" (on the grounds)).
Jumping over a Rope Which is Held by Bob and John.
Pulling Myself High on the Rings in the yard.
Playing Ball with Bob.
Going to Church with Dad and Mother.
Climbing a Mountain.
Carrying Something Home for Mother.
Planting a Tree, Anne Holding It.
Sitting on a Sled Down the Hill.
Pulling the Sled Up a Hill.
Skating on the Pond.
Recess on the School Grounds.
Climbing a Tree.
Searching for Easter Eggs in the Back Yard.
Pulling each Other.
Baseball.

Shaking Hands with Anne.

Saying Good-Bye to Mother.

Going to School.

Profile, Front view

Sitting on the Swing Holding the Rope (front view).

Going Between Mother and Dad (front view).

Holding the Umbrella in One Hand and the Bag in the Other (front view).

Playing Checkers (profile).

Eating Breakfast, Sitting Opposite Each Other (profile).

A Row of Soldiers Marching (profile).

Greeting by Shaking Hands (profile).

Space-Time representations

When I Leave My Home and Go to School.

From the Tree to the Board: Lumberyard.

From the Wheat to the Bread.

What the Early Settlers Did when They Landed.

When We Went to Visit the Market.

When We Went to Visit the Theater.

When We Went to Visit the Fruit Stands.

When We Went to Visit the Fair.

X-ray pictures

A Coal Mine (When We Were in One).

A Hospital (When We Were in One).

Going Upstairs.

In a Hotel.

In a Cave.

When We Visited the Different Floors of a Factory.

Stimulations characterized by "we," "action," and "where."

Technique

Three things are very important with regard to developing techniques.

(1) The teacher should know *that the child must develop his own technique* and that every "help" from the teacher in showing the child a "correct" technique would only mean restricting the child's individual approach. The teacher's job is to introduce the appropriate material at a time when the child is most ready to use it.

(2) Every material or technique must make its *own* contribution. If a task can be done in a different technique with a better effect, the wrong technique has been applied.

(3) The teacher should develop economy in the use of techniques. In most books on art education we find that most materials are introduced and used from the very beginning of childhood. *At a time when the child is overwhelmed by his own creativity, when he is full of intuitive power, too many different media would not only be wasteful, but would often prove distracting as well.* As has been said during the discussion of the scribbling stages, the material must fit the needs of the child and must provide the best means for the child's expression. During scribbling we have seen that the crayon serves best to express the motor activity of the child.

The child at the age level from seven to nine years is neither concerned with plane nor with the representation of depth. What is most characteristic of this age level is that the child has found a form, space, and color concept, which through repetitions develops into his schema. In the section on design, we have seen that these repetitions attain special significance in the development of design. It is therefore of the greatest importance that the child repeat the same colors for the same objects whenever he wishes to do so. A technique which does not afford the child the opportunity of experiencing mastery or self-assurance would not be a good technique for this age level.

The consistency and texture of poster paint or tempera serve this purpose best, but crayon or colored chalk can also be used successfully. There is no reason whatsoever for introducing water color at this age level as many educators suggest. Water color is transparent, runs, and changes.

The transparency of water color serves best to paint atmosphere and landscape, but not design. Its running quality introduces many "happy accidents" which do not lend themselves to repetition—happy, however, only for those who can make active use of them as a visual stimulus. Since the child in his painting is more concerned with expressing his own ideas than with visual stimuli, these "happy accidents" would turn into "sad disappointments" because the child would not gain through this experience the feeling of mastery. Since we considered this feeling of mastery of prime importance for the psychological development of the child, we must not sacrifice these important gains to some happy incidents, regardless of their beauty. An accident cannot be repeated. At an age when this desire of repetition is most definite, the inability to repeat would be disappointing rather than inspiring. We shall see that at other age levels, when the urge for repetition is not important, water color will serve to inspire the child.

This discussion has shown again that technique is closely connected with the child's development and should not be introduced merely for the purpose of changing the material.

SUMMARY   SCHEMATIC STAGE—SEVEN TO NINE YEARS

Characteristics	Human Figure	Space	Color	Design	Stimulation Topics	Technique
Discovery of a definite concept of man and environment.	Definite concept of figure depending on active knowledge and personality through repetition: "schema."	First definite space concept: "base line."				Colored crayons.
Self-assurance through repetition of form symbols: "schema."		Discovery of being a part of environment: assumption for cooperation and correlation.				Colored chalks.
In pure schema no intentional experience is expressed, only the thing itself: "the man," "the tree," and so forth.	Deviations expressing experiences can be seen in: (1) Exaggeration of important parts. (2) Neglect or omission of unimportant parts. (3) Change of symbols.	Base line expresses: (1) Base (2) Terrain	Discovery of relationship between color and object, through repetition: "color schema."	No conscious approach.	Best stimulation concentrates on action, characterized by "we" (I, John, tree) "action," "where" (characterization of terrain).	Powder paint (tempera, poster paint).
Experiences are expressed by deviations from schema.		Deviations from base line express experiences: subjective space: (1) Folding over (egocentric). (2) Mix forms of plan and elevation. (3) X-ray pictures. (4) Space-time representations.	Same color for same object.	Design forms received through repetitions, subconsciously.	Topics referring to: (1) Time sequences (journeys traveling stories). (2) X-ray pictures (inside and outside is emphasized), factory, coal mine, and so forth.	Large paper.
Use of geometric lines.			Deviation of color schema shows emotional experience.			Bristle brushes. Clay: (1) Synthetic. (2) Analytic.

Also during this age period large sheets of paper give more freedom than smaller sheets. Since the child arrives at a more detailed concept, *hair brushes* with long handles are preferable to bristle brushes. As has been said before, *clay* is an excellent means for plastic expression. In this medium also educators, who know that the process of creating is of greater significance than the final product, influence the creative concept of the child adversely by discouraging modeling merely for the practical reason that a modeling produced by the "synthetic method" of putting details together cannot be fired in the kiln. Surely it cannot easily be fired because of its slight cohesive qualities and the air bubbles in it, but it is absolutely an adult concept that products of modeling made by little children should be fired. If this concept would not have been developed by the adult teacher, the child would not care for it. During my 15 years of experience in teaching modeling to the blind, who, as a result of their handicap, model in a synthetic way, I have had no request for firing from blind individuals, who worked most enthusiastically and creatively.* From our discussion in the section on modeling, it became evident that the two modes of techniques express a different kind of thinking. *Changing the technique from synthetic to analytic would therefore mean restricting the child in freedom of expression.*

EXERCISES

(1) Collect the drawings of one second- or third-grade classroom and find out how many different schemata are used for "eye," "mouth," "nose," "body," "legs," "arms," and so forth.

(2) Collect the drawings of one child and show
  (a) Repetitions of schemata.
  (b) Deviations from schemata.

(3) Explain the meaning of deviations from schematic representations by means of several drawings.

(4) What percentage of children in a second grade are using geometric lines for their expression? Find out the percentage in a third grade. Do you find any change?

(5) Observe the relationship of reading ability and base-line expressions in one classroom.

(6) What percentage in your class has arrived at base-line representations?

(7) Do you find a difference in terms of cooperation between those who have discovered the base line as a common space experience and those who have not?

(8) Collect drawings that refer to time-space experiences.

* See tables 35, 78a, b in *The Nature of Creative Activity.*

(9) Show in drawings the meaning of "folding over."

(10) Trace the relationship between "folding over" and egocentric attitude.

(11) Collect the drawings of one child and find out whether the child uses always the same color for the same object. If he does not, analyze the reason for it.

(12) Find out in the drawings of different children how the repetition of schemata affects "design."

(13) Show the meaning of schemata in clay modeling.

(14) How many children in your classroom model analytically (by pulling out from the whole) and how many synthetically (putting parts together)?

(15) Can you establish a relationship (in terms of observation versus mechanical skills) between those who model analytically or synthetically?

(16) Analyze a child's drawing in using the following scheme (check the correct part).

Drawing Characteristics	*Personality Characteristics*
Geometric lines	Emotional, subjective
Realistic lines	Visual, objective
Base line	Cooperative
No base line	Noncooperative
Rich schemata	Intelligent
Normal schemata	Average
Poor schemata	Dull
Folding over	Egocentric
Frequent exaggeration	Emotional
Too much exaggeration	Emotionally unstable
No emphasis on particular parts	Dull
Frequent use of bright colors or dull colors	Joyous
Space-time representation	Sad

LABORATORY WORK

(1) Establish consciously through simplification a schema for "tree" and one for "house." Cut it in linoleum, placing it on a base line. By repeating both schemata and distributing them properly, design a textile.

(2) Collect pictures of designs that are based on the same principle of repetition.

(3) Collect materials of different structure of the following main groups: (a) Metals. (b) Fibers—plant, animal. (c) Plastics. (d) Stones.

CHAPTER V **The Dawning Realism**

The Gang Age (9 to 11 years)

THE CONCEPT OF REALISM

Before we discuss the special meaning of realism within the child's development, we shall clarify the term *realism*. By realism we do not understand the imitation of nature in a mere photographic way. Within art, and especially within our discussion, we shall use this term *whenever an attempt is made to represent reality as a visual concept*. The question might arise whether such a concept is desirable from the viewpoint of modern art education, which stresses the imaginative unrealistic tendencies. This would be a complete misunderstanding of the tendencies of modern progressive art education. Progressive art education stresses all tendencies that lie truly and sincerely in the development of the child. It would be a misconception to say there are no realistic tendencies in the child. We shall see that a visual concept of reality is deeply rooted in a large number of growing adolescent children. During these decisive years, the art educator must prevent the child from engaging in mere photographic imitations. A work of art is not the representation of an object itself; rather is it the representation of *the experience which we have with the particular object.*

74

THE GREATER AWARENESS OF THE SELF

This age level from nine to eleven years is usually signified in our youth by a growing feeling for independence. Group friendships or "gangs" of the same sex are common. Boys despise girls and vice versa. Orders from adults are not always taken overwillingly. Cooperation with adults is at its low peak. "The peak of the delinquent period is usually said to coincide with the peak of the gang age at ten or eleven years." * It is the time when children want to sleep out of doors, when they prefer to be among their own group and lead "wars" against each other. During this age level arises the first real awareness of the sexes. Girls are more eager to dress, and like parties; boys prefer camping, belong to secret gangs that have rules of their own, and lead wars against girls. Such wars, as we are well aware, are only compensations for awakening feelings of affection, forerunners of adolescent feelings though far from having the same meaning. These stirrings are all too clearly seen in the child's creative work.

Geometric lines, as used during the schematic stage, do not lend themselves very well to characterize boys or girls. Therefore, geometric lines do not suffice for self-expression. Indeed, the child removes quite abruptly from this mode of expression to a form of expression that *relates more to nature*. We see a definite lack of cooperation in the great number of children who *do not establish spatial correlations* in their drawings. In experiments which I conducted † 43.4 per cent of the subjects did not establish spatial relationships during this age level. The following topic was given to 400 children: "You are under an apple tree. On one of its lower branches you see an apple that you particularly admire and that you would like to have. You stretch out your hand to pick the apple, but your reach is a little short. Then you make a great effort and get the apple after all. Now you have it and enjoy eating it. Draw yourself as you are taking the apple off the tree."

The results showed, that without being influenced in any way, the children were freely able to display the pattern of their experiences. "Beautiful" trees and apples were drawn just as often as "misproportioned" people. The subject had allowed the children to be absorbed in the visual experiences of the beautiful apple hanging on one of the lower branches of the tree, as much as in the feeling of the importance attained by the apple when it is particularly desired. The body experience of grasping

* Bowley, Agatha H., *Guiding the Normal Child*. New York, Philosophical Library, 1943.
† *The Nature of Creative Activity*.

the apple could be expressed just as much as the experience of stretchin
the body while it was being picked.

I considered separately the representation of the individual huma
being, the representation of the tree and the relation of the two to on
another. This experiment has shown that at the age of nine, 69 per cen
of the children still draw according to principles of evaluation and no
according to visual observation. That is, 69 per cent of the children
this age level disregarded entirely the size of the tree in relationship t
the size of the child. However, the tendency was very strong to draw
characteristics of the tree as well as of the self. Boys made distinct boy
girls wore dresses. From the reproduced drawing it is seen that this in
creasing conceptional knowledge of the external world and its significanc
lowers the child's capacity for coordinating visual experiences with the se
in the drawing. This is borne out by the figures, for in the 10th year, 43 p
cent of the children were unable to establish a relationship between chil
and tree (Fig. 25). *This period, then, represents the time during whic
the confidence of the child in his own creative power is for the first tim
shaken by the fact that he is becoming conscious of the significance of h
environment.* Teachers and parents alike believe this period to be critica
One of the most important tasks of the teacher is to inspire the child
feeling for cooperation by stimulating a more conscious feeling of spati
correlations in his drawings. How this is done will be discussed in th
chapter on stimulation.

In the representation of the human figure

As has been noted, the mere concept of the human figure as expresse
during the schematic stage, does not lend itself to characterizations.
schema is in its nature a collective expression, like the concept for "man
In it there is no place for individual details concerned with the chara
terization of the object. It is a *generalization* of the expression "man." At
stage where the child is eager to express characteristics of sex, as boy
with trousers and girls with dresses, the schematic generalization is in
adequate for this type of expression. The concept as such and the mode
of expression are both inadequate. Geometric lines, as used before, a
unsuitable means to characterize suits or dresses. As part of this crisis th
child has discovered his inadequacy, and as a result moves toward a mo
realistic representation. It is dawning upon him that his representation
can be adjusted to nature. But the child is still far from achieving a visu
concept. The girls, in their representations, do not yet "see" that the

Fig. 25. "Picking Apples from a Tree" (ten years old). Inability to establish correlation between figure and tree caused by egocentric attitude. Emphasis on apples. (Dawning Realism.)

Fig. 26. "Man with Umbrella" (ten-year-old boy). Awareness of clothes. Stiffness due to emphasis on visual experience.

dresses have folds or wrinkles or that the hem is uneven when walking. The "hem line" is always even in drawings of this period.

This shows clearly that the drawing is not an outcome of the child's visual observation, but that the child is rather eager, merely to *characterize* the girls as girls or the boys as boys. It must not, however, be overlooked, that such a drawing is the first step toward a realistic concept. Through this concentration on the "how," the child gains feeling for details, but loses feeling for action. Indeed, we see a greater "stiffness" in the representations of the human figure in drawings of children of this age. However it is significant that henceforth *every part* has its meaning, and *retains this meaning even when separated from the whole.* This is an important means of evaluation for the teacher, since he can easily recognize whether the pupil has attained the stage of "dawning realism." As has been noted a symbol can be determined by separating it from the whole; it then loses its meaning. *Realistic or pseudorealistic lines do not lose their meaning when separated.* The child has reached the stage where the line has lost its mere symbolic significance (Fig. 26).

In expression of emotions

Through the growing awareness of a visual concept the child no longer uses exaggerations, neglect, or omissions as frequently as a means of expression of emotions. One cannot change a hand into another hand, as the child has changed symbols to express emotional binding. Other means are now used more frequently to express the focal point of the child's interest. Although at nine years, the larger number of children still use changing sizes as a definite means to express quality, their number decreases rapidly after the tenth year, as the mentioned experiment with the apple tree clearly indicates.* The child begins now to substitute means of expression by an accumulation of details on those parts which are emotionally significant. We shall talk about this important means of expression in the next chapter.

In the representation of space

THE PLANE AND THE BASE-LINE CONCEPT   In the same way as the greater awareness of the self led the child to realize that the geometric line is an inadequate expression for his needs, we also see in the representation of space a change from the mere symbolic expression, as seen in the base-line concept, to a more realistic representation. As a result of this dawning realism the child discovers that *the space between base lines becomes meaningful; the plane is discovered.* Thenceforth the base line loses its significance as the vehicle of space representations. "Folding over" is criticized as "unnatural." Trees and houses no longer stand only on the edge of the line. Though this form of representation still is in frequent use, the child also lets the trees grow from the "ground." The sky is no longer merely "above" but goes all the way down. This does not mean that the child has become aware of the meaning of the horizon.

The child of this age has not developed a conscious visual percept of depth, but he has taken certainly the first step toward such a concept. With the sky all the way down the child soon realizes that a tree, growing from the ground, will partly cover the sky. Hence he becomes aware of overlapping, and another step toward a visual concept has been perceived. Stimulated by the teacher, the child will soon apply this experience of overlapping in the sky to other experiences of overlapping. The best stimulation of this visual experience can be introduced through using the technique of paper cutting because as the different layers of papers are applied, they will cover one another. This experience of overlapping is important not only be-

* *The Nature of Creative Activity.*

Fig. 27. "Cutting a Tree" (eleven-year-old girl). Painted after hurricane ha
felled tree near her house. Notice exaggeration of tree. Awakening of visual awar
ness. (Courtesy Education Project, Museum of Modern Art, N. Y.)

cause it is a part of the growing spatial concept that leads to the represent:
tion of three-dimensional space, but also for psychological reasons. Th:
one object can cover another is an important experience, because it impli
an awareness of the existence of the other object. This is especially signif
cant during a period in which cooperation is at its low peak. Person:
experiences are important to the child because he reacts emotionally to suc
experiences (Fig. 28).

SPATIAL CORRELATION AND AN EGOCENTRIC ATTITUDE   One of th
most important attributes of this age level is the tendency toward losin
contact with groups at large. Discovery of his own personality and th
desire to be regarded as an equal to adults often leads the child into cor
flicts. Children who are misunderstood by their parents feel frustrated an
as such have the tendency to withdraw within themselves. In drawing
this withdrawal expresses itself in the inablity to establish spatial correl:
tions. The more the adult prohibits the child from following his ow
inclinations, the longer will this period of resistance or non-cooperatio

last. It is important to know that every punitive measure causes reactions that are frequently more serious than the first cause.

As has been stressed in the Introduction, art education serves a double purpose: as a means of self-expression and as a therapeutical means. The inability of the child to establish spatial correlations should for the teacher be an indication of the child's emotional state. In most cases this is due to improper handling of situations with regard to the child's growing awareness of ego. Stimulation of the child's will to establish spatial correlations in creative work will, in most cases, be accompanied by an improvement of the child's social behavior. Thus, the child may develop a greater consciousness and desire for cooperation also within his own group. Especially can this be encouraged through participation in group work. Group work, therefore, will be of special significance during this period. The teacher has to know that group work has this meaning when the child gets the feeling that *he could not have achieved singly what the group has accomplished,* and that his contribution is an important part of the whole. If the child can have the feeling that he alone could have accomplished a similar work, the group work would not have fulfilled its purpose. On the contrary, group work might even have frustrated the child.

A group of boys worked on a harbor using the technique of paper cutting. Every boy of a class of 42 worked on a special boat selected as an outcome of a classroom discussion. Since this was done in a coastal area, the boys were very "boat-minded." One cut out a sailboat, another a PT boat, a cruiser, a battleship, fishing boats, rowboats, motorboats, steamships, and one boy made a ferry. At the end, 42 or more boats were finished. A few boys cut out the docks. The whole project was pasted on blue cardboard, and the whole class helped in the final arrangement. It was a grand harbor! Every boy had his own boat that looked much better in the group than by itself. All had the feeling that they could not have accomplished such a gigantic task alone. It helped greatly to increase the feeling for cooperation. If the child feels his importance, if opportunities are given to him to work and play with his companions, if he finds emotional outlets to express what he has on his mind, if his "gang" is regarded as a social unity and therefore respected, he will soon grow out of this age into a period of reasoning and greatest usefulness.

COLOR—SUBJECTIVE STAGE

The more the child moves toward the establishment of a *visual* relationship between color and object, the more are teachers tempted to misuse his dawning sense for "realistic" colors by teaching the child "how to

Fig. 28a. "Street Scene." Group work in paper cut, emphasizing cooperation. Overlapping is an important experience.

use and to apply color." There is no place in the elementary-school class room for the teaching of color theories by means of color wheels and other "scientific" helps. Such teaching would only destroy the child's spontaneous approach and would make him insecure in his own intuitive color experiences. The only way the child can be made more color conscious is through the emphasis of the child's own reactions to color. The more emotional the character of these reactions is, the deeper will be the experience.

How then should we introduce a knowledge of color, or is this not necessary? The answer depends on what we mean by knowledge. We should certainly make the child aware of his own achievements. To state an example: we visited a slum area, and upon our return, we talked about the people living there, the unpainted houses, the broken roofs, the shattered windows replaced by wooden boards, and the back yards filled with junk. After we had discussed these living conditions and their social implications, the children painted "One Day; Living in the Slums," the feelings they would have if they were supposed to regard such a place as

Fig. 28b. "Circus." Group work in paper cutting.

their environment. Another time we went to a well-kept residential area
and saw how the houses were well painted, with differently painted
window frames, flowers in windows, curtains, nicely kept lawns, and back
yards with garden furniture. The children painted this, too: "The House
in Which I Wish to Live."

It is easily understood that the comparison of the *dull* atmosphere of
the slums with the *bright* and joyous treatment of the house in which the
child wished to live gave many opportunities to talk of *dull* and *bright*
colors, not in an abstract way, but in connection with an experience. This
certainly introduced a real, emotional relationship to the two color values
—bright and dull, or if we would like to call it "happy" and "sad." Since
the child during this period is especially open for deviations from formerly
held, rigid color schemata, he will use such emotional stimulations most
willingly. He is visually not yet ready to react more sensitively toward
colors which surround him.

The impressionistic, or visual, color scale is the last and most complex
to experience. *The child's color relationship during this stage is related
to his emotional reactions; it is highly subjective.* That is why we should

use the most different moods with reference to color—calm and excited moods as well as monotonous and changing ones because moods are related to color. For all these various moods, experiences can be found such as the one described above. Because of the highly subjective emotional reactions to color we shall call this stage the *subjective stage of color.*

DESIGN AND CRAFTS

Removal from mere symbolic expression to a more realistic treatment—that is, the conscious emphasis on dresses or suits as introduced by the growing awareness of the difference in sex, introduces the desire for decoration. Girls more and more frequently begin putting patterns on their dresses. Only then, when the child herself indicated the desire for decoration, should we proceed with it in a more conscious way. Without disturbing the emotional approach toward design, we would like to give it a sounder fundament. However, in the same way as we do not teach color theory in elementary grades by means of scientific helps, we will not introduce any formal teaching of balance, rhythm, or any other attributes of design. We might, however, encourage children to use reproducing techniques, such as potato prints or stencils. In the beginning, the simplest geometric pattern cut into the flat, cut end of a carrot will be more suitable than any complex "flower pattern." The only encouragement which the child should get by such prints, during this period, is the *conscious* understanding of repetitions. This feeling for repetition established in the former stage will readily be taken over into the emotional design and used there freely and with understanding.

It is most important for the child to get from the very beginning the impression that design, when consciously used, has the *function* of decoration. That is why it is necessary to relate design definitely to some kind of material. Printing curtains would be such a task even if the dots, or whatever is being used as simple prints, are somewhat "primitive." In this connection the child learns to understand the functional meaning and usefulness of a design. The repeating patern used for it, gives him the understanding of the nature of repetitions within design. The folds in the curtain will show how the pattern becomes dynamic through the nature of the material. This is one of the experiences the child has to get from the very beginning of the conscious design approach: *design grows out of the material!* Different materials demand different designs. If this is not recognized by the teacher he loses one of the most important aspects in design: *the specific function of each material.**

* Tomlinson, R. R., *Crafts for Children.* New York: Studio Publications, Inc., 1935.

It is entirely unsuitable to plan the design first carefully on paper and then "transfer" it to the chosen material. Planning a design implies a more "scientific approach" for which there is no provision within this period. Furthermore, a design that is determined for another material will look quite differently on paper. By doing so, the teacher has missed utilizing one of the greatest stimuli—that is, the stimulation which the child derives from the nature of the material. If the child, from the very beginning, works on the material that he wants to decorate, he receives one of the most important inspirations from the *structure* and *nature* of the material itself. The result of such established relationships between design and material will enable the child to adapt intuitive qualities for design to any material with which he is confronted. *Crafts should never be separated from design.* In our greatest cultures, skill, design, and workmanship were inseparable. Today, we see again this tendency in modern streamlined articles, from simple household utensils to furniture, cars, and architecture in general. We have to stimulate the child in time to recognize these close relationships.

In these first experiments no realistic approaches to design are recommended. To be able to use products of nature, such as flowers, leaves, and so forth, for a design, has the assumption that these forms of nature are well known to the child. There is the great danger, that instead of adapting these forms of nature to a design—that is, stylizing them, the child will make poor attempts to reproduce nature. There is no such danger in using pure, abstract forms, which, by repetition, will form a design. Even two diagonal strokes in a square, one wide and the other narrow, can make a very attractive pattern when printed on textiles. Also, paper plates or flower pots lend themselves very well for applied designs. The technique of finger painting can now be introduced since the child will be mature enough to get pleasure out of the motions, texture, and color used, not out of the consistency as we discussed it during the early stages. However, finger painting should not be done for its own sake, but for its application to useful articles, as schedule cards, simple folders, or boxes.

The most important element of design during this age level is the emotional approach toward it. Giving children paper plates and asking them to imagine themselves in the middle of the woods (using the inner circle of the plate as base line for the trees, with the self in the center, or sliding on a sled down the hill, again using the circle as a continuous base line for hill) would be a suggestion to which children react emotionally. At the same time they will carry over the experience of repetition, which they have gained with their reproducing techniques. With regard to the choice of color, children should not be disturbed by any formal suggestions or influences. We always should have in our mind that it is not the final product, but the working process which counts, and that an "odd" color scheme will not hurt the child whereas he might be disturbed by a criticism that he cannot comprehend.

With design new techniques and materials are introduced. The more inventive the teacher with the introduction of materials, the better. Open-mindedness in regard to material used for decorative purposes is one of the most important attributes of a good teacher. However, economy in its use will also be significant. But, since the mere opportunity of getting the "feel" of the material is of great importance, the mere handling of it with some simple decorative purpose in mind will establish the desired relationship. Merely twisting a strip of sheet metal for holding a candle will introduce the quality of metal. Bending two wires in wavy lines and attaching them to a wooden base will make a serviceable penholder. At the same time the child experiences the manner in which wood and metal can combine with each other. Children should then be given an opportunity to improvise on their own account combinations of materials which need not necessarily serve a useful purpose. *Getting acquainted* with the different functions and qualities of materials is the main aim. Work with different-colored wool of different textures will stimulate the children to different things in this medium. Even twisting several colors together into a knot can be a fine starting point for a discussion on the nature of weaving with regard to the different materials.

The use of clay for *pottery* will be stimulating to the child of this age level. Simple plates or dishes can easily be shaped. Even casting with a one-piece mold can be applied. This, however, is suggested only when the children make their own molds.* The following procedure is recommended: In a class discussion about the different shapes of water glasses, the one with the best shape is selected. Keeping in mind the diffi-culties in casting irregular shapes, only straight water glasses should be selected for this purpose. A cardboard box of the size of the water glass is obtained. The outside of the water glass is sized with soap. The water glass then it placed into the box and plaster of Paris (mixed with water to the proper consistency) is poured around it. After the plaster has set the glass should be removed and the box peeled off. The mold, after it has dried, is ready for use. Clay has to be mixed with water until it becomes slip—that is, clay of the consistency of thin cream of wheat. The slip is

---

* Inasmuch as this is not a book on Arts-Crafts, detailed instructions on modeling and firing pottery cannot be given. For such instructions, the teacher is referred to the many excel-lent books on the subject.

Fig. 29. Figures in Papier Mâché. (Courtesy Educational Project, Museum of Modern Art, N. Y.)

poured into the mold up to the top and after 10 minutes, poured out again. Through adhesion, enough clay sticks to the wall so as to form the thickness of the wall of the pot. Since clay shrinks when it dries (the child should watch this shrinking), the cup can easily be removed from the mold. The *cup* must be "bone dry" before it is put into the kiln. If a school does not have a kiln, the firing method used by Indians is suggested. An old iron kettle is obtained. In the back yard of the school a hole is dug in which several layers of charcoal are placed. The kettle which contains the bone-dry dishes is put into the hole upon these charcoal layers and surrounded and covered by more charcoal. Kerosene will start the fire which is kept for approximately six hours. After it has cooled off, the pieces in the kettle are *fired*. If the children have no opportunity to glaze the ware it must not be glazed by adults as it is customary in many schools, because the child would surely lose the feeling of its original production. The process of glazing will be described in the next age level under design Fig. 29).

This discussion has shown that there is no separating line between crafts and design. On the contrary, the very integration of both will give them proper meaning and significance. This is of special importance because it will also open the eyes of the child to modern means of design. Boys who are very streamline-minded when their thinking relates to cars, locomotives, or tanks, will soon apply their knowledge and understanding to other projects and materials. This is particularly significant for a time in which we encounter such varied attitudes toward design in our daily life. With regard to automobiles, the most streamlined model will not be modern enough. But the same person who could not live without this modern car chooses antique furniture or a terribly poor imitation of it. We have progressed beyond the horse and buggy, but not at home.

Great cultures have always been characterized by this unity of art and life. To create this feeling in our children from the very beginning is of greatest significance. The child cannot be exposed early enough to a proper environment. But we don't start with a conscious stimulation until the child is ready for it—that is, when his visual approach permits the conscious apprehension of the nature of good design. That is the time when the child by his own desire starts to decorate with the purpose of decoration. The meaning and influence of design on our daily life is tremendous, conscious or subconscious, and it is the duty of the teacher to awaken the innate feeling the child possesses and direct it into the proper channels.

MODELING

As we come into more advanced stages of modeling and see the child showing greater concern for formal expressions, the question of preserving the products will arise. Before answering this question, it seems important to analyze again the meaning of art, especially in modeling in the elementary-school classroom. It is important to make a distinction between modeling and sculpturing. *Modeling is the unconscious expression in clay or plasticine,* which serves as a means of self-expression in three-dimensional media. In the elementary-school classroom we use modeling, as in all other creative approaches, not as the final product, but as the educative process. This means for the teacher that he must not put the emphasis upon the preservation of the final product. If the teacher would not put emphasis on the preservation of art products, the child would never care to have it done. *Modeled pieces basically are not for firing.* Most of the synthetically modeled pieces (those that are put together from single details) would not be able to stand firing. As has been said before it is not worthwhile to sacrifice the child's individual thinking to a mere technique

The question will arise whether modeled pieces should be painted or not. This question will be especially important at this age level, when girls start to include dresses in their modelings and boys, perhaps, uniforms. The painting of modeled pieces should never be encouraged, since modeling is the expression of three-dimensional experiences, which mainly refer to the sense of touch. If a child, however, feels the need to paint his work, he should go ahead with it. Generally it is not necessary to inspire the use of paint and clay in one work during this period of age. But it might happen that, as an outcome of classroom discussions, the children would like to illustrate a scene. For example, they might want to imitate the life in an Indian village, in which they make the tents out of canvas and wooden poles, and model the Indians either of clay or papier mâché. Under such circumstances it is better to encourage the use of as many materials as possible, to have real canvas tents and the costumes of the Indians made of material rather than painted on clay or papier mâché.

As long as we use clay modeling as a means of self-expression, we stress the self as the focal point of experience. By that we do not mean that the ego must be represented in the modeling, but that the experience of the self in any form must be included. Formal aspects, which refer to the nature of composition or sculpturing, should be excluded. It is therefore entirely out of place to introduce such formal aspects as "we begin with one figure and then make two until we arrive at group representations." The child must express himself freely, and stimulation should be in the direction of the child's thinking. Since during this age the child's needs are concerned with friendship and gangs, and with greater awareness of the differences of sex and the resulting lack of cooperation, the stimulation must be directed accordingly.

ART STIMULATION

The following aspects of the child's development will stand out at this age level: Greater awareness of the self, and as a result of this egocentric attitude, a lack of cooperation. Stimulation during this period therefore must stress this self-awareness in order to give the child the feeling of importance. The stimulation must give him an opportunity to express the newly discovered importance of the difference of sex, and it also must inspire the child to use methods of cooperation as beneficial means for getting results otherwise unobtainable. In classroom discussions, therefore, we should relate spatial experiences of the newly discovered plane to the self. Playing football, for example, would refer not only to the football field (the plane on which the action takes place), but would also involve the self (boy) characterized by the special uniform of a football player. Or, sitting around a table at a birthday party would include both the emphasis on dresses and on the table with all its accessories.

To inspire cooperation, two means can successfully be used: First, the *subjective method* of cooperation which deals with the representations of individual experiences of cooperation; or *the representations of scenes in which cooperation is of importance* (Fig. 27). It is, however, vital for the teacher to know that much depends on the way in which such a stimulation is presented to a group. The atmosphere which the teacher develops during the stimulation contributes greatly to its success. Such topics as "The Help to a Wounded Soldier" or "Flood Victims" can be presented very dramatically.

The second method, the *objective method* of cooperation, *deals with group work*—a whole group works on one project.* Also here, the kind of stimulation is vital for its success. As has been pointed out, paper cutting is an excellent technique for group work. In order to be successful the organization for group work must be well-planned. The following procedure is recommended First, a classroom discussion is started about a planned topic, such as "Fair" (Fig. 28a and Fig. 28b). "What do we see at a fair?" The answers are written on the blackboard by the teacher. In the meantime a big chip board or pasteboard is prepared by some children who paint, or prepare with paper, the simple background of sky and lawn. Second, the teacher asks the children to choose from the blackboard notes: "Who would like to make the merry-go-round, the shooting gallery the Ferris wheel?" When all topics are distributed, the children start to cut out their own projects.

Third, the children are asked to bring all pieces to the teacher's table. Children who have made simple tasks will have finished sooner and should be given an opportunity to cut out other topics. When most of the children are ready, the fourth step, assembling, starts. This can be done by a committee guided by the teacher. Since the children have cut out their different objects in sizes unrelated to one another, the teacher should unobtrusively select the smaller pieces for the background by asking, "Who has done this? Please paste it on the board. Where will it look best?" The group will be interested in how and where its things are placed. A few desks should be set aside for pasting, and several things may be distributed simultaneously in order that more than one thing will be ready for pasting. After all projects are assembled, some children may complain that part of their works are covered. At this point the teacher should discuss the nature of

* Cizek, Franz, *Children's Colored Paper Work*. New York: G. E. Stechert and Co., 19

overlapping, both from the visual standpoint, as an experience of seeing, and from the social standpoint—that is, that not all can be in the foreground. Background and foreground are both important. The outcome of such stimulation must be a feeling of achievement in the children. Every child must notice his contribution to group work. But it is also important that everyone understand that he alone could not have accomplished so big a task.

Topics

As has been described in the section "Stimulation," the child's subjective relationship to man and environment has become characteristic also for this particular stage. Subject matter throughout the grades, however, is determined by man and environment. Our analysis has embraced the ever-changing subjective relationship of man to his environment. From this standpoint, the following suggested topics are indicative of the child's special subjective relationships during this period. Inasmuch as these topics are only meant to be suggestions, it is assumed that they always will be adjusted and subordinated to the particular classroom situation prevailing. It is important that the teacher surround the topics with a special atmosphere.

Clothes, dresses	Going to Church on Sunday.
	Asking Policeman on Street.
	Sailors on a Boat.
	A Birthday Party.
	Bathing.
	Working in the Field.
	The Conductor in the Train Asking for Tickets.
	The Cook in the Hotel.
	Elevator Boy Staying Overnight in the Hotel.
	A Parade of Soldiers.
Space, meaning of plane	Crossing a Street.
	Going over a Bridge.
	Playing Football.
	Playing Basketball.
	Playing Baseball.
	Policeman Directing Traffic.
	Traffic Stopping by Red Light.
	All Celebrations in Open Air.
	Boating in a Lake Surrounded by a Lawn.

Skating on a Pond Surrounded by Woods.
Farmer Ploughing His Field.
Planting a Garden.
Sitting Around a Table for Supper.

Overlapping   Looking Out the Window.
                   In the Movie Theater.
                   In the Trolley Car.
                   In the Train.
                   Also see paper cuts (below, Objective Cooperation).

Subjective   Help to a Wounded Soldier.
Cooperation   Nursing the Sick.
                   First Aid.
                   Sawing Lumber.
                   Building a House.
                   Carrying a Log.
                   Digging a Hole.
                   Repairing a Street.
                   Decorating a Christmas Tree.
                   Praying in Church.

Objective   We All Are Making a City.
Cooperation   We All Are Making a Farm.
                   We All Are Making a Circus.
                   We All Are Making a Fair.
                   We All Are Making the Ark of Noah.
                   We All Are Making a Store.

Design on   *Reproducing:* Potato print (geometric) on textiles.
Material   Finger paint: folder, card, box.

                   Emotional: Sliding Down a Hill, using inner circle of plate
                        as base line.
                   Racing Down a Hill, using inner circle of plate as base line.
                   Maypole, using inner circle of plate as base line.
                   In the Woods, using inner circle of plate as base line.
                   Picking Flowers, on a pot.
                   A Carnival, on a pot.
                   Animals of the Ark, on a pot.

                   Experiences with different material:
                        1. Decorating canes.
                        2. Bending metal to spirals (candlestick).
                        3. Work with papier mâché.

Clay

A Farmer.
A Football Player.
A Policeman.
A Soldier.
A Sailor.
A Dancer.
Two, Cutting a Log.
Digging a Hole.
Sitting at the Campfire.

Linoleum cuts

All topics as suggested applied to this technique.

Color

Rich House—Poor House, (bright—dull).
Rainy Day—Beautiful Day, (bright—dull).
Storm, (excited).
Adam and Eve Driven from the Garden of Eden.
Desert—Oasis, (monotonous—changing).

Techniques

The child has advanced beyond the use of geometric lines and base-line representations in their linear meaning. With the discovery of the plane, he now feels the need of filling in the spaces, as is seen in the representations of skies which now are painted down to the horizon. Dealing with planes renders crayon unsuitable, and this material is not recommended for use during this age level.

Poster paint is an excellent medium for filling in spaces. Thinner, prepared poster paint will give a better opportunity for mixing color, which now has become more important. Since the child concentrates now more on details, a hair brush is preferable to a bristle brush.

As has been indicated, a technique is only good if it offers a special original contribution that fits the child's needs and helps to express in the easiest way what is in his mind. Such a technique during this period is paper-cutting which offers two important stimulations not offered by any other medium. The natural way of stimulating the child to experience the meaning of overlapping (which is the first introduction into the three-dimensional space concept), has already been disclosed and cannot be replaced by any other technique. Stimulation of *cooperation* through group work is the second important technique. Also here it fulfills a specific purpose with original means. *Clay* will be used for modeling as well as for pottery. Forming with hands as well as using simple one-piece molds is suggested.

SUMMARY   STAGE OF DAWNING REALISM—NINE TO ELEVEN YEARS

Stage	Characteristics	Human Figure	Space	Color	Design	Stimulation Topics	Technique
		(1) Emphasis on clothes (dresses, uniforms), emphasizing difference between girls and boys.	(1) Removal from base-line expression.		First conscious approach toward decoration.	Self-awareness stimulated by characterization of different dresses and suits (professions).	No crayons from now on because of removal from linear expression.
Gang age.	(1) Removal from geometric lines (schema).		(2) Overlapping.	Removal from objective stage of color.	Use in connection with material.		Poster paint.
Preadolescent crisis.	(2) Lack of cooperation.	(2) Greater stiffness as result of egocentric attitude, and the emphasis on details, as clothes, hair, and so forth.	(3) Sky comes down to baseline.	Emphasis on emotional approach to color.	(1) Reproducing techniques emphasizing repetition.	Cooperation and overlapping through group work.	Flat colored chalk.
	(3) Gang age.		(4) Discovery of plane.	Subjective stage of color. Color is used with regard to subjective experience.	(2) Emotional design using the meaning of repetition.	Subjective cooperation through type of topic: "We are building a house."	Clay.
Dawning realism.	(4) Greater awareness of the self with regard to sex (boys and girls).	Tendency toward realistic lines.	(5) Filling in space between base lines.				Linoleum cut.
		Removal from schema.	(6) Difficulties in spatial correlations as result of egocentric attitude and lack of cooperation.		Acquaintance with materials and their function.	Objective cooperation through working method.	Wood.
							Metal.

For crafts, finger paint in connection with *pasteboard* work is suggested.* Work with cotton and wool of a variety of textures and colors is recommended. Acquaintance with as many materials as possible, such as wire, sheet metal, wood, and papier mâché, will stimulate the child to apply design in connection with function and structure of the material †
(Fig. 29).

EXERCISES

(1) Collect the drawings of a fourth or fifth grade. Find out how many children have introduced clothes in their drawings.
(2) Collect the drawings of one child over a period of half a year. Record your observations on the progressive change from geometric lines to realistic lines.
(3) Check the percentage of children who still depend on base-line expressions only, and those who use the spaces between the base lines.
(4) Analyze the space representation of one drawing according to:
(a) Whether or not the child adheres to base lines.
(b) Whether or not the child uses overlappings.
(c) Whether or not the child establishes proper spatial correlations.
(d) Whether or not the sky comes down to the base line (or horizon).
What conclusions can you draw from your analysis in reference to the child's ability to observe visually?
(5) Examine the children's relationship between behavior, character, and personality trends and drawings, with regard to (a) greater stiffness of figures and (b) lack of correlation in space.
(6) Do you find those children more egocentric who do not establish proper spacial correlations?

LABORATORY WORK

(1) Make an abstract design of different materials and structure.
(2) Make a simple object of wire, which shows the characteristics of the material.
(3) Do the same with (a) clay, (b) wood, (c) textiles, (d) cardboard, and (e) papier mâché.
(4) Make several abstract finger paintings, using the motions of your hand and the different structures obtained by the impressions made by the surface of fingers and palm.
(5) Make a cardboard box, using finger paint for decoration.

* Shaw, R. F., *Finger Painting*. Boston: Little, Brown and Co., 1934.
† Browne, Sibyl; Tyrrell, Ethel; Abbihl, Gertrude; and Evans, Clarice, *Art and Materials or the Schools*. New York: Progressive Education Assn., 1943.

(6) Tear a mountain chain from three matching colored papers and arrange them so that overlapping can best be seen.

(7) Make a paper cut, "City," by cutting different types of houses and arranging them properly.

(8) Make a cooperative paper cut, as suggested on p. 81.

(9) Model a mask, expressing yawning, laughing, and so forth, being guided by changes in configuration of your own facial features and muscles when yawning or laughing.

(10) Make a puppet from papier mâché.

CHAPTER VI

The Pseudorealistic Stage

The Stage of Reasoning (11 to 13 years)

PSYCHOLOGICAL ASSUMPTIONS

THE GREAT SIGNIFICANCE OF THIS STAGE CAN BE UNDERSTOOD ONLY when we regard it as a preparatory stage to the approaching crisis of adolescence. After the child has properly gone through the gang age he enters a stage in which he has developed enough intelligence to tackle almost any problem, yet, in his reactions, he still is a child. The difference between child and adult can best be seen in the diversity of their imaginative activity. This can best be observed in the different types of playing. The child plays hide and seek with the same unawareness as he uses a pencil, which he moves up and down while imitating the noises of an airplane. Such unawareness is characteristic of children. Quite obviously, their imagination transforms a pencil into an airplane. All children use their imagination in such an uninhibited way; if an adult would do the same he would be considered insane. For an adult, a pencil is a pencil and the pencil is for writing. The child's imaginative activity is unconscious. The adult's imaginative activity in its effect is controlled. This change in the imaginative activity from the unconscious to critical awareness, introduced by physical changes in the body, is one of the most important characteristics of the crisis of adolescence.

A healthy body can overcome the aftereffects of an operation much easier than a weakened body; therefore it is important to strengthen the body before undergoing a contemplated operation. We take this procedure for granted when dealing with a physical crisis, but it is all too often neglected in cases of emotional disturbances. Neither art educators nor psychologists give the necessary attention to preparing the child for the crises of adolescence. Yet this stage of reasoning is the appropriate period for such physical and psychological conditioning.

Since art education deals to a great extent with imaginative activity, the teacher has an excellent opportunity to influence and control its changes. Thus he will be able to help youth to overcome an important part of this crisis. Most commonly this change is seen in the fact that children are highly creative, whereas adults, because of their critical awareness toward their imaginative activity, generally lose their creative ability.

The important question will then be: How can we prepare the child most properly for this change that he can continue his creative production in spite of his critical awareness? Or, in other words, how can we prepare the child to create in such a way that he looks with pride on his work instead of being ashamed of it. During this stage for the first time the attention has to be shifted from the importance of the working process to an increased emphasis on the final product. Thus, the final art product becomes more and more significant with increasing age. This recognition of the growing significance of the final product is a clear demand on the part of youth, and it must be accepted by educators. The following graph might illustrate the interchanging effect of the importance of the working process upon the final product during the different age periods.

	AGE	2-5	5-7	7-9	9-11	11-13	13-15	15-17	17–
FINAL PRODUCT	Most Important								
	Increasingly Important								
	More Important								
WORKING PROCESS	Unimportant								
	Less Important								
	Important								

Another psychologically important factor comes into the picture. The closer we study adolescence, the more we see a clear distinction in the sensory reactions of the children toward their creative experiences. We see clearly that, whereas one group reacts more definitely toward *visual stimuli,* the other group is more concerned with the interpretation of *subjective experiences.* Visual experiences are defined as those which refer to our optical senses. They are concerned with the differences of color, light, and shadows, introduced through atmospheric conditions, as well as with the perspective interpretation of space. Subjective interpretations are those which emphasize the emotional relationship to the external world in reference to the body self. Visually minded individuals refer in their pictures to environment whereas nonvisually minded individuals are the expressionists. Visual types feel as spectators, looking at their work from outside. Subjectively minded people feel involved in their work. As we approach the crisis of adolescence, during which these types crystallize, we have to pay increasing attention in our stimulation to both of these important experiences. In the same way that we would discourage a visually minded person by stimulating him in referring to subjective experiences, emotional qualities, or body experiences, in the corresponding way we would inhibit a subjectively minded person if we would stimulate him by mere visual experiences. Since traditional art education is mainly built upon visual stimuli, a great part of our youth must feel not only neglected, but frustrated. Many art educators use visual stimulations throughout the secondary level, not realizing that modern expressionist art is a clear indication of the importance of nonvisual stimuli in our present-day life. The knowledge of this fact together with the increasing shift from the working process to the final product is of vital importance for art educators and educators in general who deal with this age level. A more detailed analysis with regard to proper stimulation and the psychological changes which take place during adolescence will follow in the chapter on "The Crisis of Adolescence as Seen in Creative Activity."

FIRST CONCEPT OF NATURALISTIC REPRESENTATIONS

In the human figure

From what has been said it becomes clear that only visually minded children who desire it will arrive at a realistic concept. Under realistic concept of the human figure we understand the concept that is determined by the changing optical effects experienced in different light, space, and atmospheric conditions. From this viewpoint, the drawing of clothes will become a realistic concept as soon as the changing effects which take place when we sit down are *observed*: the clothes fold or wrinkle at the bent parts, lights and shadows are determined by the changes of the sitting body, and so forth. Until he reaches this age level, the child usually employs clothes only for characterizations, to show that "this is a girl" and

"this a man." Henceforth we shall see that the visual child gradually de
velops the urge to add to his characterization the optical changes alread
discussed.

The child starts to observe visually: thus visual observation start;
where mere characterization ends. There is generally a confusion with
regard to visual experiences on the one hand and mere recognition or char
acterization on the other. Stating that the dress is red does not imply ;
visual analysis any more than the bare statement "the boy wears pants.'
Both statements are mere characterizations. They will become visual ex
periences as soon as the changes of red are observed with regard to light
shadow, and distance; or if the changing effect which the "pants" gc
through while the boy is running or otherwise in motion are recognized.

Thus, observation is not the mere ability to see or recognize. It is the
ability to analyze the visual image with regard to its changing effects ir
space. One of the first signs of the discovery of these changing effects is the
drawing of joints. Usually during this age level children develop an
increased desire to include joints in their drawings of the human figure. If
this is noticed by the teacher, it is necessary that he include it in his stimulations by pointing to motions in which the use of the joints is of impor
tance.

In later-developed stages of this age level more detailed observations
are included. The child might even observe that clothes change with different motions. Thus the visually minded child will start to concentrate more
on appearance. He will be eager to include "correct" proportions and
motions. He will use exaggeration less frequently as a means of expression.

Whereas the visually minded child concentrates more on the whole and
it changing effects, *the nonvisually minded child will concentrate more on
the details* in which he is emotionally interested. In his interpretation of
expressions he still uses the method of exaggerating important parts. The
visually minded child sees the human figure as a whole, while the nonvisually minded child is particularly concerned with the details which are
emotionally significant to him. Thus he refers more to the self and his body
feeling than to the exterior qualities. His emotional binding dominates his
art. His creative work belongs to the art of expressionism.

Since the best stimulation is the one which appeals most to the child, it
is important to stimulate the child in the direction of his thinking and
feeling. Thus, it would not only be fruitless to divert a child from his own
type, but would be frustrating to him, for it would confront him with experiences which he cannot comprehend. It is, therefore, important to notice
that mere visual stimuli would just as much frustrate the one group as
stimuli which refer to the body self and its emotions would inhibit the

ther group. In a good stimulation, values of appearance which refer to
he changing visual effects are just as important as the emphasis on body
xperiences, expressions, and emotions. That is why it is suggested that
osing models be used during this age. But a pose should never be used
nerely for purposes of imitation! Every pose given to a group must have a
lefinite meaning in order that those who are more dependent on their sub-
ective or emotional interpretation might also have an opportunity of
xpressing themselves. The pose of a beggar who stands on a street corner
hould first be discussed with regard to body motions and exterior values.
After that it is necessary to develop an atmosphere around the posing
igure by discussing the life of a beggar and all its human or social im-
lications. In such a way the teacher will be able to stimulate both types
n his group—the visually minded and the nonvisually minded. The former
vill approach the pose by drawing the model as they *see* it, whereas the
atter will draw an interpretation as they *feel* it. If we would present the
nodel merely in the common way as a visual stimulation (from the view-
oint of what we *see*), we would frustrate a considerable number of
hildren whose approach is equally important. Although both tendencies
re still not conscious to the child, it should be pointed out that this is a
ery important preparation for the stage of critical awareness, the stage
f the crisis of adolescence (Fig. 30).

THE DEVELOPMENT OF TWO DIFFERENT
SPACE CONCEPTS

Although the one group of children is most concerned in discovering
he optical space in its complexity, the other group not only fails to notice
: but retrogrades into former space representations that referred to the
se of base lines. We shall try to explain this apparent retrogression later.
At this point it is important only to note that two different concepts of
pace perception gradually develop as we approach adolescence.

The depth of the visually minded

With regard to the human figure, we defined visual experiences as the
xperiences that refer to the optical changes. In the same way, *we call the
isual space the experiences that refer to the optical changes in space.* One
f the important optical changes is the apparent diminution of distant
bjects. Closely related to this discovery, however, is the meaning of the
orizon. With the recognition of distance, space in its three-dimensional
ualities moves more and more into the focal point of interest of the

Fig. 30. "Beggar" (twelve years). Pose studied from life model. Otherwise drawn imaginatively. Stage of reasoning.

visually minded child. During this period, this move occurs almost entirely intuitively. The child merely follows his growing innate demand and power of observation. With it, light and shadows in their changing effects begin to come into the mental picture of the child. All this is done without awareness of its scientific consequences. Therefore the teacher should know that the stimulation with regard to the optical changes in space is not to be given on the conscious level of pointing toward perspective and its meaning.

Much of the precious creative unawareness of the child has all too soon been spoiled by teachers who cannot early enough see the child's taste adjusted to the adult's taste. Since it is necessary to prepare the child for the stages of critical awareness at a time when this awareness has not yet set in, such early intrusions into the child's development can be disastrous. The change from the unconscious creative approach to the stage of critical awareness has to occur gradually. The more gradually the child can move from one stage into the other, the less is the shock the child suffers from the results of the changes in his imaginative thinking. Thus, if we can *stimulate the child in such a way that he comes in his unaware stages close to the concept which he will finally attain,* we have succeeded in bridging the gap between the unconscious approaches of preadolescence and the approaches of critical awareness which start during adolescence. It is, therefore, a question of preserving the child's creative power beyond the critical stages of adolescence. *If we can do this, we have not only saved one of the greatest gifts of mankind, the ability to create, but we have also kept one of the most important attributes, necessary for proper adjustments: flexibility.* Too early criticism based only on intellectual understanding is therefore much more devastating than a stimulation which remains too long on the level of an unconscious "childish approach." Even the most visually minded child will be perfectly satisfied with stimulations that refer only to subjective observation and not to a constructive analysis of it. The child's own desire is the best measure for his stimulation.

Retrogression to base-line expressions of the nonvisually minded group

It has been observed in many cases that children who have advanced beyond the base-line concept at some point return to the very same kind of space concept. This retrogression to a former concept can only be understood if we study higher art forms of nonvisual art. There we would see that the base-line concept is no longer an unconscious "childish concept." In Egyptian, Assyrian, or medieval art expression, the base line becomes the vehicle of space representations. In this light, base-line expression represent a higher form of nonvisual consciousness, not a retrogression Indeed, the new base-line representations are the forerunners of a more conscious nonvisual art expression. The retrogression, therefore, is only apparent. It is in reality the very same step into the nonvisual sphere as the three-dimensional tendency of space representation is in the realm of visual perception.

In general, however, we shall see that nonvisually minded children concentrate in their representations more on the expression of the self and the emotions resulting from it. For them, space has significance only if it is necessary for their expression. From the very beginning, we will, therefore be able to distinguish visually minded children from the nonvisually minded merely by the choice of representations. The visually minded child prefers environment, feels like a spectator. The nonvisually minded child concentrates more on the self and draws environment only when it has emotional significance for him.

Both groups again develop a strong feeling for spatial correlations of figures in environment which was somewhat weakened through the lack of cooperation during the gang age. Since the child is now in the stage of reasoning, he has overcome an egocentric attitude that prevented him from achieving spatial relationships. If we continue to meet with such drawings we can be sure that we are dealing with children who have not grown out of the gang age. The visually minded child now establishes his spatial correlations on the basis of visual experiences, whereas the nonvisually minded child establishes his correlations mainly through the body-self The stimulation of spatial correlation is now entirely achieved through the choice of the topic. Dramatic stories set in environment are excellent means for stimulating the child's connection of the self to environment This is the age level of "Western Stories." That is why stories dramatically introduced will be very appealing to the child.

Figs. 31 and 32 show dramatic illustrations from the Bible. Moses strikes the rock that water might gush forth. Such stories should be told in such a way that environment and dramatic action are emphasized equally Strong sentiments and feelings in the characters must be developed in the same way as mood, terrain, and atmosphere. Here also the two different reactions toward experiences can clearly be seen. In Fig. 31, the painting by a nonvisually minded child, the experiences are centered in Moses alone and how in his anger he struck the rock so that water should emerge. Fig. 32, on the other hand, the painting of a visually minded child, shows us a "spectacle." How grand it is to see that water flows out of the rock! In Fig. 31, nothing but experiences of the self are embodied. The experience

Fig. 31. "Moses Strikes the Rock." Nonvisually minded representation of a thirteen-year-old boy. Experience is focussed at the self. The creator feels involved in the experience of striking the rock as the actor.

Fig. 32. "Moses Strikes the Rock." Visually minded representation of a thirteen-year-old boy. Experience is focussed at the scene. The creator feels as a spectator.

of form is intensely personal and finds its strongest expression in the linea
ments of Moses. In Fig. 32, we feel that we are taking part in this grea
moment as spectators. In the former, everything has been concentrated o
expression and gesture; in the latter, it is the arrangement of the figure
the rich colors, the motions of the people, the water, the sky, and enviror
ment—all that is visually perceivable, that has become the main probler
of representation.

We see the enormous effect the miracle had on the crowd. Some peopl
have jars with which to fetch water, others are drinking it directly fror
the earth. *Many* dramatic episodes can be seen, but all are subordinated t
the great miracle of the waterfall, the rock with the water gushing fortl
Nowhere in this picture, however, do we perceive those intense persona
sensations that hold our attention on Fig. 31, in which even the water, th
only object except the person of Moses, has been drawn in a compact mas
as though it could be grasped rather than seen. The fact that in this pictur
the arm has been added later, also shows clearly the synthetic mode o
procedure characteristic for nonvisual expression. This will be discussed i
greater detail in the next stage.

The importance of stimulating both visual and nonvisual experience
becomes evident when we look at these two pictures. We will also realiz
how differently correlation has been experienced. In the drawing by th
visually minded child, figures are correlated to landscape through the com
mon spectacle, through the visual experience which is focused on th
miracle. The nonvisually minded child, however, established correlatior
mainly through his intense body feelings and the emotions on which th
whole picture is centered. Both pictures, however, have in common th
strong dramatic effect which moved both children to realize their stron
feelings for correlations. The unawareness of both creators gave them ful
freedom for expressing the dramatic effect so vividly.

COLOR

The child does not develop in particular directions only, but does so a
a whole. If single trends are discussed separately it springs from the desir
to present a more systematic approach and from the inability to discuss al
trends simultaneously. However, space, color, and the self are fused in th
creative development of the child, and form a unity, a part of the tota
growth of the child. After what has been said, the child's tendency will be
understood if we see the same changing effects in color that were discussec
in relation to space and the representation of the human figure.

Only the visually minded children show the tendency to see color in its
anging effects. To have a visual concept of color does not mean merely
have the ability to recognize color. "This is green, red, or blue" means
ly that we can distinguish colors from one another, but not that we
ve a visual concept of color. To have a visual concept means that we
tice the *changes* color undergoes under different external conditions.
he same color appears different in light and shadow. The surrounding
lors reflect upon the focal color and make it seem different. Red in blue
ght looks different from red in orange light. Red in the distance looks
fferent from red in the foreground. Red on dull days appears quite
anged on bright days. Countless other factors impinge upon color to
ake it relative to prevailing conditions. To notice these changing effects
one of the attributes of visually minded individuals. *During this im-
ortant period which precedes the crisis of adolescence, the visually minded
hild will begin to adjust colors to his visual impressions, whereas the non-
sually minded child depends greatly on his emotional reactions toward
lor.*

Much has been written about the psychology of color, its emotional
fects on individuals. Such emotional reactions to color are to a large
xtent determined associatively, through the effect of past experiences.
hus, to one individual horror can mean red (he might relate it associa-
vely to blood), whereas to another it might be green. Psychoanalysis has
ade it evident that all rigid theories which refer emotional reactions to
olor are to a great extent outmoded. At least, generalizations should not
e applied to teaching to deny the effectiveness of the use of color theories
n leading to creative approaches. Emotional reactions to color are highly
dividualized. The nonvisually minded child uses color often in contradic-
ion to nature according to his individual emotional reaction. Color, there-
ore, becomes highly subjective in its meaning.

Also with regard to color, the main problem during this age period will
e to find means of stimulation that gradually lead the child to the stages
f critical awareness. If this is done gradually, the child will not feel the
hocks resulting from the awareness of the discrepancy between his mental
icture and his actual representation. If we now can stimulate the child
ffectively to see or feel color in the stage of unawareness, we will prevent
im from being disappointed at his "inability" to express his mental
icture. The better the color stimulation in the unaware and critical-aware-
ess stages, the more have we succeeded in bridging the gap of the crisis
f adolescence. How this can effectively be done will be discussed in the
section, "Stimulation."

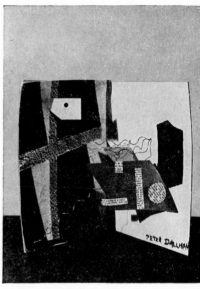

a

Fig. 33. Design in Material. (Courtesy Educational Project, Museum of Moder. Art, N. Y.) *a.* fourteen-year-old boy; *b.* fourteen and a half years.

DESIGN

With the awakening concept for reality, the conscious approach towar. design becomes increasingly significant. Whereas the visually minded chil. will more and more be concerned with the aesthetic function of design expressed by the feeling for "color schemes, rhythm, and balance," th. nonvisually minded child will more and more show the tendency to wor! either directly with materials and use them functionally or concentrat more on emotional abstractions (Fig. 33a). Both groups should be give: the type of stimulation needed for developing properly. Since the child i still in his "unaware approaches," burdening him with theories would b out of place. The only effect would be an inhibited reaction at a time whe: the child still proceeds freely in his creative work. We shall see in th. section, "Stimulation," how design and color are closely interwoven.

The visually minded child might start to relate forms of nature t design. The stylizing effect—that is, the process of simplification, migh become a part of the child's experience. Since the laws of symmetry ar more related to dogmatic periods, including periods of symbolism, it seem to be more and more out of place to include it at a time when individ ualism, emotions, and social changes dominate in our lives. Consequently dustrial forms rather than flowers should be used for design purposes, cause flowers always stimulate a desire to draw symmetrical patterns. aking block prints of symbols of the different professions, like a tele- aph pole for a telegrapher, a stylized microscope for the scientist, and forth, will not only lead to a more modern approach toward design, but ll be excellent as stimulations for the nature of stylizing.

During this period it is important to confront the child with industrial oducts as examples of good functional use of different materials. From e kitchen utensil and furniture to the streamlined car or machine, the ild should learn to adapt his design to the material. The child should be ven an opportunity to use all types of scraps creatively, even if it is only r the pleasure of working out forms or shapes in different materials thout relating them to a definite purpose (Fig. 33b).

If a potter's wheel is obtainable, the child will enjoy operating it. How- er the child should be allowed to play with the wheel without being mpered by too many technical procedures. Skill and body coordinations finitely will greatly improve the child's confidence in his abilities, which of so vital importance for the period of the crisis of adolescence. The eation of forms that can stand the critical awareness of the adolescent ll further help to bridge the gap between childhood and adolescence.

In the section, "Stimulation," there is described an approach to the use color for emotional abstractions which are a part of the design concept the nonvisually minded group.

MODELING

The meaning of modeling during this preparatory stage is of special gnificance. Here, better than in any other field, we can build a bridge tween the unconscious approach to three-dimensional expression (which e called *modeling*) and the conscious approach (which we shall call *ulpturing*). This can be done easier in clay than in painting, since the fference between modeling and sculpturing is not as great as the differ- ce in the approaches to painting, in which, especially for the visually inded, a whole transfiguration from the plane into three-dimensional ace takes place. No change of such importance can be seen in clay work. herefore, it is much easier to prepare the child in this field to face his ork with critical awareness, with confidence, and without the shock hich endangers his further creative production.

Since environment is excluded or, at least, minimized in sculpturing, sually minded as well as nonvisually minded children face the same bject matter. This also contributes greatly to make modeling a particu-

larly effective means of stimulation. The meaning of clay work during th
important period of transition is to lead the child from modeling to scul
turing in such a way that the child does not become aware of this tran
tion. This can best be done by modeling either from real or imaginati
poses. In real poses, the model is posing throughout the session. A
imaginative pose is one that the model or the student subjectively su
gests only in the beginning as a means of stimulation, but the actu
modeling is done without the pose. The pose serves then only as stimul
and control. The latter procedure, if well handled, is by far the better on
In both cases, however, it is necessary to give the pose a definite meanin
"A man carrying a heavy load," "A scrubwoman," "Tired," and so fort
The procedure of stimulation will be discussed in the following chapte
Without giving the pose a meaning, we would frustrate the group of th
subjectively minded children (Fig. 34a).

The difference of the visually minded and subjectively minded a
proaches can be seen both in working process as well as in the choice
subject matter. The visually minded group will concentrate on the chan
ing effects caused by the differences of the motions of the posing figure
light and shadows. The nonvisually minded will use the posing figu
merely as a stimulus and will model their subjective experiences of th
"man carrying a heavy load," "the scrubwoman," and so forth. Where
the visually minded child will most likely lean closer to the correct inte
pretation of the posing model, the nonvisually minded will give his ow
subjective expression. With regard to the difference of the workir
method, we shall see that the visually minded uses more and more th
analytic method of pulling out the details from the whole. Naturally, th
corresponds to visual thinking. When we think of a tree, we first think
the tree in its entirety and then of the details—the structure of the bar
the branches, the kind of twigs, and the foliage. The synthetic metho
however, will be used only by the nonvisually minded child. His thinkin
relates to the details that are of emotional significance. He builds up h
final impression out of a synthesis of partial impressions. It is therefo
of vital significance not to divert to the analytic process a child who us
the synthetic method. We would only disturb or frustrate the child
thinking.

In the same way that we encourage the visually minded child in h
modeling by directing his attention to the visual changes of form cause
through light and shadow, do we encourage the nonvisually minde
individual by stimulating subjective experiences. This way we graduall
move from the unconscious form of modeling to the conscious approac
of sculpturing. Henceforth no scenes which include environment and fig

g. 34a. "Jacob's Dream" (modeled in clay by thirteen-year-old boy). The otion was first experienced on the self.

ig. 34b. "Cow and Calf" (modeled by thirteen-year-old girl).

ures should be used. If such scenes are needed for illustrative purposes, th
should no longer be done on a creative base, but strictly as scale mode
Scenes like an "Indian Village" containing Indians no longer satisfy t
approaching critical awareness. Modeling shifts gradually to sculpturi
by eliminating all illustrative tendencies and by concentrating on moti
and expression of the human figure.

STIMULATION

Stimulation during this important period must be entirely focused up
the meaning of this stage as a preparation for the approaching crisis
adolescence. In other words, stimulation now means bridging the gap b
tween the unaware approaches of childhood and the critical awareness
adulthood. The greater the gap, the greater will be the shock which resu
from the inability to endure the coming critical awareness. Therefore t
main tendency of art education during this period should be to elimina
the gap between unawareness and awareness as gradually and as efficient
as possible. If this self-realization, which arises during adolescence,
introduced gradually, we spare children the shock that prevents the majc
ity from continuing their creative work. Since this is only an indication
frustrated feelings, the continuation of creative work not only preserv
their creative power but also influences personality growth in gener.
Especially is this true because creative thinking is closely related to flexib
ity of thinking, and the types of personalities developed by such stimul
tions will face life more flexibly, more creatively, and with better abili
for self-adjustment.

Human figure

For the visually minded, the critical awareness during adolescen
demands the drawing of correct proportions and motions with their chan
ing effects. The nonvisually minded require greater concentration c
gesture and expression. How can we stimulate these factors without doir
harm to the unaware, creative approach of the child? Three approach
are particularly valuable during this period. In "teaching" proportions
this age, the word "proportion" never should be brought into the co
sciousness of the child. Such a procedure would only inhibit his furth
creative work, since the child would start measuring proportions and app
rigid methods which are the death of any creative work. Therefore, mea
of stimulations should be found which make the child *experience* the cc
rect kind of proportion. This can best be done by the choice of topi

opics that compare the sizes of the self to environment are best suited or such purposes. Although it would not be useful to lead the child's atten- on consciously to the fact of comparing sizes, it will be important to clude this factor in the discussion. As an example, we give the special neaning of the topic, "Fighting the Fire in a Burning House." After ask- g, "Who has seen a house burning?" we will receive many descriptions f burning houses.

These many descriptions should have a proper balance of visual and onvisual experiences. Some children will be attracted by the beauty of the flames and their glowing colors, others will "feel" with the people who were living in the house and will become emotionally involved in the fate f those who lost their belongings. Still other children will be more con- erned with the technical procedures of fighting the flames. Especially the oys might become interested in this angle. But at all times we will have pportunities to direct attention to comparative proportions with questions ke: "How high did we have to climb to fight the fire?" "Did people jump ut of the window?" "How high did they jump?" "How long was the fire- nen's hose?" "How far up could they reach without climbing the ladder?" nd so forth. Such questions will inspire both groups: the visually minded ecause they become visually aware of the comparative proportions, and the nonvisually minded because they refer in their drawings to the body ctions and its emotional qualities. Many other topics like: "Sitting Under Tree," "Reaching for an Apple on a Tree," "Sitting in a Rowboat," Looking Out of the Window" and so forth, will stimulate the child to mpare sizes. However, any "correction" of proportions would only frus- ate the child. If the child does not react to the mentioned stimuli, we have o other means of making him more aware of them than by trying more imulations of the same type.

The second approach suitable to prepare the child for the coming ritical awareness of sizes and proportions is the use of posing models as a neans of stimulation. Here, too, we must give both groups a possibility or self-expression. That is why the posing model should be given a mean- g, as has been said before. As an example, we cite a particular pose: Carrying a Heavy Load on the Shoulder." "Who carries heavy loads?" Have you *seen* people carrying heavy loads?" "Have *you yourself* ever car- ed a heavy load? At what opportunity?" "Of course, workers on the ocks carry sacks of flour, or a poor woman carries a bundle of wood on er shoulder, or refugees fleeing from their burning houses." "How do we arry a heavy load?" (Let the boy or girl pose while putting a load on his r her shoulder.) "You could not go upright, very well, could you? You ould lose your balance. I also notice that you have your feet apart and

not together, why do you do that, for the same purpose of holding bett
balance?" "How do you hold the load? I notice your hands are close t
the shoulder. I see, because in this way you have a better support on th
shoulder than if you were to hold them out." "In what direction are yo
looking when you carry the load? Surely you have to look in the directio
you are walking."

All these questions will bring the pose into a higher consciousness. Th
visually minded will draw what they, now consciously, see, whereas th
nonvisually minded will refer to the experiences of the self. For bot
groups, however, it will be of benefit if the posing model does not keep th
pose. The visually minded will have to concentrate much more on the
visual experience by memorizing the image, and the nonvisually minde
will use the posing model only as a stimulus, concentrating otherwi
entirely on expression—that is, the mental picture he has formed, whic
is a resultant of his body feelings and emotional experiences (Fig. 35).

The third approach for getting the representation of the human figu
more closely related to the adolescent stages, deals with a method i
modeling. It is most stimulating to characterize first the personality of th
modeled figure and let it then go through the motion as if it were a motio
picture. For example: "A visitor (your grandpa) comes to see you. He si
down and tells you a story." The child would first model grandpa as h
arrives and would actually put him then into the position which finall
indicates telling a story. "How does your grandpa sit when he tells you
story? Does he hold a book in his hand? Does he support his head? Does h
stretch out his legs or does he cross them?" and so forth. The plasticity c
clay permits the expression of this kinetic experience. While going throug
the motions, the child will grow more consciously aware of them, and i
turn will bring himself closer to a level of creative production capable c
withstanding the critical awareness, which has to be expected soon.

Stimulation of space

The stimulation of spatial experiences again will have to be channele
in two directions. First, to prepare the visually minded child for a spac
concept that is more closely related to the adolescent concept of realizin
the visual space. Second, to prepare the nonvisually minded child for th
importance of the emotional tie-up of space and the self. We know muc
too well of the frightening effect which teaching of perspective has c
some of our children. This effect is especially frightening for children wh
have no desire for the realization of such a space concept. This group, whic
is the nonvisually minded, has no comprehension of this way of percei

ig. 35. "Thinking" (thirteen years). The child still approaches his subject
atter without critical awareness, yet his work shows a clear concept of the self.
he motion is experienced on the self.

ing space. However, *there is no need for including perspective in our art program as long as there is no demand for it* from the children.

For the visually minded, means of introducing a visual space concept should be found which excludes the teaching of constructive methods of perspective. To do that, it is most inspiring to refer even in the visual space concept to nonvisual means, to experience the different intensities of emotional experiences which are both far away and close to us. "What would happen, if one among us would suddenly die?" All children would immediately realize the tremendous intensity of this experience when it is so closely related to us. At the same time, the deaths of thousands of people on battlefields, in factories, and other places do not affect us much. The intensity of this experience grows and diminishes with the distance. Visual space, too, increases and diminishes in size and intensity, depending on the distance. However, in visual space this intensity depends only on the visual interest which we take in objects close to us, whereas in emotional experiences we can focus our greatest interest even on things that are not close to us. Thus, the intensity of nonvisual space is governed by the emotions we associate with the experience. To preclude the possibility of frustrating either experience in our stimulations, we have to refer to visual differences as well as to the different intensities of emotions.

Color

Realistic color—that is, the color of the visually minded, can only be stimulated by actual experiences with nature. The different intensities—brightness and dullness and use of colors with regard to distance, shadows and lights—can be brought into the consciousness only by observing them. Few children, and by no means all adults, can do that. We ourselves comprehend how little we see in comparison to some artist's concept of color. And some of us know that we are unable to see the "blue shadow" which we are supposed to see according to the old method of teaching. Not all of us can see the changing effects of colors, and there is no need for all of us to see them. What is a stimulation for one can mean frustration for another. There exist too many instances of frustrated children and unhappy adults, compelled to enroll in art classes in which they received visual stimuli only and in which they were forced "to see color."

Personification of color is a method that can be used for both groups, though it will appeal more to the nonvisually minded children. By personification of color is meant the seeing and dealing with color as if it were a living being. For example, the telling of some such story as the following would be effective. "Imagine you feel very happy and want to go on a hike. Everything around you is marvelous, just wonderful. Environment is beautiful, bright, and the atmosphere is happy. As you walk you see in the distance your friend, your most beloved friend. You thought how marvelous it would be to have him with you. And there he comes. Now you are talking about the most intimate things, and you become so friendly that you feel almost united with him. As you continue on your way, the atmosphere suddenly changes for the worse. It gets dark, dreary, and mysterious. And as you go on, someone stops you on the way and tells you that you are not permitted to continue; this road is not for you."

Now imagine that you are "red" in this story. How does red feel in a marvelous environment, happy and bright? What color would you choose as an environment for red to make it happy? How would you indicate to make red move on smoothly? What color is the best friend of red, whom red expected to meet? When red and his friend were talking so intimately, to which color would they unite? As they went on and the atmosphere darkened and the environment became mysterious, how would red change? How would its friend change? How would environment change with regard to red and its friend? What color would come in their way and prohibit them from continuing?

Of course there are hundreds of such stories. Almost any story can be translated into "color." This personification of color introduces it as a living symbol. No verbal theory can ever give as good an introduction into the living qualities of color as such personifications. Such an introduction into abstract design will also lead into the understanding of the nature of emotional abstract design. It is much better than music as a means of stimulation, since we have here means to refer to real living qualities. Such an interpretation of color will be highly individualized and the control by the teacher can only be in the direction of color relationships. "Is this really your friend? But he is quite different from you, isn't he?" Only such stimulations should be used to direct the child in his color intuitions.

Through such methods the child will not only gain more confidence in his use of color, but will also approach a more conscious relationship to it, which is vitally necessary for the proper adjustment to the coming stage, the crisis of adolescence.

The following list of topics should serve only as examples for the different kinds of stimulation, which all have the same aim—to bridge the gap between childhood and adolescence, unawareness and critical awareness, which so often has shown its disastrous effect on personality development.

Topics

Action from imagination

> Farmer Going Home Before Storm.
> Refugees Fleeing on Road.
> Trapeze Artist.
> Theatre Performances of Dramatic Content.
> Rowing a Boat.
> Fishing in Pond.
> Hunting Scenes.
> All Gymnastic Experiences.
> Men Working on the Street.
> Men Digging a Hole.

From posing model (not frontal posing)

> Woman Scrubbing a Floor.
> A Beggar on Street Corner.
> Woman Sweeping Floor.
> Tired from Work.
> Lifting a Heavy Load.
> A Mother Feeding a Baby.
> A Girl Reading.
> Thinking at Desk.

Stimulation of proportions

> Sitting Under a Tree.
> Burning House with Ladder Going Up on it
> Climbing a Tree.
> Reaching for an Apple on a Tree.
> Looking Out of the Window.

Dramatic

> Illustrations of books or stories.

Color

> Before the Storm on the Field.
> Impressions.
> Cold in Winter.
> Fall Storm.
> Snow Storm.
> Sunset.
> Introduce moods.
> Personification of color.

Murals

> Educational and historical related to subject
> matter signified by words *from* and *to*.

From Raw Product to Final Product (science).
From Birth to Death (history).
From Coast to Coast (geography, travel).

riezes

All topics with continuity:
Pulling Sled up Hill and down.
Fruit Harvest.
Carnival Scene.
Races.

a Design

Characterize a profession by means of symbolic
   designs (telegraph worker, tailor, shoemaker,
   cook, physician, painter, architect, railway
   conductor and so forth).

Use different materials in a functional way.
Abstract designs made from different materials
   to learn their function: wire, sheet metal,
   glass, wood, cardboard.
Knowledge of industrial designs: utensils, furniture.

a Clay

From posing model (topics as discussed).
Actions from imagination.

Kinetic motions:
   Picking up Something (potatoes).
   Mother Holding the Baby.
   Getting Tired.
   Sitting Down, Reading a Book.

Techniques

As has been said before, technique is closely related to the needs for
xpression. The technique which does not help the child to express his
articular desires is not a good one. During this period, the visually minded
iild relates his work more and more to reality. The most suitable tech-
ique will be one which easily permits the portrayal of effects in nature.
ince atmosphere and sky in nature are not opaque but have a transparent
iaracter, a medium having such transparent qualities would be most suit-
ble. This technique is *water color*. At this stage we can even encourage
ie child to make visual use of the happy accidents which occur when the
olors in a sky run together and form "clouds" in the most different

shapes. At first the whole paper may be moistened with brush or hand
before the child starts to paint. Since the child now approaches his painting
visually, such accidents as the formation of clouds or the mixing of color
will stimulate the child for his next work. Running of colors, which could
have been most discouraging at a time where linear representation domin
ated the preschematic or schematic stage, is now most stimulating.

Referring again to the quotation of Leonardo da Vinci to the effec
that an art work should look complete in every stage, will help in stimulat
ing the visually minded child in building up a visual concept. The sequenc
of how a picture is painted is here of deciding influence. For example, w
are thinking of a painting in which farmers rush home before the rising
storm. If we would ask the child to stop painting after he has finished th
stormy sky (which covers the *whole* sheet, of course), the sky as such could
exist and could be called complete. If the child then added the field with
its stormy waves and we interrupted the child again, the picture again
would look complete. The child might then add a farm or a tree and finally
would paint the farmers in the foreground as they hurriedly leave th
field. The picture has grown organically and looked complete at ever
stage. Besides that, we have the feeling that the sky is really behind th
tree or the house without appearing to cut out the part of the sky covered
by it. This *organic* growth of the picture is a vital part of a method o
approach which will help to bridge the gap to which we have referred dur
ing this period so frequently. In order to paint on the sky, the child mus
wait until it is dry; otherwise the foreground would blur with the back
ground. It is also of great advantage to use opaque colors, such as poste
paint, for the foreground. This creates a still stronger feeling for th
transparency of the atmosphere and the opaque quality of objects.

With regard to mural painting, it is suggested that either egg temper;
or ordinary poster paint be used. If possible, murals should be painted
directly, but if this is not possible, good craft paper tacked on the wall, o
stretched on stretchers while it is moist (when it dries, it tightens) wil
serve very well. For painting directly on the wall, one or two coats of fla
oil paint will serve as sizing. Bristle brushes for large spaces and hai
brushes for details are advisable. Preferably, murals should not be carefully
planned at this age level because careful planning destroys much of th
intuitive quality and reduces interest. A small sketch, which tells approxi
mately what will be on the mural, will be sufficient. Children should have
all possible freedom in painting and organizing murals. Often it is good
practice to permit two or more children to work on one mural. It must be
remembered that *a mural is a decoration of a wall and that it must tell*

tory. Sizes can differ with regard to importance. Since the child is still in the unaware creative stage, no further explanations should be given about the nature of a mural, but the teacher should have in mind that a naturalistic execution is contrary to the essence of decoration.

Techniques in clay refer to modeling, which gradually shifts to sculpturing and pottery. Also here, especially with regard to the latter, no planning should be done. Planning pottery belongs to the last stages and is most difficult. Both techniques have been discussed previously.

All other techniques as linoleum cuts or designing in different materials should be continued in the direction indicated in the general discussion on design.

PSYCHOLOGICAL CONCLUSIONS

Since this age seems to be of special significance for the further development of the child, especially with regard to the crisis of adolescence, the following generalizations will indicate clearly the issues involved. As is the case in all phases of this age level, the most important contribution art education can make toward the adjustment of personality is to help bridge the gap between childhood and adulthood. The more gradually this can be done, the less will this period be characterized by disappointments, frustrations, or even shocks. As we have previously said, one of the characteristics of adolescence is the change of the imaginative activity from uncontrolled to controlled, and can best be seen in the different ways children and adults play. If this change comes suddenly—that is, if the child becomes suddenly critically aware of his "childish behavior reactions" or his "uncontrolled imaginative activity," the usual result is a shock. As one of the consequences of this shock the child stops his creative work. He "can't draw anything" because his sudden critical awareness realizes the "inefficient" childish approach. The drawing expression seems "childish" and "ridiculous" because of the sudden awakening of an adult attitude.

The problem is how to make this change gradual. If we can stimulate the child's unaware production to such an extent that it reaches in his unaware stages a "creative maturity" which will be able to stand the critical awareness which once will set in, we have kept the child from making a sudden change, and have protected him from disappointments or shocks with regard to his changing imaginative activity. The following graph indicates more clearly the effect of proper art stimulation on personality development:

SUMMARY   PSEUDOREALISTIC STAGE OF REASONING—ELEVEN TO THIRTEEN YEARS

Characteristics	Human Figure	Space	Color	Design	Stimulation Topics	Techniques
Developed intelligence, yet unawareness.	Introduction of joints.	Three-dimensional space expressed by diminishing sizes of distant objects.	Changes of color in nature with regard to distance and mood (visually minded).	Personification of color.	Figures in dramatic environment.	Water color
Realistic approach (unconscious).	Visual attention to changes introduced through motion or atmosphere (visually minded).	Horizon line (visually minded).		Conscious approach to stylizing of industrial products (symbols for professions).	Actions from imagination and posing model (with meaning).	Mixed technique (water color and tempera).
					Relation of proportion of figures to environment.	Poster paint.
Tendency toward visual or non-visual mindedness.	Proportion	Retrogression of non-visually minded to base lines or exprssion of environment only when significant.	Emotional reaction to color of non visually minded (not related to nature).		Color moods.	Bristle brush.
					Color expression through personification. Illustrations of dramatic stories.	Hair brush.
Love for action and dramatization.	Emphasis on expression of non-visually minded.			Function of different materials, and simple designs related to them.		Linoleum.
						Clay.
					Murals ("from-to"). See design.	Materials for design (wood, metal, stone).

CHILDHOOD				ADOLES-CENCE	ADULTHOOD		
5-7	7-9	9-11	11-13	13-17	17-20	20-	Line of ←controlled activity
							Line of ←unaware activity
UNAWARE STAGES				CRITICAL AWARENESS	AWARE STAGES		

— — — — — — Meaning of good art stimulation during period of "reasoning".

—————— Normal curve without good stimulation stops far below the "line of controlled activity" thus creating a gap of indecision.

ᴡᴡᴡᴡ Characterization of fluctuation between childlike unawareness and the controlled activity of adults.

—·—·—·— Smooth curve of the "genius" who gradually moves into the stages of "critical awareness", usually at a much earlier age.

From this graph it becomes evident that the more we prepare the child during his unaware stages to develop freedom and to use approaches in his art expression which can stand the stages of critical awareness, the smoother will be his growth into the stages of adulthood. The *undecided period,* however, in which the individual feels grown out of childhood and not yet fit for adulthood, one of the most deciding periods in life, will be discussed in the next chapter.

EXERCISES

(1) Collect the drawings of a sixth or seventh grade. Find out how many children observe visually by drawing sizes for distant objects with "correct proportions" diminishing.
(2) Check the percentage that retrogresses to base-line expressions.
(3) Check drawings in which houses, figures, and trees are represented according to proportion.
(4) Relate your findings to visual or nonvisual aptitudes among the children.
(5) Group the drawings of seventh grade according to a predominance of subjective trends, referring to non-visual experiences and visual predominance. How great is the percentage of either group? How many are in-between?
(6) Analyze one drawing, using the following scheme:

	Yes	No
Proportion of value		
Correct proportion		
Uses base lines		
Diminishing sizes of distant objects		
Realistic coloring		
Coloring not related to nature		
Predominance of environment		
Predominance of figure		
Predominance of appearance		
Predominance of expression		

(7) What conclusion in regard to the child's aptitudes can you draw from this analysis?

LABORATORY WORK

(1) Model a woman scrubbing the floor, or performing some other action.

(2) Draw the same figure and think of an environment which fits best to the chosen topic.

(3) Make a cooperative design of a frieze, "Going Home from the Field," by asking each student to paint a worker with a shovel, a rake, or another tool on the shoulder. The drawing should fill the whole sheet of paper. Tack the series of drawings together around the room or along the wall.

(4) Design a symbol for a profession. Make a textile print from it by repeating the design.

(5) Make an emotional design using personification of color. (See p. 116)

(6) Make a functional form of a cup that lends itself for casting a one-piece mold.

(7) Make a one-piece mold and cast six cups.

(8) Design and execute a functional wooden knob for a drawer or door.

(9) Make a stage for your puppets.

(10) Make stage designs for a play, emphasizing different moods.

CHAPTER VII The Period of Decision

The Crisis of Adolescence
as Seen in Creative Activity

CRISIS MEANS PASSING FROM ONE STAGE TO ANOTHER UNDER GREAT
difficulty. This is true physically, emotionally, or mentally. When undergoing an operation, the time the body needs to adapt itself to the new
status created by the operation, is called a *crisis*. Since adolescence is
considered as a stage in the development of human beings, this crisis
is connected with the difficulties of passing from one developmental stage
to another, from the period of childhood to that of maturity.*

Because the crisis of adolescence is connected with bodily, as well as
with emotional, changes, we deal here with a complex crisis in which
body, emotions, and mind have to adjust to a new situation. Indeed, we
can, therefore, say that this is an *important period of decision* in human
development. That it is a period of decisive changes can be seen in the
different behavior reactions and attitudes of people before and after adolescence. How often do we experience such sudden changes from happy,
open-minded children to shy and serious-looking youths. Much of this
change is due to the degree of difficulty under which the individual has

* Munro, T., "Adolescence and Art Education," in *Methods of Teaching the Fine Arts.*
University of North Carolina Press, 1935.

passed the crisis of adolescence. The less the child is affected by the changes of body and mind, the easier he can adjust to the new situation. The greater the difficulties were, the less was the child prepared to face the crisis properly. The question is, how can art education help to ease the crisis of adolescence? This can best be studied if we investigate the psychological changes which directly refer to the changes of the creative concept.

THE PSYCHOLOGICAL CHANGE IN THE IMAGINATIVE CONCEPT

If we attempt to investigate the psychological change of the imaginative concept, it is necessary to consider the facts which determine it before and after adolescence. It is especially important to stress those facts that cause this change. They can best be observed in the intermediary phase of representations expressing the pre- and postadolescent stages. For this purpose the topic "Playing Tag on the Schoolground" was given to a number of elementary-school children of the first three grades, high-school boys and girls of the junior high school, and college students, approximately 300 of each group.

Children and students were under no compulsion to draw the topic, but did so only if they wished. Individuals without prior special training in art were selected for this study. Of interest are the different ways of expressing the experience of catching and being caught, on the one hand, and the spatial representation of the school ground, on the other. But it was also important to note that 95 per cent of all elementary-school children made some attempt to represent this experience, whereas only 3 per cent of the college students tried to depict this well-known game. Both facts—the different kinds of interpretation and the small percentage of the high-school, and the still smaller percentage of the college, students who attempted to draw the given topic (in contrast to an almost 100 per cent participation by the elementary-school children)—will give us a deep insight into the nature of this part of the crisis of adolescence.

In looking at the *children's* drawings, two striking features are apparent. (1) We see no attempt at realistic representations, neither in the representations of the human figures nor in the representations of the school ground. (2) The lower the age of the group, the less the attempt is made to indicate environment.

Let us select one drawing and describe it in greater detail, stressing some of the attributes more or less characteristic of all the representations of this age group. The child, a boy six years and six months of age, intro

Fig. 36. "Playing Tag on the Schoolground" (six and a half years old). Notice the exaggerated arm of the catching boy and the omitted arms of the captive. (Geometric lines. School ground is expressed by base line only.)

duced a representative symbol for "boy," an oval for "body" and a circle for "head." "Arms" and "legs" are expressed differently in the representation of the catching boy and the captive. Whereas the arms of the captive are omitted entirely, those of the captor are very much overemphasized, indicating the importance of the subjective experience of reaching out to catch. This finds its strongest expression in the exaggerated symbol of "the grasping hands" (Fig. 36). We also see a difference in the length of the legs in both figures. Looking at the other drawings of this age group, we frequently see the same difference in the representation of this part of the body—shorter legs for the captive and longer legs for the captor. We can conclude that "shorter legs" indicate "slower running" whereas "longer legs" mean "faster running." This confirms only what we have discussed in the chapter dealing with preschematic and schematic stages. The school ground is indicated by a base line only, which shows that the subjective feeling of being a part of environment is the only spatial experience the child has.

Fig. 37. "Playing Tag on the School Ground" (nine years old). Slight exaggeration of important parts. Characterization of environment (still base-line concept). "Clothes" replace geometric lines.

From this description as well as from our study in general, it is apparent that the child's creative expression is mainly connected with such subjective experiences as bodily feelings, muscle sensations, and touch impressions. It also is obvious that the child's way of perceiving space is determined by his subjective relationship to it, since the child's perception is derived from bodily, not from visual, experiences. The proportions in the child's representations are proportions of value, not the result of esthetic evaluations. That is why it can be assumed that *the child's world of imagination is mainly bound up with the self,* with subjective feelings and subjective relationships toward surroundings.

Let us look at another drawing which will lead us a step further toward the period of adolescence. It is the drawing of a nine-year-old girl and is another characteristic example chosen from the 300 of its kind. This drawing (Fig. 37) compared with the other, most obviously shows a greater relationship to "reality." The girls wear dresses. There even is an attempt to portray the flying hair of the running girls. Although unimportant details can be seen, there still is a clear overemphasis of the arm of the catching girl, thereby expressing the importance of this part. There distinctly is a greater emphasis on environmental objects. The school ground is indicated by trees and by a fence which surrounds the field. The space in the picture is divided into three sections. On the base line of the upper section there is the above-mentioned fence crossing the paper horizontally; then the middle section with the girls, as the focus of the experience; and the lower section with a fence standing on the bottom edge of the paper, which represents the base line. Although the fence is in the visual foreground, it is represented smaller than the girls, almost half the size. But if we consider the motion of the figures, we see a greater stiffness, even a lack of correlation between them. This is typical for the representations of this age group (see chapter on "Gang Age"). On the other hand, a greater emphasis on single details, as the flying hair, shows the interest in things of significance. The nicely designed dresses of the girls, both in front view, hardly touch each other. If the somewhat exaggerated arm were not drawn, the topic would scarcely be recognizable.

From this representation we can assume that a definite *tendency exists to replace mere symobls ("oval" for "body") by a representation which is more related to reality.* But as we have seen in our general discussion of this stage, this approach toward a realistic representation is due to a greater consciousness of the self deriving from the thought "I am wearing a dress," but is not a result of a visual concept. The proportion of value seen in the size of the girls which, compared with the trees, are drawn according to the degree of importance, still shows the lack of visual experiences, or at least a strong dominance of a subjective attitude toward the representation. Another fact seems important: the percentage of children who did not want to depict the topic has slightly increased, which shows decreasing confidence in self-expression. The temporary lack of spatial correlation is a result of a more egocentric attitude which, as we have seen, is typical for this age level, which we called the "gang age."

When we turn our attention to the drawings of the postadolescent college students, we see first of all that only a very limited number of students voluntarily depicted this topic (35 per cent). Those who did, tried to represent it as *realistically* as possible: some by the real movement of running with "well proportioned" figures including a part of the campus; others with the emphasis on the figures only, stressing the muscles and the function of the body (Fig. 38).

From this experiment it becomes clear that the closer the child approaches adolescence, the more he loses the strong subjective relationship

Fig. 38. "Playing Tag on the School Ground" (fifteen years old). Attempt at realistic representation.

to the world of symbols. The growing consciousness of his own body introduces a more critical awareness of the self. In some cases, the higher consciousness of the self leads to a more detailed and determined expression of the body, whereas in other cases, this growing critical attitude stimulates very strongly visual observation. *A conscious critical awareness now dominates the creative production of the postadolescent individual.* Two types are evident: the one who focuses all experiences on the *self*; the other who concentrates more on environment, using the eyes as the intermediaries for creative experiences. Since each of these types has its own definite reaction, we shall call each by its own characteristic designation. The child who refers mainly to visual experiences, we call the *visual type*; the other, who refers more to subjective feelings as body feelings, muscle sensations, or kinesthetic experiences, we call the *haptic type.**
Because of the importance of these two types and their proper stimulation and personality development, a more detailed analysis of the two types follows in this chapter.

There is, however, an intermediate stage, in which the individual has already lost the connection with his childish way of symbolic representa-

* *Haptic* derives from the Greek word *haptikos* and means, able to lay hold of.

tion and has not yet found confidence in his own conscious approach. Through the strong desire of establishing a conscious approach, however, the child loses temporarily the subjective attitude toward his own creations. With this loss, the confidence in his world of imagination is shaken. Consequently, the drawings show this feeling of insecurity as a visible expression of the battle between the two impulses. This period in which the youth has neither an unconscious childish nor a conscious approach of self-expression is marked by a very profound crisis which sometimes shakes the whole self-confidence. This is the reason why so many individuals stop their creative work at this period. In the study of adolescence this particular phase of the crisis hardly has been recognized.

From the foregoing report it becomes clear that one of the most important tasks of art education during this vital period is to introduce means and methods of stimulations which would prevent the child from losing self-confidence by encouraging each type in its own way to produce creatively. Proposals on how this can be done is the main thesis of this chapter.

THE DEVELOPMENT OF TWO DISTINCT CREATIVE TYPES

We can now clearly distinguish two types both by the end products of their artistic activities and by their attitude toward their own experiences. When we investigate the artistic products of these two types, we find that the visual type starts from his environment, that he feels always as spectator, and that his intermediaries for experience are mainly the eyes. The other, the haptic type, is primarily concerned with his own body sensations and the subjective experiences in which he feels emotionally involved. In *The Nature of Creative Activity* I have demonstrated the existence of these two distinct creative types based upon two different reactions toward the world of experiences. In the course of this study it was found that imaginative activity, including the ability to give objective reference to creations of the imagination, by no means depends upon the capacity for perceptive observation. Furthermore, it was shown that the inability inspectively to notice "visual" objects is not always an inhibitory factor in creative activities. On the contrary, the very fact of not paying attention to visual impressions may become the basis of a specific creativeness of the haptic type. This is of greatest importance for art educators, especially for those who still are concerned with visual stimulations only.

A visually minded individual would be disturbed and inhibited were he to be stimulated only by means of haptic impressions—that is, were he asked not to use sight, but to orientate himself only by means of touch, bodily feelings, muscular sensations, and kinesthetic fusions. So much is clear, but what is not as obvious is that "seeing" may also become an inhibitory factor when forced upon an individual who does not use his visual experiences for creative work. Both facts are established by numerous experiments reported in the work referred to before.*

An extreme haptical type of individual—who is by no means rare—is normal-sighted and uses his eyes only when compelled to do so; otherwise he reacts as would a blind person who is entirely dependent upon touch and kinesthesis. An extreme visually minded person, on the other hand, is entirely lost in the dark and depends completely on his visual experiences of the outside world. This distinction is true for creative types as well as for individuals in general, as it has been reported elsewhere.†

Most people fall between these two extreme types. Investigations have proved, however, that only few individuals have equal amounts of visual and haptic predisposition. Seventy-five per cent have an appreciable tendency toward one or the other. Since the tendency toward these two antipodes of experience is important not only for the proper stimulation in creative activity but also to life in general (especially, as we shall see, in the proper choice of occupation), we shall discuss this aspect of the problem in a separate chapter.

The result of an investigation in which I tested 1128 subjects by means of specifically designed tests for visual or haptic aptitude was as follows: 47 per cent were clearly visual, 23 per cent were haptic, and 30 per cent either received a score below the line where a clear identification was possible, or were otherwise not identifiable. In other words, approximately half of the individuals tested reacted visually, whereas not quite a fourth reacted haptically.

Thus, it would appear that one among four individuals depends for his subjective reactions upon touch and kinesthesis rather than upon vision. Aside from its far-reaching significance in other fields, for art teaching this fact means that only half of the population can benefit from visual stimuli. The others either are not reached or become frustrated by this type of stimulation. Each type should therefore be stimulated in the directions of his experiences and thinking. To do this, we should become acquainted with the nature of these two creative types, particularly because during the crisis of adolescence the individual is most unsure of himself. The kind of stimulation that is able to inspire him will not only contribute to his

---

* *The Nature of Creative Activity.*
† Lowenfeld, Viktor, "Tests for Visual and Haptical Aptitude." *American Journal of Psychology,* Vol. 58, 1945.

creative development, but will also instil the self-confidence necessary for a wholesome personality development.

Visual type

The main intermediaries for visual impressions are the eyes. The ability to observe visually does not depend entirely upon the physical conditions of the eyes. Inferior visual awareness is not necessarily determined by a physical defect of the eyes. On the contrary, as experiments have proven, the psychological factor of having the *aptitude* to observe is of deciding significance. This is of special importance because it implies the fact that being forced to observe might possibly create inhibitions. Before one can remove inhibitions it is necessary to recognize them as such. Superfluous as this statement may appear, it should nevertheless be emphasized at the outset of the discussion on the two creative types. To be observed, for example, is that it would be completely wrong to attempt to set free the creative powers of a nonvisual type of individual by trying to remove his "visual inhibition" and anxiously attempting to familiarize him with visual impressions. One would in fact achieve the exact opposite, just as one would inhibit creative ability by forcing a visualizer to pay special attention to tactile impressions. *Not being able to see, or rather not noticing visual impressions, is not always an inhibitory factor.* On the contrary, we have seen that the very fact of not paying attention to visual impressions becomes the basis of the specific creativeness of the haptic type. Therefore, before the way is cleared for the development of creative ability, it is essential to ascertain which creative type is involved. From this it follows that naturalistic modes of expression should not be used as the only criterion. The use of such a criterion actually inhibits free creative expression. To ascertain the type being dealt with, the specific attributes of each have to be determined.

The *visual type, the observer,* usually approaches things from their appearance. He feels as a *spectator.* One important factor in visual observation is the ability to see first the whole without an awareness of details, then to analyze this total impression into detailed or partial impressions, and finally to synthesize these parts into a new whole. The visual type first sees the general shape of a tree, then the single leaves, the twigs, the branches, the trunk, and finally everything incorporated in the synthesis of the whole tree. Starting with the general outline, partial impressions thus are integrated into a whole, simultaneous image. This is true not only psychologically, but also for the act of creating. Thus, we will notice that visual types usually begin with the outlines of objects and enrich the form with details as the visual analysis is able to penetrate deeper into the nature of the object.

This visual penetration deals mainly with two factors: first, with the analysis of the characteristics of shape and structure of the object itself; and second, with the changing effects of these shapes and structures determined by light, shadow, color, atmosphere, and distance. Observing details, therefore, is not always a sign of visual-mindedness; it can be an indication of good memory as well as of subjective interest in these details. For visual-mindedness it is necessary to see the changes which these details undergo under the various external conditions as mentioned above.

Visually minded persons have a tendency to transform kinesthetic and tactile experiences into visual experiences. If, for instance, a visual-minded person acquaints himself with an object in complete darkness, he tries to visualize all tactile or kinesthetic experiences. "How it looks" is the first reaction to any object met in darkness. In other words, he tries to imagine in visual terms what he has perceived through other senses. A visually minded person who encounters an object in darkness thus tries immediately to visualize the object he has met. From this analysis it becomes evident that the visual approach toward the outside world is an analytic approach of a spectator who finds his problems in the complex observation of the ever-changing appearances of shapes and forms.

Haptic type

The main intermediary for the haptic type of individual is the *body-self*—muscular sensations, kinesthetic experiences, touch impressions, and all experiences which place the self in value relationship to the outside world. In this art, the self is projected as the true actor of the picture whose formal characteristics are the resultant of a synthesis of bodily, emotional, and intellectual apprehension of shape and form. Sizes and spaces are determined by their emotional value in size and importance. The haptic type, therefore, is primarily a *subjective type*. Haptically minded persons do not transform kinesthetic and tactile experiences into visual ones, but are completely content with the tactile or kinesthetic modality itself, as experiments have shown. If a haptically minded person acquaints himself with an object in complete darkness, he would remain satisfied with his tactile or kinesthetic experiences. Since tactile impressions are mostly partial only (this is true for all impressions of objects that cannot be embraced with the hands, where the hands have to move) the haptic individual will arrive at a synthesis of these partial impressions only when he becomes emotionally interested in the object itself. Normally, he will not build up such a synthesis and will remain satisfied with his haptic experience. If he encounters an object in darkness, he will merely withdraw, perhaps, with some feelings of the surface structure of the obstacle or with partial impressions of those parts that he has touched. Since the haptic type uses the self as the true projector of his experiences, his pictorial representations are highly subjective; his proportions are proportions of value.

In art education it is therefore of prime importance to consider these attitudes toward the world of experiences as significant as the visual approaches toward art. Thus a stimulation will be effective only if it includes haptic sensations as well as visual experiences.

THE DIFFERENT CREATIVE CONCEPTS
OF THE TWO TYPES

To be able to separate pure optical perception from other sense impressions we need an object of contemplation that cannot be influenced or disturbed by other senses. But associatively almost everything in our surroundings somehow influences all of our sensations and experiences. We can therefore hardly ever speak of pure optical perception of things. Even color, regarded in isolation from any object, awakes in us dark, bright, cheerful, or warm feelings, and it seems self-evident that, for example, a tree waving in the wind awakes in us some knowledge of the elasticity of the wood, the nature of the leaves, and so forth. Thus Van Gogh writes in a letter to his brother, "Yesterday evening I concerned myself with the gently rising terrain of the wood, which is completely covered with dry, dead beech leaves. . . . The problem is—and I find this extremely difficult—to bring out the depth of the color and the enormous strength and firmness of the soil. . . . Out of this soil grow the trunks of the beeches, which are a shining green on the side on which they are brightly illuminated, while on the shadow side the trunks show a warm, strong blackgreen. . . . I am affected and intrigued to see how strongly the trunks are rooted in the ground. I began to paint them with the brush, and was unable to bring out the characteristics of the soil, which had already been painted in thick colors. The new brush strokes simply disappeared. Therefore I pressed roots and trunks out of the tube and modelled them a little with my brush. There, now they stand in it, grow out of it, and have firmly taken root." *

We see here how the optical impression has been influenced and formed by other sense impressions, how intellectual apprehension of shape and form fused with optical and emotional experiences. Can optical per-

* Van Gogh, Vincent, *Letters*. Berlin: Bruno Cassirer, pp. 14, 16 and 17.

Fig. 39. "Youth Imploring." Sculpture by a seventeen-year-old girl, who has been blind since birth.

ception, therefore, be adequately perceived by means of seeing with the eye alone? We shall have to conclude that optical perception in its purest form is only an extreme case of visual perception in general. We must therefore use the term "visual perception," when impressions coming from other senses are subordinate to those coming from the eye, and when visual impressions are the *dominant* feature in a percept.

The artistic representation of visual impressions always starts from optical perception. It is concerned with the subjective experience of the self only in so far as any creative activity is an individual mental act. "Being bound to the self" in this sense is not what we shall understand by the term later, because it does not seek its experience in bodily sensations, but *outside the body*. The self merely evaluates the experience.

"The further optical experience recedes into the background, the less important does the eye become as the intermediary of the concept. To the same extent the importance of the environment diminishes, and experience is more and more confined to the processes that go on in the body as a whole—bodily sensations, muscular innervations, deep sensibilities, and their various emotional effects. As the importance of the sense of sight diminishes, so that of the senses derived from the body as the intermediary between sensations and the concept increase. In what follows, we shall mean by "haptic perception" the synthesis between tactile perceptions of external reality and those subjective experiences that seem to be so closely bound up with the experience of the self." *

From the discussion it can clearly be seen that visual and haptic concepts are fundamentally different in their basic experiential content. Although we have pointed out that pure haptical or visual concepts are rarely to be found, in our teaching experiences the tendency toward the one or the other can clearly be seen. As we are able to recognize them, we will be able to encourage the individual *in the direction* of his thinking, and thereby provide the guidance he sorely needs during the crisis of adolescence.

Human figure

For the visual type the human figure is a part of the environment (Fig. 40). As such, the human figure is exposed to the same phenomena as environment. The main experiences related to the representation of the human figure are the qualities that can be discovered with our eyes. "Correct proportions and measurements" are, therefore, of prime significance for the visual type. The changing effects of lights and shadows in the

* *The Nature of Creative Activity*, p. 82.

Fig. 40. "People Look at the Battleship Missouri" (twelve years old). Representation of a visual type. (Courtesy Educational Project, Museum of Modern Art, N. Y.)

different motions are necessarily a part of the visual image. In art stimulation, therefore, the posing model is of different significance for the two creative types because the visually minded individual is mainly concerned with the visual analysis of his optical impressions.

The haptic type, however, uses the human figure as the interpreter of his emotions and feelings (Fig. 41). Since different parts of our body have various functions and importance, the proportions given these parts will assume the emotional significance assigned to them. The wounds on the hands of Christ are of such significance in a Byzantine mural that the hands dominate in size and in importance. Another experience related especially to haptic types is the intense body feeling expressed in the desire to get one's body transferred to another place (that is, when late; related to the wish of catching up with time and space) or the desire to catch something that is already out of reach by throwing one's arm after it. These typically haptic experiences are in strong contradiction to visual observations. They spring from body experiences and kinesthetic sensations. Since these experiences are highly subjective in their interpretations,

Fig. 41. "People," Representation of a haptic type. No environment is repre-sented. Experience is completely focussed at expression. (Courtesy Educational Project, Museum of Modern Art, N. Y.)

The haptic representation of the human figure and its meaning is a highly subjective one.

In my *The Nature of Creative Activity* I have called attention to numerous examples of the works of the blind among whom haptic ex-pression is much more common. In this book, I have demonstrated the meaning of autoplastic sensations, the sensations of drawing all experi-ences from the body, and the significance they assume. The figure of a "Youth Imploring" modeled by a girl who has been blind since birth will illustrate these viewpoints. Its most striking characteristic that we feel to be closely connected with the title is the over-emphasis on the imploring hands. We feel the strength of the elemental forces embodied in this figure when we regard the gradual increase in its proportions. It starts from the slender basis of the delicate legs and rising like a hymn to heaven finds in the great hands its mighty closing chord. The base has, as it were, been dematerialized: it is no longer earth-bound, and we have before us only the feeling "I implore!" (Fig. 39). In almost all sculptures by the blind we find that those parts of the body that have emotional

significance are greatly exaggerated. We find, however, the same principle
of representation in all epochs and cultures in which expressive qualitie
are of greater importance than visual ones.

In Egyptian murals the kings and other prominent persons are mad
larger in exactly the same way as in Byzantine paintings. In these case
large and small cannot be regarded as visual qualities: they are expressive
evaluations; visual experiences have to make way for impulses lying out
side of the visual sphere. This is especially true for modern art in which
the emphasis again is on the side of expressive qualities. Then we wil
understand the true meaning of the complex creations of Picasso in which
space and time fuse, in which profile and front views are expressed simul
taneously, in which the arm of a horrified mother becomes separated from
the body as an expression of the intense feeling of reaching for he
bombed child.* The nature of this art expression is at least as deepl
rooted, historically and psychologically, as the visual interpretation of th
world which surrounds us.

Since the stimulation of these subjective feelings is of prime impor
tance for art educators who deal with the stage under discussion, ther
will be developed, in the chapter on stimulations, methods for bringing
out and encouraging these important feelings without neglecting the ir
dividual personality.

Space

Space cannot be conceived in its totality. Its infinity is irrational an
it becomes accessible to our senses only when we circumscribe it. At th
centre of space, with nothing whatever to surround us, space itself woul
be infinite and therefore nonexistent. The self would cease to be a measur
of value in space. It would vanish to nothing in infinity. Our senses an
our psychological attitude set limits to space, and each in its own wa
enables us to grasp space. *Visual space,* for which the eyes are the inte
mediaries, we perceive as the widest space. *Haptic space,* for which ou
organs of touch and our bodily sensations are the intermediaries, is th
most restricted. Both spaces achieve a magical significance whenever th
self is included in them through value judgments. In what follows w
shall discuss the difference in the ways in which these two sensory spac
are pictorially represented. The direction of our investigation is dete
mined on the one hand by the difference in the modes of sensory perceptio
of these two spaces, and on the other hand, by the "restriction" of th
extent of haptic as compared with visual space. Both points of view a

* Mural "Guernica," by Pablo Picasso.

ecessary for understanding the kind of stimulation that the art educator
as to use during this deciding stage in order that he will neither neglect
or frustrate either of these types.

In relation to its environment, the self grows or diminishes in size and
a importance. Next to children we seem large, next to a skyscraper, small;
nimportant in the world at large, important in our own circle; most im-
ortant, perhaps, when we are quite alone. These attitudes vary according
o our psychological state. The narrower, the more restricted, three-
imensional space or the space of our psychological experiences is, the
nore importance is assigned to the self. Haptic space is of necessity re-
ricted. In it, therefore, the significance and the importance of the self
re very much emphasized.

Among the differences produced by the eye in the visual image, is the
pparent diminution of distant objects. In drawing, this apparent diminu-
on of distant objects is achieved by using laws of perspective. The outer
mits of visual space are represented by the boundary of the horizon line.
low are distant objects represented in haptical space? Distant objects, in
ais kind of space, do not produce differences in size to the sense of touch
r to emotional reactions. Thus, the visual image receives a decisive cor-
ction. When space is being explored tactually, distances can only have
ifferent values attached to them or seem of greater or less emotional
gnificance. In haptic space, therefore, we find a predominance of sub-
ctive value judgments. In visual space (the space of appearances) dis-
nce is expressed by a progressive diminution of distant objects. The
nging for freedom, however, grows with its remoteness. An individual
ithout restrictions is unaware of boundaries. His eyes can easily rest on
ie horizon. The horizon of the share cropper is his cotton field, the horizon
f a laundry woman her tub. *The perspective of haptic space is a perspec-
ve of values.*

None of the creative interpretations of these spaces is true in a realis-
c sense. Both spaces are "distorted" by individual interpretations. Al-
tough philosophy has generally considered visual space as the more
ralistic, nevertheless it has less validity than the space of touch. Distant
ojects do not actually change in size, and the sense of touch truly records
ais truth. Visual experiences show an apparent diminution in the size
f objects in space, but this is in strong contradiction to reality. Bushmen,
ho were confronted with photographs or reproductions of paintings of
tree-dimensional qualities, were unable to orientate themselves in the
ngle of visual foreshortenings.* For them sizes do not differ with regard
o distances. Their spatial interpretations, however, are not "true interpre-

* Frobenius, Leo, *Kulturgeschichte Afrikas.* Zürich, Phaidon-Verlag, 1933.

tations" either, since by them objects in space are evaluated according to
significance. Interesting to note, however, is that we are completely one-
sided in our judgments relating to the validity of our own visual space
interpretations. Our civilization has become so accustomed to the photographic interpretation of space that we have to change completely our
concept if we shift to the "unconventional" interpretations of haptic space
although these have been the conventional interpretations among historica
cultures in which *expression* dominated in the realm of art.

THE TWO CREATIVE TYPES ARE PSYCHOLOGICAL

When we sit in a train, watching the swiftly passing landscape, we
may or may not realize that the impression of the landscape as a whole
exists only in our minds. In reality we do not see the whole thing, but
only many little strips of landscape about the size of the window, each
one quickly replaced by another. Some of us are quite satisfied with these
many partial impressions and would even feel dizzy if compelled to
integrate the fleeting glimpses into a whole. Others, however, do not need
to be stimulated to put this "picture puzzle" together. While moving, they
fuse all these strips together and see in their minds a whole landscape
more than that, they orientate themselves quite well in it.

Members of the first group not only lose contact with the parts of the
landscape that are left behind, but often become irritated by the "ever
changing" picture. Many of us have experienced how this irritation contributes to the discomfort of train travel. It is not only the fresh air that
makes riding in an open car a pleasure, or the smoothness of high-altitude
flying that makes it more pleasant than the take-off; it is also the enlarged
visual circle which permits better orientation and a fuller sense of physical
security. The body likes to know what is being done to it. The driver of a
car does not feel the sudden stop as much as the passengers do.

The traveler who sits either comfortably or painfully in his compartment seldom realizes that this ability or failure to produce a single, unified
picture out of the many successive impressions of the landscape may
classify him according to a definite psychological type, which differs from
other types on this and many other points, as we shall see.

Since definite trends and behavior patterns are clearest seen when they
are deprived of "cover," they can best be observed and investigated in
extreme cases. In order to investigate the relationship of our visual sense
to the determination of the psychological type, it was necessary to experiment with the totally blind. The problem was this: If there are haptic and
visual types among normal people, can both types also be found among

the blind? If so, it would be proof that the two types were psychologically distinct.

Most blind sculptors do not model in the usual way, with the statue facing them; they stand parallel to the statue or behind it, with the face turned in the same direction as the face of the worker. The reason for this is that the impressions of the outer world do not reach the blind in a mirror-like projection, which is the way these impressions reach the normal eye. The experience of the totally blind is primarily derived from the forms they observe and feel on themselves. Accordingly, the sculpture is formed in the same direction, with the sculptor usually working on the face of his figure as though he were embracing it from behind. This was true of both the individuals, A and B, whose work we are considering (Figs. 42 and 43). But how extremely different are their approaches.

Sculptor A (Fig. 42) starts with the general outline of a head (a). Then he pulls out the nose (c), adds eyes (d) consisting of eyeballs and lids (e, f), mouth, and features (g). Finally he has completed a sculpture in which all single features are fused in a unified and closed surface, very much like a "normal" head (Fig. 42j). Sculptor B (Fig. 43), however, starts with the chin (a), puts in the teeth (and even the tonsils) (b), and prepares the hole for the nose and sticks it on (c, d). Then the eyes are added, from the inside, and the hollow of the head is closed (e). Finally such expressive features as wrinkles and tears (the sculpture represents "Pain") are added (f), but they remain isolated on the finished product (Figure 43g). One feels as if they could easily be removed. They are still partial impressions, isolated from the main form instead of being fused into a "complete" image as in the head in Fig. 42. They are like the many single impressions that we get in looking out of the train, without fusing them into a whole image of the landscape.

I led the two blind sculptors into a room, escorting them along the window side, past the two other walls, and back to the entrance. Then I asked both to point toward the direction of one particular window. A, who made the sculpture with the "smooth" surface, immediately knew the accurate direction, whereas B could not orientate himself at all. B had only the partial impressions in his mind received while moving along a wall. He could not unify these impressions into a whole impression of the room. Since a vital part of orientation consists of the ability to gain this unity, B was completely unable to orientate himself.*

These two attitudes may be further observed in two self-portraits, C

* Similar experiments on a larger scale are reported by the author in *The Nature of Creative Activity*. Also Reves confirms these observations: Reves, G., *Die Formenwelt des Tastsinnes*. The Hague: Martinus Nijhoff, 1938.

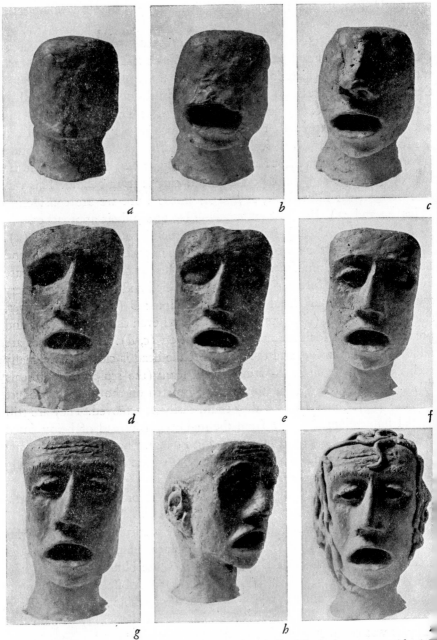

Fig. 42. "Pain." Visual-blind sculpture. Congenitally blind sixteen-year-old girl

a). General outline
b). Cavity of the mouth is formed
c). Nose is added
d). Eye sockets are hollowed out

e). Eyeballs are put in
f). Lids are pulled over
g). Wrinkles are formed
h). Ears are added

i). The head is finished. All features are incorporated into a unified surface. Typical for the visual type.

Fig. 42j. Finished product. "Pain."

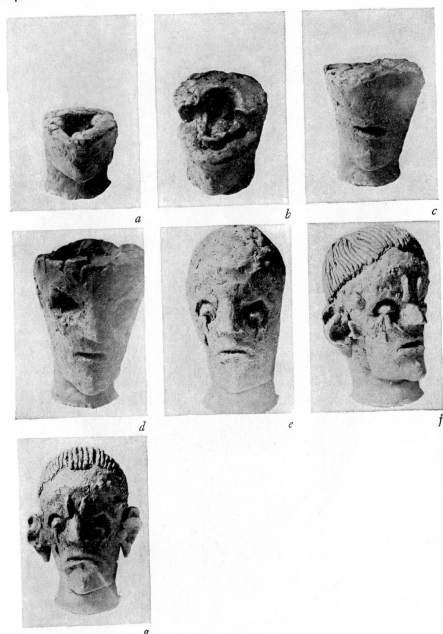

Fig. 43. "Pain." Haptical-blind sculpture. Sixteen-year-old blind boy.

a). Start with the chin
b). Teeth, tongue, and so forth are put in
c). Mouth is closed, nothing can be seen of inside features
d). Nose is added, eye sockets made
e). Eyes are put in from inside, head "closed"
f). Features and hair are added
g). Finished head with all features still isolated as partial impressions. Typical for the blind, haptic type.

Fig. 43b. All single features, like wrinkles and tears, hair or temples, still remain isolated on the final product.

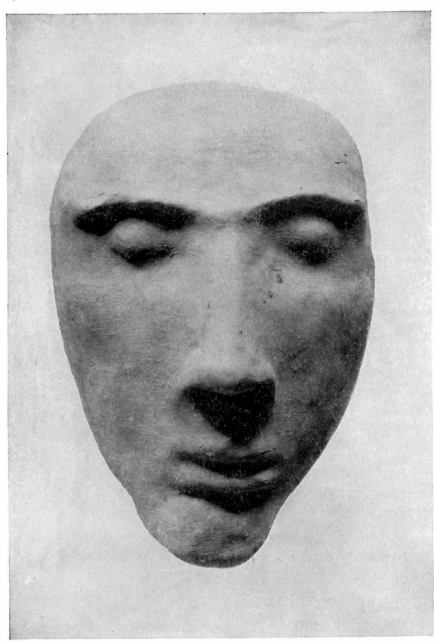

Fig. 44. "Self-Portrait" of visually minded blind sculptor. Notice unified surface appearance.

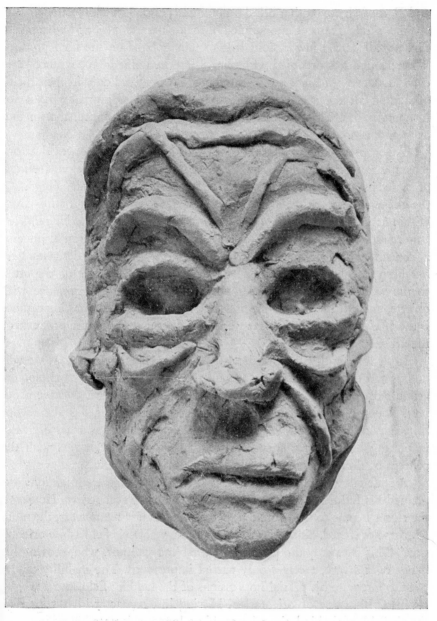

Fig. 45. "Self-Portrait" of haptically minded blind sculptor. Features are very expressive, but remain isolated.

and *D*, made by two other blind individuals (Figs. 44 and 45). In Fig. 44, all the single features are unified into a "natural vision," whereas in Fig. 45, all partial impressions still remain isolated on the final product. Whereas one was occupied with expressing the unified "appearance" and even "likeness" of his portrait, the other was involved only in the process of adding all the surface features which seemed to him important for his personality. This, in fact, is a manifestation of impressionism and expressionism.

The impressionist world is the world of appearances, the world of our senses. The world of expressionist art is the world of expression, feelings, of subjective processes. In impressionist art, as in "Self-Portrait" (Fig. 44), the *surface structure triumphs*, whereas expressive art, originating from within as in "Self-Portrait" (Fig. 45), places the *self in a value relationship to its environment*. That which is perceivable in the external universe is contrasted with that which is experienced by the "inward senses." As has been said before, art consists in depicting the relations of the artist to the world of his experiences—that is, depicting his experience with objects, and not the objects themselves. Again, what is of final importance is the *kind of experience;* this is what decisively determines the products of the artist.

If we look in this light at the self-portraits (Figs. 44 and 45), we will understand the different forces at work; we see that it is the psychological attitude of the individual which determines the style of his creative products. The same applies, not only to our creative impulses, but also to our thinking and doing. While one person thinks in details and has difficulty in putting his thoughts together into a whole, another begins with the concept of the whole and finds it difficult to go into details.

An air-pilot training candidate who failed in his examinations explained his failure as follows: "In high altitudes I feel secure. However, the closer I come to the ground, especially in landing maneuvers, the more I become confused. Since I cannot take in the whole air field I lose orientation." This is exactly the problem of the blind sculptor, who, moving his hands over a face, receives only partial impressions. The inability of the pilot to integrate his partial impressions of the landing field into a whole, confused his sense of orientation. Having lost contact with the part of the air field left behind, the pilot could no longer orientate himself.

In primitive, haptic, and expressive art the same attitude toward the experience of senses can be observed; however, with one striking additional factor. As a man sitting in a train loses contact with the area he leaves behind him, so does the haptic artist. But the train passenger, like the artist, may suddenly become bound up with something that quickly passes his eyes and strikes his personality, such as an old shack, or a hawk circling in the air. From this time on, the hawk will circle with him and grow in his mind as one outstanding, isolated impression of the many he has perceived in succession.

A blind person who made himself acquainted with a room became very much interested in a desk lamp. He could feel the bulb growing warmer when he turned on the light, and when he was asked afterwards to model the room in clay, the lamp was the most conspicuous part, even overshadowing the desk. This impression became outstanding and most of the others disappeared. The lamp may have been for him a symbol of the "unattainable," or better, the "unperceivable," which can easily change for the primitive man into any magic symbol. The creative result, however, shows the same expression for it: proportion of value.

Reference is again made to the sculpture "Youth Imploring" (Fig. 39) described previously (page 139). The world of expressionist art is one of expression, feelings, subjective processes: *of haptic experiences.* Bodily feelings, kinesthetic experiences, muscular sensations are clearest examples of subjective processes. The bodily feelings of these uplifted hands have become incorporated into the magic content of the expression of the whole sculpture. The same kind of expression can be seen in the works of modern masters such as William Lehmbruck, as well as in the exaggerated hands of primitive African sculptures. Or we might better say it can be seen in every art that originates in haptic rather than in visual experiences.

Thus, the two creative types are psychological which, independent of physiological factors, exist in their own realms. We have found that there are completely and congenitally blind individuals who react visually or haptically in the same way as normal-sighted people react both ways. We now know from "Self-Portrait" (Fig. 44) that a blind person reacts "visually" if he is able to receive out of his touch impressions (which are partial impressions) a simultaneous image of the whole, like the visually minded, normal-sighted person who sits in the train and fuses all partial impressions into a simultaneous image. *Both final products are distinguished by the same visual attributes of emphasizing the external appearance.* Blind as well as normal-sighted haptic types, however, create entirely "from within." Their inward feelings are expressed in disregard of any realistic external qualities.

It becomes evident that imaginative activity and even the ability to give objective form to the creations of the imagination by no means depends on the capacity to see and observe things. This is of vital importance for art educators because it will be an important factor in determining the

Fig. 46. "Street Scene," painted by visually minded sixteen-year-old adolescent youth. Light and shadow, atmosphere, and visual proportions, determined by the law of perspective, govern this representation. (Courtesy Educational Project, Museum of Modern Art, N. Y.)

methods of stimulation discussed in the following section (compare Figs. 46 and 47).

SIGNIFICANCE OF A PROPER ART STIMULATION

Proper art stimulation is always determined by the factors that influence the growth and development of the individual during a particular age period. During the crisis of adolescence the individual has to battle for many far-reaching decisions. He stands on the threshold of adulthood, reached under circumstances which often affect his life very definitely. Adjustment from childhood to adulthood usually occurs under difficulties, physiologically and psychologically. Neither one can be separated from the other because the body is closely related to our mind, and affects it greatly. We shall, however, be concerned only with the psychological effects and how we can influence them or, better, help the individual to overcome them by means of creative activity. Creative activity will thus become the natural outlet and means of expression for the individual. Art education

Fig. 47. "Lying on the Bed," painted by a haptically minded seventeen-year-old adolescent youth. Everything is focused around the self. Color has a subjective meaning; so have lights and darks. (Courtesy Educational Project, Museum of Modern Art, N. Y.)

during this important period should by no means be offered to only a selected group, but should be a natural means of expression for everyone. This conclusion is not in accord with common practice in the American high school, where art is taught to a small group of artistically "gifted" students. "Gifted" usually refers to skill, and conventional interpretations of objects of nature. If we can eliminate this attitude toward "art expression" and at the same time develop self-confidence in the individual to accept *art as self-expression according to individual needs,* we have succeeded in our chief aim of making art a common expression of mankind. In order to be able to do so, we will have to study the psychological needs for the proper stimulation during this crucial period of decision.

Psychological methods

From our previous discussion three important criteria stand out as vital considerations for the proper stimulation of creating self-confidence in the individual and thus making art a common expression of all: (1) The change from an unconscious approach to a critical awareness. (2) The change of the imaginative concept. (3) The crystallization of two different creative types or concepts.

During the discussion of the stage of reasoning, it was emphasized that the closer the unconscious approach in its intellectual and emotional apprehension can be brought to the stage of critical awareness, the easier can the child bridge the gap created by the crisis of adolescence. This gap, as we said, consists mainly of the undecided attitude of the individual, who feels torn in two directions: childhood and adulthood—childhood in his play and adulthood in his intellectual awareness. How often have we had the opportunity to see this contradiction in the attitude of youngsters who, while playing with airplanes and imitating sounds and motions, suddenly bring themselves short and become ashamed because they are no longer supposed to engage in such childish antics. This distorted attitude can best be seen in creative activity when youngsters want to apologize for their "childish" drawings by an assumed mere "lack of skill." If discouragement did not as a rule accompany these "false" apologies, it would not be a harmful matter. But the apologies are usually symptoms of lack of self-confidence which is the end of creative expression. To avoid such discouragement we should introduce teaching methods that counteract this trend.

Before considering methods, the characteristics of a good method should be indicated. Methods that restrict the individual instead of making him free are poor. Methods having no relation to the individual needs of the student are rigid, and as such do not lead to the establishment of freedom. At the other extreme is the trend in progressive art education to throw overboard all teaching methods and to regard the unhampered creation by the individual as the only possible creative outcome of good education. Although such an approach may be applicable to some, it cannot become a basis for art education, especially during such a difficult period as the crisis of adolescence.

Other teachers try to avoid the basic difficulties by saying that the youth during this stage is particularly receptive to learning new skills and techniques. As a result of this attitude, they teach skills and techniques in order to cover the "poor creativity" of the pupils during this stage. Acquiring skills and techniques is an important aim of the teaching of art during this period because we should give the individual adequate means for competing with the creative approaches of adults. But if the techniques are not used as *means* to an end, but become ends themselves, they will only be facades without structure. Techniques should be developed, not taught; they must be born out of the need for expression.

With the complexity of expression the need for a more complex technique grows. This need can be satisfied by the individual only in his own individual desires. Techniques copied by students from teachers are taught, not grown, are rigid means of expression which obey inflexible rules. They are entirely unsuitable means of self-expression. What *can* be taught is the basic use of a painting or drawing material. Every student will find his own way of using materials according to his needs. As we shall see, oil painting will be used differently by visually minded and by haptically minded individuals. The one group prefers to use the complexity of an impressionistic color scale, but the other group is more concerned with the expression of "local colors." Within the visually minded group are numerous different approaches, as we know from the difference of pointillistic art of Signac and the paintings of Whistler or Manet. In the same way, we find extremely different approaches in the techniques of haptic art. Techniques of art will be discussed in greater detail in a subsequent chapter; what needs emphasis here is that teaching skills or techniques without the necessary emphasis on the creative foundation would be only an escape from the real problem.

A method of art is good if it brings out the innate qualities of an individual by developing self-confidence and the desire to go ahead. If the method is not applicable to a large group, it is of no use for our educational system. If the method does not grow out of the psychological development of the child, it is an artifice.

This statement characterizes the problems with regard to a good method. Generally, the first indication of critical awareness is in the inability of establishing close correlations between imaginative thinking and the drawing on the paper. There are two important criteria in this connection: (1) the confusion in the kind of imaginative activity, and (2) the lack of visual and muscular coordination when making a line. The confused attitude toward the type of imaginative thinking necessary for pictorial representation results in an attitude of "I can't draw" in much the same way as the inability of guiding a line according to one's visual determination. The discussion, consequently, can now be crystallized in these two questions: (1) How can we clarify the kind of imaginative activity which lends itself to pictorial representation? (2) What means do we have for establishing a close visual control over motor activities?

IMAGINATIVE ACTIVITY FOR PICTORIAL REPRESENTATION   Much of the confusion of adolescent critical awareness is due to the fact that in adolescent thinking, art must by all means establish a "realistic" relationship to environment, a relationship which develops a "true" (photographic) picture of the external world. The concept of "truth" should be established from as many angles as possible, especially with the help of works of art, of different epochs and cultures. It will then become evident that "truth" is relative, and that the word should be replaced by "sincerity." An African sculpture is as "true" to its creator as was the "David" to Michelangelo. The experience, however, which the African sculptor had with his work is vitally different from the experience Michelangelo had when he created the "David." Thus it is the difference in the experience that determines art expression, whether it be painting, music, architecture, or any other art form. To show and demonstrate this relationship between experience and art work in the greatest possible varieties is one of the most important educational means that may eventuate in an unhampered interpretation of experiences.*

A work of art is not a product of nature; it is a product of human spirit, thinking, and emotions, and can only be understood when the driving forces which lead to its creation are understood. These driving forces are of essential significance and everything else is only a by-product. If these driving forces are lacking, not even the most developed skills can ever replace them. That is why the works of the Primitives can be great works of art, while most skillfully executed works are not necessarily works of art if they lack the driving forces, the inner spirit that determines the greatness of an art work. They are like beautiful wrappers around nothing. It is therefore important to show the different qualities of these driving forces on the most diverse works of art of different epochs and cultures. It is important to show how in a Greek sculpture the highest adoration of the beauty of the body has been expressed. This can be understood only if we imagine that even a mother subordinated her feelings to the concept of beauty by disposing of a baby for the mere reason that its body was not perfect, as was the custom among the Spartans.

The driving forces which determined the expression of the "ideal" form and shape must be entirely different from those which determined religious expression (the medieval). "Ideal forms" disappear when expression dominates. When we cry, we do not care whether we cry beautifully. The driving force represents the need to incorporate all experiences deriving from expression into the single work of art to make it a symbol of expression. That is why, as we shall see, that in times when a general idea of expression was universal, like the general idea of religious expres-

---

* Munro, Thomas, "Creative Ability in Art and Its Educational Fostering," in *Art in American Life and Education*. Bloomington, Ill.: Public School Publishing Co., 1941.

sion during medieval times, the tendency toward symbolism or the general validity of expression, is great. If the driving force, however, is individualistic—that is, when expression derives from personal experiences, art expression will be highly individualized.

From this angle we have only to compare Picasso with Rouault to see the strong differences in their individual expression based on the difference in kind of experience (compare Fig. 57a and Fig. 57b). Whereas many of the experiences of Picasso can easily be traced to body sensations and kinetic experiences (as the desire to paint dynamically, front view and profile in one interpretation of a head) Rouault concerns himself greatly with associations of past experiences in which medieval art is often brought into a new light. Its greatest and most powerful expression is found in the dark outlines as seen in the medieval stained windows. How different is the origin of the driving forces in an impressionistic picture in which the external appearance, the changes of light and shadows, the illuminating qualities of surfaces, the complex idea of the breaking of colors, reaches its climax. How contrasted to such external structures and appearances are the driving forces which make an African sculptor carve his idols, or an Indian his totems. An analysis of these forces leads the student directly away from the mere imitative urge of reproducing nature.*

Youths during the period of adolescence are eager to give their thinking an intellectual backing. Although they will readily absorb those differences in the nature of the driving forces which determine the art experience, such a stimulation would not be enough for creating self-confidence in their shaken personalities. It would not be sufficient to awake in them the desire to express themselves in their own individual way. The personal experience in our everyday life must be included in the discussion of the difference of the driving forces which determine our imaginative experiences—that is, when we see a burning house, the driving forces which determine our experiences related to it will be quite different for different individuals. The one might be affected by the beauty of the blazing flames flaring skyward, their reflections, and the dancing shadows cast by them. The other individual is deeply touched by the fate of the people who are now without a roof over their heads, suddenly deprived of everything they could enjoy a few moments before. This individual sees the weeping mother holding the only thing she had been able to save: the baby in her arms. Still a third individual might leave the scene thinking only of what he would have done in the same circumstances.

* McMahon, A. Philip, The Art of Enjoying Art. New York: McGraw-Hill Book Co., 1938; Downey, June E., Creative Imagination. New York: Harcourt, Brace and Co., 1929.

From these different attitudes toward the same experience it becomes evident that the driving imaginative forces which determine pictorial representations are quite different. Whereas the one would merely approach the accident as a spectator (emphasizing visual experiences) the other might become involved in the struggle for existence, setting the ego as a value relationship into the focus of the experience. Haptic sensations determine his world of imagination.

How can we use these differences among imaginative experiences in a more systematic way—that is, starting with simple stimulations and proceeding to more complex ones? This question is of decisive importance, since we know that a youth whose confidence has been shaken so that he has the attitude of "I can't draw" will not start merely with the foregoing stimulations. He will need to know also that art experiences can be most diverse, depending upon the driving forces which determine them. He will need to know that art experiences are not necessarily "true reproductions" of nature, since "truth" with regard to art expression is a relative expression and changes with the times and for different individuals. As important as this basic attitude is, it is insufficient for giving the student, who has no confidence in his abilities, a "start" in his own creative activity. For this purpose we must give him the correct means and tools to create in him the desire to go ahead. But since technique and expression are so closely related that they cannot be separated, a discussion is needed on method and technique.

ESTABLISHING VISUAL AND MOTOR COORDINATION   It quite often happens that we have to go through the same stages twice, but never does development repeat itself. If we learn a new language as adults we might have to go through stages that are similar to learning to speak in childhood. Whereas the child gradually develops the ability to form vowels and consonants *without a purpose* in mind, the adult when learning a language uses *conscious* methods for correct pronunciation. Although we repeat certain stages of progress and apprehension, the repetition is on the level of consciousness. When the child establishes a coordination between his motor activity and his mark on the paper (during the stage of scribbling) it is done unconsciously. Such coordination, when lost during adolescence, can be regained only on the level of consciousness with a purpose behind it. A method that can introduce such a lost feeling would then be psychological, which is in conformity with human development. It would not be a system or a rigid way of learning "how to draw." On the contrary, such a method has nothing to do with drawing or art since it involves only the psychological factor of establishing visual and motor coordination. Since this factor is one of the most important assumptions for artistic activities, it is an indirect approach toward establishing confidence in self-expression as related to pictorial representation.

From what has been said, it follows that no talent or special abilities should be necessary for the establishment of such a psychological factor. If there is no serious physiological disturbance, we have simply to relate two sensory activities: the motions of the arm and the seeing of the lines produced by the motions. Not a single student in my experiences has been unable to establish such simple coordinations. It can be established by swinging a black crayon over a smooth paper, starting from the left corner of the paper and moving in motions to the right corner, repeating these motions with ever-greater certainty until we are so much at ease that no effort is used for the control of these motions (Fig. a). This occurs when we feel quite relaxed while making the swinging motions back and forth. We may raise the motions, gradually making a higher and higher arch (Fig. b). If this can be done gradually we simply demonstrate that we are able to control more differentiated motions. Raising the motions gradually, without forgetting that we start and end at the corners, means a more complex coordination than simply moving in a monotonous fashion.

Coordination gains in complexity if we change the motions and vary the pressure on the crayon. Since the varying pressure applied on the crayon is a part of motor control, too, it still has no relationship whatsoever to art expression. It is only one of the psychological assumptions necessary for gaining freedom and self-confidence in creative expression. Starting with bold, heavy motions on the bottom by putting much pressure on the crayon, and raising the motions by decreasing the pressure, will result in a shaded arch, dark on the bottom and gradually becoming lighter on the top (Fig. c).

 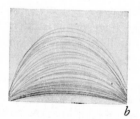 

a   b   c

Separating layers of different intensities might introduce a greater consciousness with regard to motor control. This greater consciousness can even be increased by adjusting vertical lines (or motions) of different intensities to the corresponding layers (Figs. d, e).

d   e

Here we could already start to move gradually from the mere psychological factors of motor control by merely asking for a proper distribution
of dark and light lines, the width of the different perpendicular motions,
and the different spaces between them. Although this is irrelevant to the
establishment of visual and motor coordination, it adds to the interest in
the subject matter. If we follow this method, we will discover a close and
quite organic parallel development between the unconscious development
of motor coordination in childhood and the one gained on the conscious
level. Since the child at some point will discover that there is a relationship
between his drawing and his experience with the outside world, so will
most students go through these stages and will quietly add "branches" to
the vertical motions. They have demonstrated by this act that they, too,
have related their motor activity to their visual experience with environment.

Once this relationship has been established, the most important psychological transformation has occurred. Now the use of the acquired confidence of visual and motor coordination for *expressive qualities* is of
greatest importance. And here we turn to the continuation of finding a
system which leads from simple stimulations of imaginative concepts to
more complex ones.

For the proper approach toward art experiences it is of vital importance
to distinguish between what is essential and what is unessential for the

expression of an experience. *Everything is essential which directly relates to the expression of the experience.* Unessential are those factors which have no direct relationship to the creation of the work. To use these essentials as a guide for the complexity of a stimulation is the key for the "system" of a proper art stimulation.

For example, our experience may be derived from a body motion: we were intrigued by a worker who carried a heavy load on his shoulder. Carrying a heavy load is now the most essential experience that we would like to express. Everything else becomes unessential. Thus, we do not care whether Mr. Smith or Mr. Jones carries the heavy load. Their faces might only detract from the essential expression in the same way as the face of the "Man with the Helmet" by Rembrandt would have contradicted his experience if it had overpowered the helmet. Rembrandt illuminated the helmet as the essential part, and put the face in deep shadows as if he wanted to say "under the helmet all faces look alike." It is not the portrait of Mr. Jones, it is the "Man with the Helmet." The helmet overshadows the face of the unknown soldier. If we compare this great painting with one of Rembrandt's portraits in which the face has to stand out and the headdress is almost a silhouette we will more definitely experience the meaning of these essentials.

Thus, while concentrating on the act of carrying a heavy load, we shall omit everything that does not contribute to "carrying a heavy load," and concentrate more and more on the experience itself. Although we are quite aware of the meaning of carrying, especially when going through the experience ourselves, we will soon discover that it is the lack of active knowledge which prevents the student from portraying his experience. "What are we doing when we are carrying? Are we bent or upright? Do we have our legs together, or apart from each other, to gain better support? How do we hold our load? Do we need to bend our arms or do we have them straight? Do we look at the ground or forward?" Such questions will activate the passive knowledge of the individual and at the same time stress the essentials necessary for the expression of carrying a heavy load (Fig. 48). It will help those who have no definite concept and will not disturb or restrict those who have the natural gift of expressing themselves. It is much more stimulating and easier not to start to draw from nature but to use the experiences derived from the self.

The complexity of nature, its details and lights and shadows, deflect the attention from the essentials and may in the beginning be too complex and confusing. This way, we also will avoid imposing visual stimulations upon the whole group. Visual and haptic types will apply their individual application to this stimulation, which starts from the self. The visually

Fig. 48. Sketching from posing figure interpreting a topic.

minded individual will include environment in his visual concept and will project the experience of the self into this environment, whereas the haptically minded student will become absorbed solely in the qualities deriving from his own subjective experiences.

At some point, however, it might become essential to include more than one motion into a representation—for instance, if the repetition of a motion is essential for the atmosphere of the working situation. Digging potatoes and putting them into bags is a continuous activity requiring repetition. We would not do justice to the essentials to exclude this act of repetition. Sometimes monotony is one of the essentials; then we would not much vary the motions but would place them parallel. Another time it belongs to the essentials to show the type of motions workers go through while executing a job. Then we would find it necessary to show the characteristics of the motion by representing characteristic phases showing the rhythm, or working process, in one representation: "The Rhythm of Workers on the Road Swinging Their Picks."

The essentials might even become more complex if we include social atmospheres or emotional reactions. However, with gaining confidence the urge for expression grows, and the guidance of the teacher may diminish.

'hus we shall see that the quality and sincerity of art expression are in ose relationship to the urge for expression we were able to stimulate. ustice to details must grow out of the desire for expression, otherwise we re not dealing with creative actiivty. The study of a detail must never be n aim in itself, and in this respect art education often fails. The academic method, which used rules for creative production, starts with details. A mouth separated from its environment loses its meaning and becomes an anatomical part unrelated to art. A mouth is a dynamic part of the face nd ceases to exist as such when separated from the whole.

Form and expression are a unit and can never be separated from each ther without doing harm to either part. If a student who paints a picture f a man pulling a boat gets "stuck" because he cannot express the essen- ial quality of a pulling hand, the study of a pulling hand grows out of the esire to incorporate this hand into the whole experience of a pulling man. He will then proceed with his study, not as a separated, isolated detail, ut as a part of the whole which becomes fulfillment only when it unites vith the rest. Studying details in the academic meaning becomes quite uperfluous within a curriculum of modern art education. *The urge for tudying details develops from the individual need for expression.* This eed, however, is very diverse, individual, and highly subjective. The isually minded will be more concerned with matters of appearance, tructure, and form, whereas the haptic type will deal with subjective experiences that place the ego in value relationship to environment.

Proper stimulation for the further development of the individual

From the foregoing discussion, it becomes apparent that proper art timulation relates as much to personality development as to creative expression itself. This double function of art teaching signifies its im- portance within this decisive period of development, and shows clearly why art should not be confined to a selected group but should become a means of expression for everyone.

To understand proper art stimulation during this age with regard to the further development of an individual, we have only to consider indi- viduals who did not receive the benefits of such a stimulation. They not only have lost the urge for creative expression, but also their creative and flexible responses to the outside world. Surely, many have regained these responses in a field other than art. However, it is still an open question whether even the latter would not benefit from art as a means of relaxation and of escape into a world that is completely different from their daily occupation. Those, however, who have not regained confidence in thei creativity (and this applies to the great majority) are searching for inade quate outlets, rigid or static (or rather diversions) which neither contribut to personality development, nor enrich the life of the individual. Art in an form, as a dynamic outlet, will not only confront the creator with evei changing problems, but will enhance the flexibility of his thinking an feeling.

We have discussed the direct influence of proper art stimulation oi the crisis of adolescence. As a direct result of this influence, the individua will not only carry on with his desire to express himself, but will evolv freely and flexibly. This unfolding process, which takes place durin, adolescence, is dependent upon the use of proper stimulation in creativ activity. This stimulation will reflect on the mental and emotional develop ment of the individual and play an important part in influencing efficienc in daily occupations. No occupation can be successfully performed withou creative thinking. This is true for the carpenter who creatively deals wit his material, in the same way as for the businessman who has to find new means to attract the buyer; or for the scientist; or for the physician wh has to deal with his problems from ever-changing assumptions, flexibly inventively, and creatively. Furthermore, creative activity under the guid ance of an enlightened teacher can become an important means for helpin young people in selecting life occupations that fit their psychologica aptitudes.

Guidance in the selection of vocations

As we have seen, it is the kind of experience which decisively deter mines the art product of the individual. Among other properties, the kin of experience will be greatly influenced by perceptual attributes. Visually minded individuals will concentrate on different experiences than wil haptic types. Although most individuals fall between these two extreme types there are few individuals who have no preference for the one or the other type. In creative work, this preference reveals itself very definitely not only in the choice of subject matter but also in its interpretation. Thus the teacher will, with some experience, be able to diagnose preferences of pupils from their work.

In some occupations visual control is impossible and would interfere with the efficiency of the worker. Among such occupations are mechanica jobs that are done inside a case with the hands as the only control; work in the darkness, which requires close body coordinations; work on switch boards; typing in which the control of the eyes would only decrease effi iency; work on the assembly line in which motions must become mechan-ized; and all occupations that demand a close control of touch impressions nd kinesthesis.

Other occupations place main emphasis on the use of the eyes because ney deal with ocular observation, such as estimation of distance, orienta-ion, and surveying. Certainly a great number of occupations require both bilities, yet it is often possible to determine which of these aptitudes is ominant and of greater importance.

The teacher's judgment should be based on a number of drawings pread over a period of time. Only then will he be able to diagnose justly ne aptitudes of his pupils. If there are still doubts concerning which is the ominant aptitude, a test can be given,* which determines the degree of ptitude. Usually the creative work over a certain period should be quite onclusive. It shows quite definitely whether the choice of subject matter determined by visual or subjective experiences, whether it is related to nvironment or the self. To what degree are visible impressions preferred, r haptical experiences represented? Do we deal with extreme types who lways concentrate on visual or haptic experiences only? Do we see a con-nuous sequence of drawings in which the external appearance, light and nadow, depth and distance, is expressed, or do we see occasionally a pref-erence for expressive features that refers to a subjective interpretation of n experience, not derived directly from visual experiences? How fre-quently do we see such interruptions in the dominance of visual interpreta-ions? If we have enough work over a sufficiently long period, we can lmost state the degree or percentage of the predominance of one or the ther aptitude. We might, however, also see both trends appear contin-ously in all works of one individual. However, this is rare. We usually an see whether the interpretation of subjective feelings or the representa-ion of the visible world was of greater importance to the creator.

THE MEANING OF AESTHETIC CRITERIA

Questions of aesthetics or composition cannot be separated from the reative development as a whole. They, too, develop according to the pecific need of the individual. Questions of aesthetics or composition annot or, better, *should not* be taught, but must grow out of the individual work of the student. They are closely bound up with personality. If com-osition is taught academically—that is, as a subject matter in itself de-ached from the work, it becomes dead knowledge which will inhibit

* Lowenfeld, V., "Tests for Visual and Haptical Aptitudes." *American Journal of sychology*, Vol. 58, 1945.

rather than help an intuitive urge. Thus teaching of composition will b
more harmful than useful at precisely the time when freedom is mor
important than rigid rules. If, however, composition grows out of indi
vidual needs, if it becomes a means of expression that helps the student t
express what is in his mind, it will be an important tool, more for th
teacher than for the *student*. It is not the student but the teacher wh
must learn the meaning of composition, and understand it, in order t
guide the student. In this way, certain qualities or needs of expression o
aesthetics can be achieved with the least effort and discouragement. There
fore, we shall proceed with a discussion of those problems of compositio
the teacher must know for guiding his pupils. Although compositio
unifies all elements of expression as a whole, we shall not be able to under
stand and analyze this unification without knowing the meaning of th
single elements. We, therefore, start with a discussion of the meaning o
the single elements of line, space, color, and their different relationship
to one another.

The elements of composition

We have seen that the explanation and the understanding of a work o
art as a product of human spirit and emotions must start from assumption
other than the explanation of a product of nature. Without any risk o
being misunderstood, we can experience nature subjectively, everyone i
his own way. We will all experience a sunset differently. One individua
is deeply impressed by the bright colors, another is attracted by mood an
atmosphere. This is very different with regard to a product of art. An ar
work is a product of the human spirit. In a human work, only those thing
are essential that are made by the intention of the author, the artist. W
can speak of a basic understanding of the work only if the understandin
is related to the essential intentions of the artist. That is why it would b
wrong to try to find our Western aesthetic principles in African sculpture
We would also approach a Gothic picture with entirely unsuitable mean
if we would search for an impressionistic depiction of space. Sometime
we think that art and our feeling for aesthetic values are so closely relate
that we can measure the greatness of an art work by its "beauty." But the
again we see that different cultures and epochs had quite different opinion
on "beauty"; so we must assume that "beauty" also is a relative valu
judgment. People often say, "I would not hang such a picture in my room."
We must know that to be hung in a room is not the ultimate destiny of
picture and that not all pictures lend themselves to decorative purpose
In fact only a very few do, and these are not always the best. Great work

of art are too much filled with tension and emotions to lend themselves to decorative purposes only.*

Then again some people think that the complexity of content of a picture determines its greatness, and feel betrayed when they recognize that greatest works of art often have the simplest contents, whereas greatest ideas do not necessarily have to be expressed artistically. Even portraits, where a realistic interpretation in terms of a likeness might claim particular validity, cannot be judged solely by realistic standards. Leonardo da Vinci has this to say in this connection: "In painting a portrait, a good painter has two chief objects to paint: man and the intention of his soul; the first is easy, the latter hard." Or: "The painter who draws by practice and judgment of the eye without the use of reason is like a mirror which reproduces all the objects which are set opposite to it, very similar but without knowledge of the same; he is like a parrot which talks words without understanding." The photographic camera was not invented at that time, otherwise, I am sure, Leonardo da Vinci would have replaced the mirror with a camera.

Rather than showing the elements of which a composition consists, our discussion heretofore has tried to eliminate the negative factors that do not contribute to the understanding of a work of art. A creative product of a student or a work of art can be understood only by its own means, by studying the basic elements, such as the line and its relationships, space and its relative meanings, and color and its individual interpretations. To do this, we shall first discuss the meaning of the single elements, and later bring them into relation with one another.†

THE MEANING OF THE LINE AND ITS RELATIONS   If we draw a line, it would be a creation—very primitive, but a creation nevertheless because this line expresses something related to our feelings or ideas. The line might be bold, black, and direct, starting and stopping at definite points and thus showing *decision* of character. The line might be timid, dainty, wavering, *indefinite* like a child just starting to take his first steps, not knowing where he will end. Or the line might be *dreamy,* as it seems to us when we are suddenly at a place without knowing how we reached it; or the line might be *sketchy,* consisting of many parts, whose synthesis finally might approach the mental image which it followed step by step; or it might be an *intellectual* line, well thought over and carefully controlled;

* Chandler, A. R., *Beauty and Human Nature, Elements of Psychological Aesthetics.* New York: D. Appleton Century Co., Inc., 1934.
† Munro, Thomas, "Powers of Art Appreciation and Evaluation," in *Art in American Life and Education.* Bloomington, Ill.: Public School Publishing Co., 1941.

or it might be a *calm* line in which everything is quietly and carefully but determinedly drawn like the uniform waves of the calm sea; or it is an *excited* line in which no motions can be predicted, ever-changing as our emotions change when we live through great excitements; or a *felt* line drawn unconsciously, just *intuitively* following an emotional drive; or we might have drawn the line with a *utilitarian* purpose in mind, perhaps to separate two areas, as an architect who wants to indicate that this space has to be divided; or did we have in our mind a *symbolic sign* like the "minus," thinking only of its function or meaning, which through repetition has received general validity? Or were we aware of its *quality* as it flowed from our pencil as we can see it in the signatures of *vain* persons, who play with the line like a lady who never can handle her powder puff elegantly enough when she feels conscious of being observed? Or is it an *interrupted* line, drawn in two or many continuations, showing thoughts which are not spoken out as we do it in letters in which we like to express continuations of thoughts by merely adding a few interrupted lines? Or is the thought so important that we have to *underline* it; or did we draw entirely *mechanically* as we do it when doodling while waiting at the telephone for an important call; or did we want to emphasize *rhythm* by placing one line parallel to another weighing carefully the different widths of the lines as we do it when designing; or were we finally *unsatisfied* with the whole approach and crossed it with two bold strokes indicating that it no longer exists?

These are only some of the distinctions of lines which will lead to a better understanding of the individual and his work; however, we would not do justice to the meaning of the line within a composition without discussing the different relationships of lines among one another. Such a discussion of merely the meaning of the line itself without its relationship to environment would be like a life story that is concerned only with the facts which deal directly with the person, and not with the interdependent causal connections that determine the life of an individual, like: "Up to this date Miss X was a student at this college. She could not continue her studies." That really is like an interrupted line. But why is it interrupted? Was she compelled to interrupt her studies or did she do it voluntarily? Will it be merely an interruption or won't she come back at all? What tragedy sometimes lies behind such simple words as "she could not continue her studies." Lack of money, illness, death, or whatever the reason, we never would be satisfied with a life story that only mentions the facts. The circumstances under which she interrupted her studies will make the fact interesting and dramatic to us. In the same way that we would like to see the accompanying lines in her life, we also would like to see the circum-

ances under which lines are interrupted, or in general, the relationships
f lines to one another.

Two indefinite lines that finally meet at a definite point after long and
any interruptions are like two friends who, after long interrupted con-
act, meet again. If, however, these two lines are definite, starting at a
efinite point, steering consciously toward the meeting point from the
ery beginning, their meaning is quite different. It is the same as if two
ersons would reach for something they already have in mind. The more
his something is removed from their reach, the more inaccessible it be-
omes. It is the same with the two converging lines of a Gothic arch whose
leaning has gone into the realm of inapproachable religious faith. People
nd ideas can meet under diverse circumstances; so can lines. The line
ecomes a living symbol, and as soon as we have reached this point, we
eed no longer ponder over this symbol's meaning, because we can draw
ur experiences and relationships directly from life.

We know from the very beginning of creative activity, from scribbling,
vhat *repetition* can mean. In scribbling, repetition meant a greater con-
ciousness. But we know from life how different the meaning of repetition
an be, depending upon the circumstances under which something is
epeated. If a bold line is repeated by a dainty sketchy line, it might mean
mere imitation, like one who tries to imitate the original but is not quite
ure of himself. However, repetition that is done over and over with the
ame degree of certainty might have the same effect as the uniform ticking
of a clock which creates a monotonous rhythm that is noticed only when the
lock stops, or when the rhythm changes. Thus it might mean equality or
oure rhythm depending upon the circumstances under which the lines
epeat themselves.

If I have lost something valuable to me, and I ask someone to help me
earch for it, we both would do the same thing—we would search for the
ost article. The emotions, however, with which both are participating are
of different intensity, since the lost object belongs to me. Thus parallel
ines would not do justice to such an expression. We would both search
differently. How different it would be if the emotional factor would be
cut out, as with the workers in a field who harvest potatoes or grain all day
long! Here, the parallel lines would get their real meaning: of an *ever-
lasting* repetition. If we would interrupt these parallel bent motions by
upright figures, these interruptions would then introduce a pause, as Millet
did it in his famous picture, "The Gleaners." The more upright the line
(or the figures), the more definite is the interruption as shown in the
illustration.

If, however, we deal with parallel lines that are in perpendicular rela-

tionship to a base line, the meaning of the parallel lines changes again
(|) The perpendicular line, the most *absolute* line which is neither influ
enced from the left nor from the right, expresses the same *stability* that
flagpole expresses as the bearer of the symbol of the country. If thos
lines of stability are repeated in equal intervals, they will have the sam
meaning as soldiers, in whom *equality* and *stability* are unified. If, how
ever, *one line stands out* from this uniformity, it immediately catches ou
attention like one civilian in the midst of a row of soldiers. The circum
stances under which this line is standing out will determine its meaning
It might be an odd line with a little slant, as a felled tree falling in th
midst of a forest of skyward-growing trees has *lost its stability;* or it migh
stand out in height overlooking all other lines like the officer on horseback
We might, however, just as well raise the base line in a convex curve lik
a hill overlooking the valley, or we might introduce a *protecting* line,
concave line like a protecting hole.

If the relationship of lines is well balanced, if one line takes care of th
other, as in a building in which all stones hold together, we speak of *stati*
lines; if, however, one stone is removed all other stones start moving. W
then speak of *dynamic lines,* lines that are no longer balanced but moving
Lines might be *open, receiving* like our arms when we meet again after
long separation. But just as we might not be quite sure whether the person
we are about to greet is indeed the long-unseen friend, since he ha
changed during his absence, so will the circumstances determine the mean
ing under which the open lines are drawn. Or lines might *be closed.* This
could mean *protection* as well as *prison,* depending on the kind of lines
expressing the meaning of closing. If they are bold, rough and determine
like bars of a cell, we surely associate them with "prison"; if they are
round, carefully surrounding the hole, they will be protecting. If, however,
one *line breaks through* such a protecting line, like the arm of Adam by
Michelangelo which reaches out from the earth to communicate with God,
the circumstances under which the line breaks through will determine
its meaning; it might be a tree breaking through the horizon, reaching
skyward, or it might be the hand of Adam.

In this connection the different height of the horizon in a picture might
receive its real significance. A high horizon which because of its height will
not be interrupted, serves as a protection, whereas a low horizon makes the
landscape stand out, and with the frequently interrupted horizontal line,
introduces a more unquiet and restless atmosphere. A high horizon may
include all people living in this space as a protecting line. A low horizon,
however, exposes man to the elements.

Although this discussion on the meaning of the line and its relationships is by no means exhaustive—since life can never be discussed exhaustively—it has shown the close interdependence of line and experience and has thus demonstrated that the line, as a vital element of expression, can be understood only as a part of it.*

THE MEANING OF SPACE AND ITS RELATIONS   As long as space is not defined in its qualities, it can generally have four meanings: (1) in its unlimited quality, (2) within a restricted boundary, (3) the relationships of spaces of different significance, and (4) we in the space, or our subjective relationship to space.

The unlimited space cannot be conceived in its totality. Its infinity, the universe, is irrational. Space becomes accessible to our senses only when we circumscribe it, or when we assign to it a definite meaning. As long as we think of the inaccessible space of the universe, space remains irrational. As soon as we think in terms of "sky," we relate the sky to a definite atmosphere or mood, we have assigned to space a definite meaning, and as such, it becomes accessible to our senses, especially to our optical sense. If we think of restricted space, like the space in a room, it becomes accessible not only to our eyes but also to our kinesthesis or acoustic reactions. This space can be measured and, therefore, objectively determined in its sizes. The quality of this space, however, depends upon our subjective relationship to it. *Objective* space is space perceived *optically*. Its pictorial representation is governed by the law of perspective. Its clearest depiction is produced by the photographic camera. *Subjective space* is the space in which we include the self. In it, therefore, we find a predominance of subjective interpretations or judgments of value. They can refer to sizes and their subjective values, or they can refer to the qualities of spaces as expressed through different emphasis on light and shadow and color.

A simple story will illustrate the meaning of these subjective relationships and their interpretation in art. You and your friend are standing in front of a door not knowing what or whom you will meet when the door is opened. Your present relationships to the space inside of the door, therefore, is *undetermined*. The only thing you know is that you and your friend will soon enter a room. In art we would say that a *definite* space experience is contrasted to an *indefinite* one, thus creating the same tension and interest that we feel now as we are waiting in front of the door. The door opens! We enter a small, low room. The room is bare and empty. No one is living there; people have not yet moved in. This room has two doors.

* D'Amico, Victor, *Creative Teaching in Art*. Scranton: International Textbook Co., 1941.

Your friend goes through one, you through the other. You enter a very small room, almost the size of a closet; your friend, however, enters a big hall. Both of you are compelled to stay in your rooms for some time without being able to leave them. After you have lived in these rooms you come back into the room from which you entered. Your impressions will be different. You will find this "small room" very large; your friend, accustomed to his big hall, will find it smaller than before. Your subjective relationship to the size of the room has changed. Through the inclusion of the self the spatial relations to the sizes of the different rooms have become subjective.

In art these subjective interpretations of value relationships in space are of prime significance. Not only does the significance, which is assigned to the self, change with regard to the importance it has in relation to environment, but the spaces also change with regard to the emotional significance they have to us.

Before discussing this experience of spatial relationships with regard to sizes in its pictorial representations, I would like to continue the story about the rooms, adding to the subjective relationships of sizes the relationships of qualities.

Again you and your friend are standing in front of the same door. The difference in your impressions then and now consists of the fact that you both have now *different* but *definite* feelings of what will meet you when the door opens. Having lived in the "closet" for such a long time, you will have in your mind a comfortably sized room, whereas your friend, having lived in the big hall, will remember this room as small. The door opens and how surprised you both are when you discover a very nicely and comfortably furnished room with a fine rug and well-designed furniture. Again you don't stay in this room, but each of you enters one of the two doors that lead into the rooms well known to you both. Again how great is the surprise to find your very small room as beautiful as you ever could imagine a room to be. It has changed to a perfectly designed room, a room as comfortable as you never could have dreamed it, and at once you feel quite at home. Every glance reveals something new, gives more satisfaction of well-spaced and perfectly designed environment. Your friend, in the meanwhile, entered his room. The big hall has not changed except that it now appears barer and grayer than before. The walls have become dirtier, the atmosphere more gloomy. He feels quite lost in this big hall and anxiously awaits the time when he will be allowed to leave. How different are your impressions when you both return to the middle room. To you, coming from your most perfectly designed room, the middle room, though larger than yours, will appear quite common, neither attractive nor distinctive in any respect. How different is the reaction of your friend. He will be delighted with everything in this room; everything will appear wonderful to him. Though he comes from his big hall, the middle room now seems to him better than anything he could imagine.

We conclude from these two stories that *big space* may mean *much space* and *freedom*, as well as *being lost* and *restricted* (in one's comfort). *Small space*, however, may mean *restriction in space* and in *freedom* as well as *greatest satisfaction* in being in a world of one's own. These problems could be further complicated by the addition of the problem of different personalities and their emotional reactions. The latter is the problem of Beethoven who wrote, "I hate the world at large, with its grimaces; how well I feel in my four walls"; as well as the problem of the little dancer who sits at home weeping because she cannot find the way to the world at large.

How are the subjective relationships expressed in art? To concretize the discussion, these compositional elements will be analyzed by means of three pictures representing the same subject in different space relationships. The topic is the same, "A Wood Chopper," and we shall see how his spatial relationships determine not only the meaning of the pictures but also change his character and emotional relationships.

a   b   c

Fig. 49. "Wood Chopper."

The problem is the same as with the rooms. Like the entrance room in the former story, here the woodcutter remains in fact unchanged. What does change is his relationship to the surrounding spaces. Fig. 49a shows the relationship between sky and earth; in Fig. 49b, the immediate space in which he lives becomes characterized by a higher horizon; and in Fig. 49c, the space around him becomes restricted. If we investigate these changes we shall find phenomena closely parallel to the problems developed in the story of the rooms. Vast space, as expressed in Fig. 49a, means here *unrestricted freedom*. The space surrounding the woodcutter is almost unrestricted. In this space, in which he is uplifted by the convex line of the hill (see discussion on "line"), he stands out as a symbol of power, a master over nature, cutting wood, chopping trees at his own will. No one interferes with him. How different is the effect of Fig. 49b, where he is no longer surrounded by free air in free space. Through the raised horizon he has become a part of the earth, of his earth, characterized by stumps of trees and lumber. It is his earthy life that surrounds him. In Fig. 49a we were able to forget that woodcutting is a job with which to earn one's living, but in Fig. 49b we definitely are not only reminded of that but become aware of what it means to cut wood all day long. The self is struggling with its environment. No one is victorious, and the only thing standing out above the horizon is the axe, a reminder that in it lies power and that with it the man earns his living. The subjective relationship of the wood chopper to the space that surrounds him has changed. It has narrowed his field of vision and has brought him down to his daily occupation. How this relationship has changed in Fig. 49c! Now even the horizon has disappeared. The trees stand like the bars of a prison. The man has become the victim of his occupation, perhaps of society, a prisoner of the trees, which seem to take away from him air and freedom. How small he appears now; how beaten down by his environment, especially if compared with Fig. 49a.

However, as we have learned from our story about the different rooms and their relationships, much space not only means freedom but may also mean the feeling *of being lost,* whereas restricted space may mean greatest satisfaction derived from the feeling *of being in the world of one's own.* These relative value judgments in art are of great significance They help in understanding the works of art and provide the teacher with the proper perspective for criticizing and evaluating art products of children. How often do we see a student struggle for a definite expression, without even being aware of the problems involved. Being aware of such psychological principles in the use of the elements of composition will help the teacher to protect his students from such unnecessary struggles. How this different expression of much space with the meaning of being lost, or of restricted space with the meaning of feeling happy in one's own world is shown in art, is demonstrated by means of the following three illustrations. Again the central figure remains unchanged. The topic is "Coming Home."

a
b
c

Fig. 50. "Coming Home."

Fig. 50a, which corresponds to Fig. 49a, shows the person standing out from the horizon and exposed to storm in the vastness of space. But here, unlike Fig. 49a, where standing-out meant power, the same spatial relationship means loneliness, the feeling of being lost in the vastness of almost unrestricted space. In Fig. 50b the horizon is moved up as in Fig. 49b, and characterizes more the immediate space of action. But unlike Fig. 49b where it meant more restriction, it now has the significance of greater protection. The man can no longer feel as lonely and lost as in Fig. 50a, for he is surrounded by protecting elements. This feeling of security is increased in Fig. 50c, "Home-Coming," where the space is completely restricted. It is not the restriction of a prison as it was in Fig. 49c; it is now complete protection, which creates the feeling of happiness, in contrast to Fig. 49c.

How can the same space relations create such divers impressions? It is exactly as in the story of the rooms. Here also, all depends on the circumstances under which these space relationships occur. If we compare Fig. 50c with Fig. 49c, we will immediately recognize that in Fig. 49c restriction in space is expressed by lines that are determined—determined and bold because they start and stop at definite points, going over the whole length of the picture, as the trees do. They are dynamic and excited lines because we cannot predict where they will start, where they have their base. This gives us the feeling that even trees might come closer and closer, thus expressing *unlimited* restriction. How different are the lines used in Fig. 50c, where restricted space expresses obviously the feeling of protection. Here we have the restricted space expressed by utilitarian static lines, lines symbolizing the boundaries of the room; by lines that are not in contrast to the central figure (as the trees are contrasted to the woodcutter), but which unite with him. They find in him their continuation, as it can be so well seen in the arms of the boy and the motion of the woman All lines either *unite* or *protect*.

The very same difference in the use of lines holds true for Fig. 50b and 49b, and Fig. 49a and 50a. Whereas in Fig. 50b the lines are all curved around the central figure as if to frame him almost like a protective umbrella, in Fig. 49b the lines are all opposing the central figure, stinging against him, as it were, pointing swords toward him irregularly.

From this discussion it becomes clear that the means of expression determine the particular meaning of spatial relationships.

THE MEANING OF LIGHT AND SHADOW   Throughout the history of art the meaning of light and shadow has gone through the most interesting and divers phases. If one were to write a history of art, based only upon the changes in the meaning of light and shadow during the different epochs and cultures, he might produce one of the most dramatically written histories of art. The use of light and shadow in art in its different meanings and qualities not only indicates a different creative concept, but allows us as we shall see, to draw conclusions concerning different attitudes toward life and their psychological implications. A period which has not yet "discovered" the existence of light and shadow must be quite different from one in which light and shadow are accurately used according to our visual percept. How different must be a period that not only uses light and shadow but accentuates it by exaggerating light and deepening shadows How different from such an epoch must be a period in which light and shadow are used as *effects,* as *illuminations,* dramatically as on a stage And again how different must be a time in which light is used only as *source of light,* in a *utilitarian meaning,* as it were to turn on the light in dark room only for the purpose of better visibility. And how different must be a period in which light and shadow are used independently from realistic laws, through their own forces, governed only by intuitive means, thus creating a mysterious atmosphere. Or we see an epoch, perhaps on the opposite end of the scale, that is not only satisfied with the visual recognition of light and shadow but analyzes the way the impressions of light and shadow reach our eyes. Again, how contrasted is the experience with light and darks if we exclude external visual impressions and emphasize the *expressive* qualities of the *warmth* of light, or the *frightening* attributes of lightning or the *emptiness* and *loneliness* of darkness; and how different would be a period that deals with light and dark only in their qualities as *design*—that is, the proper distribution of both values.

Of course, we have shown here only a few meanings of light and shadow; many more may be found, especially when we consider the fact at rarely does one of these attributes appear independently. The more omplex mixtures of different attitudes toward light and shadow give specially a deep insight into the struggle for the predominance of certain xperiences. In order to get such a deeper insight into the nature of the meaning of light and shadow (or, better, lights and darks), we shall discuss the psychological origin of these different concepts. Such a discussion is important not only for the understanding and appreciation of the works of art of different cultures and epochs, but also for the proper stimulation and understanding of students who want to express something definite by means of light and shadow but, unaware of their real significance, use lights and darks in a conventional way. A teacher who knows these most diverse origins of the experiences with lights and darks will be able to direct the students' thinking into adequate channels and avoid discouragements, which always result from a discrepancy between the mental image and its actual representation.

If we perceive an object without using our eyes, the impression we receive from this object is not at all connected with lights and shadows, or only associatively. If we try to perceive a head by touch impressions only and glide our hand along the profile, our impression consists of the contour of the profile, of a line along which we move our fingers. Indeed, we speak of psychology of the touch line, meaning the main line of touch impressions which characterize the object. This line has a kinesthetic origin, the meaning of moving along the outline. Only the line can have this meaning. Consequently, we should find in all nonvisual or haptic epochs of art or art expressions an emphasis on the line as a means of representation. In other words, an artist who is more concerned with subjective experiences, the haptic artist, will predominantly use the line as a means of expression and not the visual experience of light and shadow. Lights and shadows in their real meaning are expressions of the three-dimensional qualities of space. The line as a boundary, however, can also become a mere symbol of expression of the most essential representation, of the condensed abstract of the thing itself. The three-dimensional qualities become meaningless in comparison to the importance of the expression of the essential meaning of the object (Fig. 51). These essential qualities are neither connected with the surface nor with the substance of the thing. Therefore, neither light nor shadow will be able to signify them. The line, itself of abstract quality (we do not see lines in nature), will be the best representative for these spiritual values.

Therefore it can be easily understood, that in periods of art in which the spiritual forces diminish, the meaning of the substance and surface increases. It is possible, however, that the meaning of substance is so

Fig. 51. Byzantine mural emphasizing unrealistic meaning of the line.

subordinate that light and shadow indicate only the three-dimensiona quality of the thing and nothing else. Light and shadow have merely th meaning of characterizing the representations. In such works of art, ligh and shadow are confined to the objects which are of expressive importanc (Fig. 52). The visual experience, which always needs a source of light, i such works is highly subordinate. Therefore, all works of art, in whic either expression or the mere abstract characterization of form and sub stance is predominant, show light and shadow only as means of emphasiz ing the meaningful parts. If, however, a visual experience is reported— that is, characterized accurately, light and shadow go beyond specifi objects and include environment as well. These realistic representation (reports on nature) use light and shadow to characterize nature itsel without accentuating our subjective relationship to it. The more the desir grows to give an exact report, as connected with utilitarian purposes, th more light and shadow obey laws related to the laws of perspective. Thes tendencies are best seen in creative works of individuals who emphasize i their work their realistic or utilitarian relationship to the object. If the ex perience of light and shadow becomes a dominant experience, if the three dimensional quality of form becomes the main discovery in a work of ar light and shadow appear exaggerated. This can often be seen in drawing

PVS·KAROLI·CRIVELLI·VENETI

ig. 52. Madonna. After a painting by Crivelli. Bache Collection. Metropolitan
Museum of Art, N. Y. Light and shadow merely characterize form. (Courtesy
Bettmann Archives.)

Fig. 53. Entombment of Christ. After a painting by Caravaggio. Vatican, Rome. Exaggeration of light and shadow. (Courtesy Bettmann Archives.)

Fig. 54. Adoration of the Shepherds. After a painting by El Greco. Dramatic illumination. (Courtesy Bettmann Archives.)

Fig. 55. Painting by Rembrandt. Magic mystical light.

of youths or in periods of art in which the discovery of light and shadow
has the quality of a first experience. Such a discovery often leads to the
need to find and indicate the source of light. In such works of art, not
only light and shadow in their relationship are shown, but also the source
from which the light comes (Fig. 53). Paintings of interiors, therefore,
deal with this kind of discovery of a special meaning of light.

Fig. 56. Haystack and Sheep. After a painting by C. Pissarro. Light and shadow express atmosphere, surface appearance and distance. (Courtesy Bettmann Archives.)

Epochs and cultures that are dynamic and not content with the mere visible experiences, use light and shadow to give expression to this dramatic quality characteristic of this epoch. In such cultures the work of art is more like a gigantic stage design. Neither life nor atmosphere is real. Both appear in the dramatic illuminations of baroque art in which the fight of earthly with spiritual qualities is deeply symbolized by this specific use of light. When light and shadow lose the quality of dramatic interpretations as well as of realistic representations, they no longer obey the laws of nature. The artist, the Lord as it were, then freely determines lights and shadows. He creates his own laws, which are governed only by the relationship of his intuitive forces to the world outside (Fig. 54). The atmosphere created by these forces is necessarily magically mystic. The best representative is Rembrandt in his latest works. His greatest strength, and his most precious gift to mankind, is his light vibrating in the darkness and his power of dealing with lights and darks in unlimited and absolute freedom (Fig. 55). The antipode to this most mysterious way of directing lights and shadows intuitively is an art which not only prefers the bright

Fig. 57a. Painting by Picasso. Meaning of darks and lights are entirely different from visual impressions. (Courtesy Museum of Modern Art, N. Y.)

daylight in which nothing can be hidden, but tries to analyze these daylight impressions with regard to quality of light, shadows, and color (Fig. 56). Visual experiences like atmosphere, the different qualities and intensities of surface appearances, celebrate their triumphs.

Impressionistic art is visual art in its extreme meaning. Light, shadow and color are no longer means to an end, but ends themselves. In this art

Fig. 57b. Painting by Rouault in which lights and darks are emotionally determined. (Courtesy Museum of Modern Art, N. Y.)

the evaluation of lights and darks obeys only the rules of visual perception. Directly opposed to this art we shall find those creations which use lights and darks no longer in connection with visually perceivable appearances. This type of art in which light sometimes is an *expression* of happiness, another time has a mere symbolic meaning, is *purely expressive.* It places light and dark in value relationship to each other, using it *emotionally,* *expressively,* and *symbolically.* In this art, lights and shadows are neither governed by rules nor do they obey any external laws (Fig. 57a and b). How different is the significance of lights and darks if we finally look at the art in which lights and darks seemingly have the purest meaning because in design its significance is not connected with any subject matter. The meaning of light and dark in design is nothing else but their proper distribution.*

From this discussion it follows that lights and darks must be treated differently according to their special meaning. It would be entirely wrong to stimulate an individual who intends to express his inner relationship to lights and darks by means of visual methods referring to the outside appearance of lights and shadows. It would be just as wrong to stimulate an individual who is mainly interested in the impressionistic qualities of lights and shadows by means of his emotional responses to darks and lights. It is of great significance, therefore, that we know the different meanings of light and shadow as important elements of a composition, because only then will we be able to understand its meaning as a creative force.

COLOR, AN ELEMENT IN COMPOSITION   Color, as an element of composition, is a means of artistic expression. Therefore, we shall deal with it, in this framework, from this angle only. Thus, we exclude the science of color which is just as remote from our discussion as the teaching of "right measurements" as seen in the "golden mean." * Only our subjective relationship to color, the meaning color has to the creator, will be discussed within this chapter.

Color can have as many meanings as line, space, or lights and darks. The simplest is the meaning of mere characterization. Color merely characterizes the object: the grass is green, the sky is blue, the bark of a tree is brown, the foliage is green, and so forth. An artist who uses color merely to characterize objects must put his creative emphasis elsewhere because he must be concerned with other means of expression more than with color. Color has for this artist a subordinate meaning. It is a mere *descriptive* meaning which finds its parallel in the early stages of speech development. The main aim of this descriptive meaning lies in the establishment of a relationship between color and object, or in speech, between word and

* Compare with Schoen, M., *Art and Beauty.* New York: The Macmillan Co., 1942; Opdyke, George H., *Art and Nature Appreciation.* New York: The Macmillan Co., 1933.

* The golden mean is a "most desired proportion" according to the geometrical progression: 8, 13, 21, 34, 55 . . . and so forth or 13/8, 21/13, 34/21 . . . and so forth. This was already known to the Egyptians and Greeks. Hambidge, Jay, *Dynamic Symmetry.* New Haven: Yale University Press, 1923.

meaning. The origin of this relationship in art can be visual or haptical—visual when the description is done according to our visual percept, which uses the eyes as the intermediaries; haptical when the description is an outcome of emotional or body reactions. Both relationships can be *general and bold* or *individual and sensitive,* depending upon epoch and culture, and artist personality. The more differentiated these relationships between object and color grow, the more complex becomes the problem of color. The most general and bold visual relationship is the assignment of one local color always related to the same object (see "Objective Stage of Color p. 62). The visual percept is thus general and undifferentiated, and is satisfied merely by the process of distinguishing objects roughly by relating them to the color to which they pertain. The most general and bold haptic relationship between object and color is the repetition of one and the same color for the same emotional experience. Thus a rigid relationship between emotion and color represents the most primitive haptic color experience. Through such a general validity and repetition, the color becomes a symbol of expression. *Color symbols thus are the most primitive haptic means of color expressions.*

The more differentiated visual color experiences grow, the more we see the need to refrain from using local color tones. With the increased desire *to see* and *observe* color, the quality of color assigned to the objects and the relationships of the colors to one another become more differentiated and complex. Visual relationships of color deal with the optically perceivable influences of one color on another. Red will appear different in a blue or yellow environment. The reflections of colors on one another may, however, assume such importance that local colors cease to exist. In this art, the relationship between object and color has shifted its center of gravity from the importance of the object to the meaning of color. In impressionistic art, the visual percept has attained its highest significance.

The more differentiated haptic color experiences grow, the more we abstain from color symbols of general validity. Color expression becomes a highly subjective experience. Associations with past experiences become fused with emotional reactions to present experiences. Also, with the increasing differentiation of haptic color experiences, color relationships assume major significance. Haptic color relationships are determined by the emotional effects colors have on us. A blue within purple might have a lonely, sad effect, whereas a purple within a bright-yellow environment will create the mood of solemnity. A green close to a shrill yellow might mean "fear," whereas it might calm us down if we place it close to a soft blue. Although much has been written on the emotional meaning and significance of color, color relationship will always be a highly subjective means of expression. Expressionistic art, therefore, is the art in which haptic color experiences receive their highest meaning.

Maitland Graves provides a brief summary of the conclusions on the psychological effects of color "reached by investigators and psychologists as a result of experiments upon thousands of people.*

"The warm colors, yellow, orange, and red, are positive and aggressive, restless, or stimulating, as compared to the cool violets, blues, and greens, which are negative, aloof, and retiring, tranquil or serene.

"Color preference is as follows, in the order named (pure colors): a. Red, b. Blue, c. Violet, d. Green, e. Orange, f. Yellow.

"Pure colors are preferred to shades and tints when used in small areas.

"In large areas, shades and tints are preferred to pure colors." †

Although these conclusions are reached "on thousands of people," they have no general validity for teaching purposes. That they are reached on thousands of people means only that the majority reacted to these colors in the way the summary shows. Since the majority of an average population is visually minded, the haptically minded minority is neglected if we apply the results of this "summary" rigidly. In a classroom situation the haptically minded group may need more attention than the visually minded. In this case, such summaries must be interpreted with great care.

In his *Characteristics and Symbolism of Color,* Maitland Graves refers to historic and present-day symbolisms of colors. He discusses pleasant and unpleasant associations without undue dogmatism. In his analysis of the majority of the colors, he provides interesting and valuable information. But Graves also emphasizes that such information is subjective and is not generally valid. He says, "Yellow, for example, is a sacred color, not only in China but also in European Christianity. On the other hand, it is sometimes used to signify treachery and deceit. This is confusing unless it is remembered that yellow is, and has been, loosely applied to many hues, tints, and shades, ranging from the clear and brilliant cadmium and lemon yellows to the ochers and bilious greenish yellows. . . . Bright clear yellow is emblematic of the sun and is cheerful, gay, and lively. . . . The darker and the more neutralized yellows and greenish yellows are the most unpopular and disliked of all colors. These yellows are associated with sickness and disease, indecency, cowardice, jealousy, envy, deceit, and treachery. The yellow flag is flown on quarantined ships and sometimes hospitals. In tenth-century France, the doors of the houses of traitors and

---

* Graves, Maitland, *The Art of Color and Design,* p. 256. New York: McGraw-Hill Book Company, Inc., 1941.
† *Ibid.,* p. 257.

criminals were painted yellow, and Judas was pictured as clad in yellow garments. . . . Today the terms 'yellow dog' and 'yellow streak' convey the ideas of treachery and cowardice. Nevertheless, these yellows, although unpleasant by themselves, may be satisfactory and even beautiful when properly related with other colors." *

Valuable and important as these color associations may be for the proper knowledge and understanding of colors, color itself in art is meaningless unless related to its environment. And, again according to Graves, "colors unpleasant by themselves may be satisfactory and even beautiful when properly related with other colors. That shows that there is no general validity or rule in color reactions in art, but that relationships determine their meaning just as they do in space and line."

Instead of discussing the possible meanings of the single colors, we shall, therefore, discuss the meaning of color relationships within a composition. Depending upon period and culture, and artist personality, color relationship can be based on aesthetic or expressive assumptions.

In the visual and decorative arts, color relationships are based mostly on aesthetic functions. Color relationships, therefore, are dependent upon the principles given in color harmony. These principles can best be understood if we compare them with music, especially with tonal music, the music in which the longing for resounding chords is one of the main driving forces. In some of the tonal works of music the interest in the work of art is increased by the dramatic tension under which sounds approach one another under different circumstances, until the longing for the chord is so great, that the chord finally has to resound. Of course, the type of experience underlying this "battle" is different with different works and composers.

In the representative arts we do not deal with different time sequences as we do in listening to music. We can see a picture simultaneously. In color, however, we can draw close parallels with music, if we regard the single colors as tones and a color harmony as chord. In a picture, as in music, the resounding of a color harmony can be interrupted by colors which are interpolated in order to increase the tension or interest for the "resounding" color harmony. In the same way that rhythm in music is produced by the principle of repetition, it is also produced in color. In music as well as in color compositions the interest in repetitions is created by varying them, either by different emphasis with regard to the intensity of tones (dynamics) or through different intervals (harmonies).

If the longing for the resounding of a chord is subordinated to the expressive quality, disregarding whether it is produced by discords or

* *Ibid.*, p. 259.

chords, we deal with the type of music which can be compared with color compositions in which aesthetic are subordinated to expressive values. In this realm color relationships assume a different significance. Subjective value relationships dominate this type of color composition. There are no absolute bright or poor colors. Everything depends upon the meaning of color with regard to its environment. We may compare this experience with a girl who looks beautifully dressed in her dull environment. As soon as she has to compete with others on the dance floor, she will be submerged in the mass of color and brightness. Bright colors may become dull when overpowered by environmental influences. Bright colors may no more seem bright but monotonous when repeated by equally intensive colors.

The significance attached to color can be apprehended by imagining the feeling of a student who could not graduate but has to sit in her "beautiful" evening dress amongst her graduate colleagues wearing their black baccalaureate gowns. If she would have to paint this picture, the bright colors of her evening dress would not assume the meaning of brightness or significance. Visually bright colors, then, do not necessarily refer to emotional contents of the same meaning. Colors receive their emotional content through the relationships in which they are represented. Since these relationships are an outcome of subjective experiences and associations, color relationships in expressionistic art are highly individual.

UNITY, OR COMPOSITION   Unity, or composition, in a work of art we call the integration of all the previously mentioned properties in a sum total in which all compositional elements are interwoven into one consistent pattern. "The purpose of composition is to organize all the physical elements which make up a work of art into a coherent pattern, pleasing to the senses." * However, "pleasing to the senses" is a relative value judgment. We all know that many people would oppose our calling Picasso's mural, "Guernica" pleasing to the senses. We have, however, a simple means to prove this "consistent pattern" by attempting to change the unity in a work of art. The greater the work of art, the less is the possibility of making the slightest change in any of its compositional elements. Any attempt to change any one of the compositional properties must subsequently result in a disunity of all other elements. If we would change the arm of "Adam" in the mural by Michelangelo, the whole mural would fall into pieces and would lose its "consistent pattern." The same result would attend an attempt to raise the line that separates Adam from the Lord. A

* Read, Herbert, *Education Through Art.* London: Faber and Faber, Ltd., 1943.

work of art contains the highest and most complete organization of its elements. In such an organization there is nothing superfluous. It represents the highest form of economy. Every part is related to the whole and the whole is related to every part. The foreground supports the background and the background brings out the foreground. If one can exist without the other, the work of art is incomplete.

In recognizing this unity of composition as the highest form of organization and economy in which nothing can be changed without doing harm to the whole, an important means of criticism is placed in the hands of the educator. He will no longer look exclusively for balance and rhythm, the aesthetic properties in a composition, but will become aware of the integration of all elements and their expressive qualities. He will use as a criterion the possibility of changes as well as the necessity that each part is a part of the whole. He will furthermore steer toward this highest economy in which only the most necessary things are expressed. *Necessary,* however, also is a relative value judgment. Necessary for a visual work of art are other properties than for a haptical one. This again is an important principle of which the educator must be aware. In both realms of art, however, he will not succeed if he does not place the individual above rules, if he does not consider unity of composition the most *integrated outcome of personality and creation.**

USE OF TECHNIQUES IN THE SECONDARY SCHOOL

What has been said in the foregoing section concerning the meaning of economy in a work of art can also be applied to the art of teaching and to the use of techniques. An enlightened teacher, therefore, will introduce the correct stimulus at a time when the student is psychologically receptive and has acquired the needed skills. All techniques should not be presented simultaneously without first introducing the student to the organic meaning of these techniques, and without establishing first a relationship between representation, personality and technique. With regard to the use of techniques, Goethe remarked, "In the limitation the master reveals himself." The most economical use of techniques and their application will be the best. The most definite use of them will be the most direct, outspoken, and *forceful.*

The relationship of an individual to his technique is more an outcome of his experiences in the world which surrounds him than a result of learned skill. As long as technique is separated from individual expression, tech-

* See also Evans, Joan, *Taste and Temperament.* New York: The Macmillan Co., 1939.

nique is only a handicraft which may even restrict the individual instead of encouraging him. If, for example, a haptically minded student is introduced to oil painting by being shown impressionistic methods of painting in nature, he will soon become discouraged because he will not see in nature the complex colors which are the results of visual analyses. His thinking and experiencing might be more related to the expressions in line than in color. *Technique and individuality are closely interwoven*: therefore, techniques should be *developed,* not taught. Technique is an expression of individuality, and as such, must contribute to, not hamper, the development of individuality. Consequently, the best technique will permit the individual to express himself most easily.

Since, as we have seen, art education in the secondary- and elementary-school classroom does not prepare for a profession but rather serves as a means to develop the mental and emotional growth of the individual, the teaching of techniquese must be focused upon the problem of finding the kind of expression adequate for the student personalities. All techniques, therefore, must be introduced with the purpose of fostering free expression by the student.

An introduction to painting materials will be helpful at this point in our discussion. Every paint material consists of the color pigment (usually paint powder) and the binding media, or the materials that hold or bind the color pigment and cause it to adhere to the painting surface. The color pigment is for all techniques theoretically the same. It can be produced from different types of earth, from plants, or by chemical processes. Depending on the different techniques, the binding media will be different. Pigment mixed with wax and pressed into the correct form (old molds for candles can be used) will provide adequate wax crayons. If gum arabic is used as binding medium, the result will be water colors. Gum arabic is used because it is soluble in water. For practical purposes, mix color pigment and a solution of 1/10 gum arabic in water so that it becomes saturated with pigment. Pour it into little flat dishes, and let the water evaporate. What remains is a button of water color. If we would like to produce oil paints, color pigment and oil are mixed. For practical purposes mix linseed oil, or better poppy-seed oil, with pigment to obtain excellent workable oil paints. Tempera is the kind of paint which can be thinned either with oil or water. The binding medium, therefore, must be of such quality as to combine with both. Only an emulsion can do that. Tempera, therefore, consists of color pigment and an emulsion. For practical purposes, it is easiest to use the yellow of an egg as the emulsion (the protein of the egg serves as emulsifying agent). Then add one part of water and mix it with color pigment. To keep it fresh, add one drop of oil of cloves. There are many

different types of tempera colors in trade, with different kinds of emulsions: casein, egg, or tempera made from synthetic emulsions.*

The following table will simplify the explanation of the nature of the
different types of painting material:

		Wax	Wax crayons
		Gum Arabic	Water colors
Color pigment	+	Oil	Oil paint
		Emulsion	Tempera

The following discussion of techniques that are suitable for the secondary-school classroom, will be confined to the nature of the techniques
as related to personality development and expressive qualities. Only the
most essential technical procedures will be emphasized, since purely technical matters can more adequately be found in books dealing with art
materials and techniques.†

Sketching techniques

LINEAR   As long as the line is emphasized, the *expressive* quality is
predominant. The line as such is an abstract expression. It can have *kinesthetic* origin but can also stand merely as a *symbol*. If it has kinesthetic
origin, the line has more the character of *motion* (repeated lines with flowing character) ; if the line is an abstract of a form (an outline), it is determined mainly by expressive desires. The line which interprets visual experiences is usually a *sketchy line,* emphasizing the three-dimensional qualities
of the form. For linear drawings, wax crayon (trade name, "Marking
Crayon") is a good material. Since erasing is impossible, the student is
compelled to concentrate more definitely on his concept. In expressive art,
every line has significance. Even unintended lines have expressive qualities,
perhaps the quality of "Fehlleistungen," ‡ which play a major role in
psychoanalysis. In expressive linear sketching, therefore, nothing should
be covered or erased: everything should remain in its genuine original
"handwriting." Wax crayon or lithographic pencil leads the student
directly to this understanding, since he finds it impossible to "change" his
concept within one drawing. If a concept does need a basic change, a new

---

* Clannon, Edward, *Making Your Own Materials.* New York: Museum of Modern Art,
Committee on Art in American Education, 1943.

† Doerner, Max, *The Materials of the Artist and Their Use in Painting.* New York: Harcourt Brace and Co., 1939.

‡ According to Sigmund Freud, "Fehlleistungen" are unintentional actions which are
revealing with regard to the individual's subconscious reactions. Misspellings often belong
to this category.

Fig. 58. Sketch of motions in black crayon. Free expression in lines.

drawing must be started. This, however, is important too, because it gives the student as well as the teacher an opportunity to see the growth of a concept, which is often revealing of the student's thinking and provides the teacher with a source of guidance (Figs. 58, 59, and 60). Since the character of the expressive line is in its truest one-dimensional meaning, smooth paper is preferable to paper with a rough texture because the latter would divert from the smooth, gliding, one-dimensional character of the line. This technique can be followed by brush and pen drawings; long-haired sable brushes and black drawing ink or drawing pens lend themselves very well to this purpose. Since the use of brush and ink demands more technical skill than that of wax crayon, the former should be introduced only after the student has gained confidence in the use of wax crayons. This technique leads directly to etching or aquatint, which will be discussed under the heading of "Graphics" in a later section.

THREE-DIMENSIONAL   Sketching techniques that include shades of different intensities are usually techniques emphasizing visual reactions toward experiences. The essence of these techniques, therefore, is the emphasis on the quality of the visually perceivable appearance of the objects. Consequently, the technique must permit the easiest approach toward a visual image. Since the visual image changes with regard to mood, atmosphere, light, shadow, and distance, a technique must be chosen which is more flexible and changeable. Such a technique is *charcoal*. Charcoal, because of its adaptability to easy changes, is the material which can best be used where quick adjustment to an impression or an image is needed. The visually inclined student will, therefore, feel at ease with charcoal in his hand; whereas the expressively inclined, haptically minded student would feel unhappy with this "smeary" material. Charcoal can be followed up with graphite sticks or with soft pencil, in which the adaptability is no longer as great as in charcoal. For these techniques, coarse paper is preferable, because it diminishes the linear character and gives more easily through its texture the effect of depth and atmosphere. These techniques lead directly to the techniques of lithography, which will be discussed in a later section.

Easel painting

IMAGINATIVE   An easel painting is an intimate expression of emotions, ideas, or experiences in nature. It reveals the artist's direct relationship to his world of sensations. An easel painting, therefore, usually is not illustrative like a mural, which tells a story or an event, but is more the artist's direct approach to the world of his experiences. It is the most subjective approach in painting techniques.

Depending on personality, subject matter, and method of approach, different techniques will lead easiest to the desired expressive qualities. It devolves upon the teacher to recognize and guide his students into the kind of techniques that are most adequate to their desire for expression. Some

Fig. 59. Stiff, academic representation of head by Frank Stewart.

Fig. 60. Free representation made by the same student, Frank Stewart, after applying correct stimulation.

students need models for visual inspiration. Other students are hampered
by what they see, since they use means different from visual stimuli as starting points for their creative experiences. Their world is bound up with imaginative experiences which can basically be visual or haptical, the world of
appearances or the world of subjectve expressions. For both groups, however, different techniques will lead to their aim.

   In general, for imaginative paintings—that is, paintings that are not
done from nature, but purely from imagination, techniques must be
chosen that lend themselves to a building-up process, to the possibility
of going over the painting again and again without technically tearing the
picture into uneven, heterogeneous parts. There are different techniques for

utilizing such processes. They can be divided into techniques that can be carefully planned, layer by layer, and techniques that are not built up gradually, but are applied emotionally.

Techniques that are applied emotionally—that is, directly, without planning or contemplation, are technically the easiest to use. The aim of such a technique is to preserve the paint stroke in its original quality. Such pictures are usually painted *alla prima*—that is, in one sitting. "Painting alla prima aims from the very start at the final effect of the finished picture, and attempts to arrive at that effect in the shortest and most direct way." * If oil paint is used, the painter has to paint wet in wet to keep the homogeneous character. If the picture cannot be painted in one sitting, the binding media has to be of such quality that it permits only slow drying. In order to keep the painting from drying, a mixture of oil of clove (1 part) and poppy seed oil (5 parts) is recommended. If, however, tempera is being used, it is suggested that the picture be sprayed slightly with thin emulsion or with water before continuing to paint on the dry picture, especially when casein tempera is used. Tempera gives sharper, clearer, and more illuminating qualities. Sharpness suggests the emphasis of the line— expressive rather than visual quality. Indeed, tempera does not lend itself well either to studies of nature or to "atmospheric" effects. An attempt to use tempera paint for realistic effects would, therefore, mean a waste of energy. Tempera will be an excellent medium in the hands of haptically inclined students, but will be a poor one in the hands of purely visually minded individuals. Of course, here also the teacher's understanding of the desires of his students should be the deciding guide.

If the desire for careful planning is great, two techniques are suggested which truly satisfy this urge. The one technique is the use of oil paint in different layers in which the opaque and the transparent quality of the paint is effectively used. The other technique is a mixtechnique in successive layers. This is the technique of the old masters, and is best seen in Il Tintoretto, El Greco, and Titian. It is the technique that uses the illuminating and sharp quality of tempera paint as well as the quality of depth of oil paint. One layer is done in opaque tempera paint. When this is dry, a transparent wash or glaze is painted over it. This can be repeated again and again until the desired effect is reached. The wash—that is, the transparent layer, usually consists of resin, dissolved in turpentine. Mastic resin is excellent for this purpose. Since in this technique the final concept is built up layer by layer, this approach will be used by artists who prefer

---

* Doerner, Max, *The Materials of the Artist.* New York: Harcourt, Brace and Co., 1934. Hiler, Hilaire, *The Painter's Pocketbook of Methods and Materials.* London: Faber and Faber Ltd., 1937.

"scientific" planning and are otherwise more intellectually inclined. This technique is in contrasting effect to the emotionally used alla-prima technique in which the student has the immediate desire to give his emotions form and expression.

The *ground* used for oil and tempera paintings should be prepared. Whether paper, cardboard, pasteboard, canvas, or wooden panels (plywood) are used, the important job of the sizing material is to fill in the pores and prevent the sinking-in of the paint. Glue (1/10 in 9/10 water dissolved in a double boiler) will in most cases prevent too much absorbtion of paint. If the student wishes a gliding ground with a smooth and luminous surface, the ground must not be absorbent. For this purpose, the best material to use is heavy white paper on a stretcher, sized with a coat of glue. Works of great artists are painted in oil on paper and have kept perfectly. Before the paper is placed on a stretcher, it must be well moistened. In this condition it is glued to the stretcher. After it has dried, it stretches perfectly. Other smooth grounds can be achieved by painting a coat of white (titanium white or zinc white) over the coat of glue (oil ground). This especially is necessary when canvas is used. Gliding grounds are necessary for carefully planned work in which the brush stroke must have a clear and distinct character. If a rough impression is desired, the ground must be soaky (absorbent) in order to soak in the binding media as quickly as possible. Mixing some fine chalk or gypsum into the glue or oil paint will make the ground absorbent.

FROM NATURE   In painting from nature a quick approach is desirable. The technique, therefore, must be one in which final results can be obtained in the shortest possible time. That is why no technique that involves a building-up process in which one layer supplements the other lends itself for painting in nature.

Several techniques can be used for this purpose. Water color is good because its luminous effect lends itself very well for painting atmosphere. However, there is a difference between painting wet in wet, or wet on dry ground. If colors should merge into one another, wet in wet is the desirable technique. If sharp outlines are wanted, the ground has to be dry. Disregard of these quite obvious facts very often leads to failure and discouragement. Although much stimulation can result from accidental fusions of colors, the teacher should use such accidental happenings for explanations of what can be done consciously and how it is to be done. The ground (the type of paper) used for water colors depend on the desired outcome as well as on the approach. The more the student is inclined to give a rough and sketchy impression of a visual image, the coarser the paper can be. The more the student depends on the detailed effect of the scene—that is, the more he depends on the subject matter he wants to paint, the smoother the paper should be. Technically inclined students, who receive more enjoyment from the accuracy of depicting the subject matter than from painting impressions of nature which refer to mood and atmosphere, will therefore prefer the smoother ground. If these different attitudes toward depicting nature spring from the type and character of personality, students should not be diverted from their own approach. On the contrary, in both approaches there are strong values: each should be recognized and used to the fullest extent. Although the latter type, the one who is more dependent on subject matter, might be the less "artistic" type, it is of greater importance to foster personality trends than to "make" of everyone an "artist."

Pure tempera paint does not lend itself very well for painting in nature because its contours are too sharp and its colors not "atmospheric." Although there exist fine studies of nature in tempera techniques, its use for this purpose is not recommended. If more opaque colors are desired, a mixed technique of water color and tempera is suggested. If only tempera white is added to water colors, the technique is called "gouache." Although it is not customary to mix tempera and water color in one painting, there is no reason for not doing so if the student gets enjoyment out of the transparency of water colors and the contrasting effect of opaque tempera paint. In fact, many students through this contrast have come to a quicker and lasting understanding of the painting of "atmosphere." The experience of the changing colors with regard to distant objects has nothing to do with a surface experience of these objects. The main experience refers to atmosphere. Therefore, this can be best expressed by a technique that emphasizes the transparency of the air. A student might, however, become interested in the surface structure of a near-by object and there is no reason why he should not use a technique, like tempera, that permits an easier approach.

In oil, alla-prima techniques are the only ones which can be used in nature. There are two possibilities, depending again on the nature of the student. The one, mixing the desired colors on the palette and then applying them to the canvas; the other, using clear colors either with brush or with palette knife and putting them close to one another on the canvas. The final effect is reached through optical fusion in our visual apparatus. For visually inclined students who do not depend on detailed impressions, but rather depict mood and atmosphere, this technique is strongly recommended, since it permits the exercise of greater freedom in color and expression.

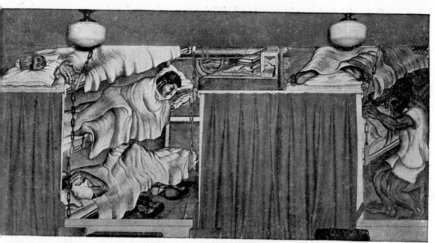

Fig. 61. Section of mural painted as part of architecture by John T. Biggers.

Also here, the student who finds most of his relief and enjoyment in detailed representations will prefer a smoother, nonabsorbent, meager ground. However, the student who prefers quick and rough sketches without details will find the rougher texture with some chalk or gypsum mixed into an oil ground more satisfactory. The teacher's understanding of the technical needs adjusted to the individual desires of his students will greatly contribute to their free and uninhibited development.

Mural Painting and Its Techniques

THE NATURE OF A MURAL   Whereas an easel picture is an intimate expression of emotions, ideas, or impressions, separated from its surrounding by a frame which intimately closes it off from its environment, a mural is a part of "another whole"—architecture. The painter has to adjust to whatever problems arise from architectural conditions. This is the first decisive difference between an easel picture and a mural. No restrictions whatsoever are related to an easel painting with regard to size, technique, and subject matter. In a mural the size is determined by the architect (actually, the size of the wall). The technique has to be adjusted to the purpose of a mural—that is, its decorative effect, and the subject matter often depends upon the meaning of the building in which the mural is painted (Fig. 61).

Let us consider more closely these three characteristics that are decisive in distinguishing between an easel painting and a mural. The architect determines size and shape of the wall space for a mural. The first problem in designing a mural, therefore, is to adjust the composition to the architecture for which it is determined. This should not be felt as a restriction. On the contrary, it might become a basic stimulation, an inspiration, or at least a challenge to use a given shape for a composition. In a good mural, architecture and mural composition must be so closely interwoven that the one cannot be separated from the other. As soon as the architecture is felt as a restriction, the mural is as out of place as when the mural overpowers the architecture. Only when architecture and mural go together so well that one improves the other does the mural fulfill its purpose.

The second problem is technique in a broader sense, not merely as it is related to material. This problem can best be understood if we remember that the mural has to be a *part of the wall,* of the architecture as a whole. The painter must not work at cross-purposes with the architect by painting "a hole" in a wall, which would be the case if the painter emphasized distance or depth in his composition. The architect says, "There is wall." This wall is important in his architectural concept, and the painter must support this idea. Therefore, a mural cannot stress foreground and background effects, but should regard all parts as equally significant and distribute the composition over the whole wall space. In this sense, the mural is a decoration of the wall and should not conflict with its architectural meaning. That is why the mural technique must emphasize the line and its decorative meaning, and stress the luminous, expressive quality of the paint, not its atmospheric attributes. Finally, the mural must permit the emphasis of the surface of the wall as such, whenever it seems necessary.

The third problem relates to content. An easel painting can be removed from a wall whenever desired. It is something in itself, existing for no other purpose than for its creation. A mural is painted as a part of a whole and must be adapted to the purpose of the whole. The subject matter of a mural depends upon the space for which it is determined. This, too, can be felt as a restriction as well as an inspiration or challenge. Surely, confines of space on a wall were not regarded as a restriction during the early medieval age in which religious subject matter dominated in mural expression. Since murals are painted as part of a whole architecture serving a definite purpose, a mural is destined for a larger audience whose members often (like in the churches) receive the impression simultaneously. A mural is, therefore, much more than a picture: it is a means of communication: it tells a story or transmits an idea. Also, from this point of view we will understand its technical approach toward a clear and definite depiction.

After this brief discussion of the nature of the mural, we shall proceed to a consideration of the different types of murals appropriate for the secondary-school level.

Fig. 62. Murals painted as a part of architecture. Group work. Hampton Institute.

THE PLANNED MURAL   A mural that is planned for a definite architecture, painted either directly on the wall, and intentionally of lasting
character, must first be planned in detail. A scale plan of the wall must
first be made, and the mural composition adjusted to this plan. If the mural
is painted directly on the wall, two techniques can be chosen: the "fresco"
painting on the wet mortar, or the mural (or "secco") painting on a dried
plaster ground.

Fresco painting is done on wet mortar, and on wet lime plaster in
which lime is used as binding medium and white color. "The water evap-
orates, and at the same time the lime absorbs carbonic acid gas from the
air. On the surface of the picture is formed a glassy skin of crystalline
carbonate of lime, which incorporates the colors with the ground in such a
manner as to make them absolutely insoluble in water, and at the same
time gives to them the fine sheen peculiar to genuine fresco painting." *
Although fresco technique is the most durable among all mural techniques,
its application is too complicated for use in the secondary-school class
room.

A technique that is easily applied is commonly called "mural painting"
(formerly, "secco painting"). A plaster ground is sized with a wash of
lime. The binding medium is egg yolk or casein. Glue water can also be
used in the proportion of 1 to 10. Two parts water for one egg yolk is the
best mixture. The paint can be mixed before each painting session, or
better, the paint pigment may be mixed with water to form a thick paste
and then mixed with egg yolk whenever it is needed for painting. In this
technique no white is necessary, since the white of the wall will be used
not only to keep the feeling for the wall surface but also as "white," when
ever it is needed.

The planned mural has tremendous educational values, which are
partly due to the fact that the student has to adjust to given conditions
such as architecture and subject matter; and partly to the fact that almost
any subject matter that lends itself for illustrative purposes is suitable for
a mural. Thus, historic, social, religious, or scientific themes can be used
very successfully for mural paintings, thereby providing an excellent
opportunity to integrate learning in other fields with art (Fig. 63).

THE DIRECT MURAL   In contrast to the planned mural, in which
every detail must be known before its final execution, the direct mural is
applied directly to the wall without sketches or with only rough sketches

---

* Doerner, Max, *The Materials of the Artist*. New York: Harcourt, Brace and Co., 1934,
p. 265. Mayer, Ralph, *The Artist's Handbook*. New York: Viking Press, 1940.

Fig. 63. Planned mural. Section from "Evolution of Architecture" by Arthur Carpenter. (Educational Project, Penn. State College.)

These murals are for special occasions, rather than for lasting memorials. Thus, theatre decorations, dance-hall decorations, or murals for special receptions come under this category. The best technique for this purpose is a casein ground and glue water or casein as binding medium. Transparent oil paint on white ground can also be used successfully. A rough sketch of the whole plan is designed first. This sketch, however, does not go into details, but leaves them open to special "inspirations" during the process of execution. Thus the direct mural gives the student considerable freedom for changes and permits him more flexibility than does the planned mural. Such a procedure corresponds to the environment and the purpose for which the direct mural is painted. Whereas the carefully planned mural is painted into a permanent architecture where it will remain as a part of the building, the direct mural will adjust to the occasions for which it is painted. It will be removed after the occasion is over and will be replaced by another. Its subject matter can relate to specific occasions whose rationale is unfamiliar to outsiders. The direct mural, conducted by enlightened leadership, can make an important contribution to the school life and its art consciousness. Because of its popularity and its direct approach it will be much easier understood and appreciated by the general audience. This, however, increases the responsibility of the art teacher for good guidance and leadership.

Both of the mural types described lend themselves also to group work.

THE GROUP MURAL   The fact that many students can participate in the creation of a group mural has distinct social values. Every participant subordinates his own contribution to the whole, yet all have the feeling of cooperative accomplishment. These values are modified by loss of artistic unity inherent in such a group project. The strongly creative individual can be hampered by "cooperation" with others. The planned mural, whose self-consistency and adaptation to the architecture to which it is related must be unimpaired, lends itself for group murals only when different students paint on different walls or panels. Students of mine executed several panels in the Department of Sociology, depicting the theme "Freedom" in various aspects: "Freedom Through Achievement," "Freedom Through Religion," "Freedom Through Evolution," "Freedom Through Revolution," "Freedom Through Expression," "Freedom Through Science," and so forth. Architecturally each window was a kind of niche, which we used for the different individual panels (Fig. 62). A few students painted the remainder of the wall, which surrounded the panels, with industrial designs, thereby integrating the individual panels into the whole architecture. In this way the planned mural lends itself to group work. If, however, such a subdivision into different separated wall spaces is impossible, the disadvantages of lack of unity and the overpowering of one student by another are much greater than the educational advantages derived from the cooperative project. Even when separate wall spaces can be obtained in one unit, there is still the problem of creating a unity among all panels.

The direct mural is the type to be preferred for group work. Since this mural is not planned for lasting value, lack of unity will not be disturbing. Usually determined for a specific occasion, it is subordinated to a definite "spirit." Whether the mural is for a reception, a dance, or a play the student has from the beginning the feeling that all students will subordinate themselves to a specific task. Proper organization is of prime importance. Group work does not mean that everyone can paint everywhere. The teacher or a committee should distribute the work properly. In this work the advantages of cooperation and social adjustments are very distinct. It is, however, important that all students participate in some functions, otherwise the effect might easily be negative.

Sculpturing in the Secondary School

The three-dimensional expression of emotions, thoughts, or impressions of nature deals with methods of sculpturing. Naturally, this type of expression is more restricted in the choice of subject matter than painting, since it excludes the representation of environment. This restriction, however, is only superficial because many students who have little desire and understanding for expressing themselves in painting will find much relief and enjoyment in the realm of three-dimensional expression. Sculpturing lends itself to a choice of "living things," animals or men, as subject matter. The more visually inclined the student is, the more will he refer his work to nature and its appearance. The more haptically he is inclined, the more will he deviate from nature and concentrate on his subjective relationship to nature or the expression of his own feelings. The three-dimensional stimulation relating to subject matter and technique will, therefore, be different for those whose desire it is to approach surface appearances and for those who want to express their subjective relationships to their experiences. Whereas the former group receives its best stimulation from nature, the latter group will draw its stimulation from its own feelings.

The stimulation for the visual group, therefore, will refer mainly to appearance or aesthetic evaluation, dealing with structural differences as well as with the meaning of sizes and proportions. The stimulation for the haptic sculptor will consist of directing his attention to the feeling of muscle sensations, kinesthetic experiences, and emotional relationships. However, the chief aim of teaching sculpturing in the secondary-school classroom is to promote personality growth through self-expression, not to give special professional training. We will, therefore, discuss those technical questions only that lend themselves for this purpose.*

SCULPTURING VERSUS MODELING   A distinction has already been made between sculpturing and modeling, especially in the more advanced stages and grade levels. The expression of an unconscious approach, the stages without critical awareness has been called "modeling," whereas the conscious expression in three-dimensional media has been called "sculpturing." In modeling, the working process is of greater importance. In sculpturing the emphasis is laid upon the final product. In modeling as well as in sculpturing, two definite techniques, which are closely related to different kinds of thinking, can be observed: (1) The building up of partial impressions to a synthesis of a conceived form—that is, the synthetic tech-

* Putnam, Brenda, *The Sculpture Way*. New York: Frederick A. Stokes Co., 1939.

nique and (2) The process of gradually cutting out from the whole form all unnecessary parts until, through this analytical process, the final form is reached—that is, the analytic technique. Synthetic thinking refers to a concept in which the partial impressions add up to a unity, whereas analytic thinking approaches the outer surface as a whole in its appearance. The difference between modeling and sculpturing, as has been pointed out, is that in sculpturing the thinking is consciously related to the technique ("building up from single part" or "cutting out from the whole" in clay wood, or stone), whereas in modeling the working process is purely instinctive.

This means that in the secondary-school classroom we will deal with techniques of *sculpturing* only, since the student should approach his media with the proper understanding and knowledge of its meaning for expression.

SCULPTURING IN PLASTIC MEDIA   The number of plastic media on the market has grown considerably during the past few years. Although clay is still the most popular material, it is by no means the most satis factory, especially for use in the secondary-school classroom in which facilities for keeping clay in moist condition are not always available. If sculpturing is done only once or twice a week, as in most of the country's secondary schools, constant attention is necessary to keep the clay and the unfinished products workable. There is another disagreeable attribute of clay: it needs to be stiffened or supported by "armatures" (wire structures that hold the sculpture in the desired position). This technically necessary evil keeps the student from making spontaneous changes. It also makes casting necessary, because the clay sculpture cannot dry with the enclosed armature. Since clay shrinks during the process of drying and the wire maintains its volume, the clay would break. Furthermore, wire and clay are of such different nature, that often when the student prepares the armature he gets involved in the creative process of dealing with a "wire sculpture" and thus forgets that *his concept should grow out of the clay.* This is one of the basic criticisms of the use of an armature. It diverts the student from one of the most important creative principles. *The creative concept must grow out of the material from which it is created.* In this respect a clay sculpture and a stone plastic involve different creative principles. Thus the most organic clay sculpture would be one which is solidly built, with no parts standing out, so that an armature is superfluous. Certainly in ceramics sculptures, which are fired and glazed in the kiln, wire structures cannot be used.

If plasticine can be obtained in large enough quantities, it has some advantages over clay. It is stiffer and therefore does not need support by armatures. It does not dry out. This, of course, is an advantage for schools in which art is taught only once or twice a week. Furthermore, plasticine does not shrink, hence it can stay on an armature indefinitely without cracking. Plasticine has, however, a disadvantage in that it is not of a permanent character. Either it must be used for experimentation purposes only, or it must be cast into another material.

Victor D'Amico reports * a new cohesive clay invented by Arthur Baggs, ceramic artist at Ohio State University, that "holds together at the slightest contact and needs no firing" Only experiment and time will prove whether this is the great invention that makes casting unnecessary. Certainly with the growing needs for plastic materials, sooner or later we will arrive at the final solution of how to preserve the sculpture in the form and material in which it was created. It is to be hoped that such a badly needed material soon will be discovered, but in the meanwhile, casting, or the transference of a clay sculpture into another medium, will remain necessary.

CASTING   Casting is a very old means of reproducing three-dimensional objects in different media. The simplest example of casting is the seal. The seal is the equivalent of the negative or mold, whereas the impression of the seal on the sealing wax is the reproduction of the positive in the different medium. Casting always has been considered as a mere craft, a skill necessary to put a sculpture in a more permanent form. We speak of a plaster cast if the material used for casting is plaster of Paris; we speak of a bronze cast if bronze is poured into the mold; and so forth. Casting, however, is in strong contradiction to a functional relationship between creative work and material. In modern art we emphasize again and again that the work of art should organically grow out of the material from which it is created. Especially in architecture, where we deal with so many different materials, do we want to give each material its specific function. We have definitely given up wearing wigs and making wooden columns appear like stone. If we build a frame bungalow we emphasize instead of hide the beauty of the wood. When we build a brick or stone building, we desire to show the function of the materials. From this point of view, the practice of pouring a clay sculpture in plaster or bronze (materials having different attributes than clay) on which we cannot see the imprint of our hands or tools, is to be condemned. With such a cast

* Creative Teaching in Art.

Fig. 64. Masks. Facial expression as organic start for sculpturing and casting.

bronze sculpture we pretend it is possible to treat this material as we do clay. This is incompatible with a functional concept of creative activity in relationship to the material used.

As long as casting is treated as a mere technical transference into another material, casting itself is not an art form. If, however, casting is technically treated as an art form in its own right, it will become a new form of sculpturing. A stained window, for example, has an art form of its own in which the lead, while holding the glass pieces together, determines the linear composition. In casting, the creative concept should also grow out of the technique, or vice versa, thus representing a new form of art. In this new form of sculpturing the seams which heretofore have been carefully removed on the final product, would become a part of the creative concept. Instead of removing them, one should allow them to fulfil their linear function in the same way as does the lead in the stained window.

The simplest approach is to cast a piece without undercuts.* A piece without undercuts needs only to be cast with a one-piece mold. A mask, in which facial expressions can best be studied and taught, would therefore be the most organic beginning for casting (Fig. 64). Over the clay mask plaster of Paris is poured to a thickness of approximately three inches. If many pieces are made from the same mold, it is advisable to build in a

* Daugherty, John Wolf, *Pottery Made Easy.* New York: Bruce Publishing Co., 1940.

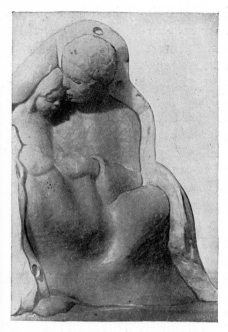

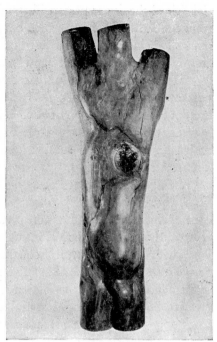

Fig. 65. Casting of a clay sculpture showing good characteristics of clay. (Sculpture by Samella Sanders.)

Fig. 66. "Victim." Wood sculpture by Henry W. Bannarn, showing excellent use of the structure of the material.

screen to hold the plaster together and prevent it from breaking. When the plaster is dry, the clay can easily be removed. The mold is then carefully cleaned and sized with sizing soap, a substance which fills up the pores completely, thus preventing any material from sticking to it. After this is done, the casting material (in secondary schools only plaster of Paris is advisable) is poured into the mold. To facilitate the removal of the finished product from the mold when it is hardened, it is suggested that a handle of thick wire be built into the casting material. If only one piece is to be poured, the original mold can be chipped off. This is called a "waste mold."

If a piece has undercuts, which is to be expected in any round sculpture, the mold must consist of two or more pieces. Before casting is done, the sculpture has to be divided into sections with no undercuts (Fig. 65). These sections must be marked by clay walls approximately one inch high and then each section has to be filled with plaster. Before an adjacent section is done, the clay wall must be removed until the whole sculpture is enclosed with plaster. The more organic a clay sculpture is made, the more simply can it be cast. The more the clay sculpture grows out of the material "clay,' the fewer parts will stand out, since clay in itself has too little firmness. Such sculptures, which have no separated or "attached" parts are naturally "closed" as a functional outcome of the dealing with the material from which they are formed and lend themselves best for casting.

If casting is included in the secondary-school curriculum, it is most important to relate it from the very beginning to sculpturing itself. If this is not done, serious disappointments will result from the many obstacles that may arise from too many undercuts or pieces that stand out from the sculpture. I have seen students of college classes develop a horror, or almost a class psychosis, when too many pieces which were too difficult for casting were destroyed or damaged in the process. When a cast is well done, *nothing should be corrected on it*. If whole sections have to be made over again, the unity of the creative work suffers, while the creator feels frustrated owing to technical insufficiency which has spoiled his work. The work with armatures greatly contributes to such frustrations, since armatures represent factors working against the spirit of the material. If casting is introduced (and in my opinion it should be, because it offers not only creative but also industrial stimulations) armatures should not be used. They only offer obstacles, technically and creatively. What should be done if a student insists upon representing motions that cannot be formed without "stiffening" the clay? If, for example, a student would like to have the arm standing out, we can only tell him that his creative concept is not suited for execution in clay. He should either execute it in a different material, or create the same expression in a concept that grows out of the clay. Similarly, an architect of the medieval period could not have built Gothic towers out of wood. The modern architect will not build a stone building with the concept of a frame bungalow. He will not even plaster wood in order to give a wrong impression of the nature of his building material. To stress this point also in sculpturing is psychologically important because it is another way of emphasizing "truth" in the creative concept. A clay sculpture should be modeled so that it looks like a clay sculpture. This is not a new idea, but a neglected one in the creative concept of modern "functional" art, which emphasizes again and again the interdependency of material and creative concept without doing justice to this particular material. If the concept of a clay sculpture is really adjusted to the qualities of clay, casting is a simple matter.

Although I have seen classes which were disgusted from the frustrating effects of poor results of casting, I have also seen groups that became enthusiastic about the wonderful and inspiring process of transferring a clay sculpture into a work of durable material. It all depends on the way casting is presented. It is most important that the student receive his inspirations for good sculpturing in clay from the way the sculpture lends itself to casting. This experience, therefore, is a vital art experience, and by no means should be turned over to "professionals" but must remain a part of the student's experience.*

CARVING IN WOOD AND CUTTING IN STONE   Carving in wood and cutting in stone have their places in the secondary-school classroom if they are used merely as an inspiration for working in a different medium and a means of feeling out different approaches. From this angle, however, it should be noted that there are decisive differences among the processes offered in clay work. In plastic material, the student may either choose to build up a sculpture out of partial impressions or to form it from the whole. In carving or cutting, the student has only one possibility, one psychological approach, and this is the analytical one, which starts from the whole and arrives at the final product by the process of elimination. Not all students are able to form such a concept; therefore not all students can be asked to do work in carving or cutting. The analytical mind works differently from the synthetical one. Whereas the analytical mind has from the beginning the impression of the whole simultaneously before him, the synthetical mind gradually builds up a sculpture into a whole. Thus, a student who very efficiently builds up a sculpture of numerous parts might feel frustrated during the process of carving or cutting, since it is contrary to his thinking and concept.

Carving in wood and cutting in stone must again "grow out" of the special material in which it is done (Fig. 66). Carving in soft wood is different from carving in hard wood. Not only do the different woods have different grains, but they also have different cutting qualities, which should be used to the fullest extent in a wood sculpture. There is no good reason for cutting small details with great difficulty in a kind of wood which lends itself best for subjects of rough texture. Using the grain as a part of the wood sculpture is an outcome of the relationship of the creative concept to material. To neglect this quality of wood means taking the beauty from the wood. Most commonly used woods for carving are apple, oak, and yellow pine. Walnut, mahogany, pear, and chestnut are also excellent for wood sculpturing. Very often the shape of the wood block or the branches or the log itself can be inspiring to the student. The material must be dry because carving in moist or damp material would be too difficult and discouraging.†

* Toft, Albert, *Modelling and Sculpturing*. Philadelphia: Lippincott (J. B.) Co., 1936; Glass, Frederick James, *Modelling and Sculpture*. New York: Scribner's (Charles) Sons, 1929.
† For more technical information, see Leland, Charles G., *Woodcarving*. New York: Pitman Publishing Corp., 1931; Jackson, James, *The Handicraft of Woodcarving*. New York: Pitman Publishing Corp., 1921; Sowers, J. T., *Wood Carving Made Easy*. Milwaukee: Bruce Publishing Co., 1936.

The process of cutting in stone is psychologically the same as carving in wood. It is the process of elimination, an analytical process. However, the material and the tools are different. Here, too, the creative concept should grow out of the material. A work in granite will naturally not lend itself to fine and detailed executions, since the texture of granite is rough and its spotty surface may divert attention from such delicate detail. This stone is most effective for colossal statues, or for sculptures that have the effect of a rock. The fine and smooth surface structure of marble, however, lends itself excellently for delicate work.

Although working in stone is considered as sculpturing in its best meaning, it is rarely used in high schools because of the many difficulties connected with the material and the use of tools. Cutting in plaster can, however, serve as an adequate substitute, although plaster itself is not very beautiful. Soap sculpture, although popular, is not recommended because the smallness of the size often results in the feeling of restriction.

The question often arises whether sculptures can be painted. From what has been said, it is quite clear that painting a sculpture would be the same as making a wood building look like stone. Emphasizing the beauty of the material and its special characteristics is an important practice of modern art. A sculpture must be so convincingly done that nothing need be added, particularly painting, because sculpturing is entirely in the realm of three-dimensional expression.

However, when a figure is used for purposes other than that of mere self-expression color may be added to it. When three-dimensional works are used in relationship with another functional whole, as in theater decorations, or as a group in an altar (during the medieval age), the sculpture loses its intimate meaning as an expression itself and becomes a part of another symbolic or realistic form of expression. In this relationship surface structure or beauty of the material becomes entirely subordinated to the literary or interpretative meaning of the work of art (Fig. 67).

In this connection, mention should be made of the educational meaning of puppets, which can be carved in wood, made from clay, or formed out of papier mâché and painted—a most inspiring and useful art form. The educational value of puppets is not only great because they lend themselves so very well for the integration into other school subjects (English, history) but also because of their wide range of expressive qualities. Successful, satirical self-portraits have been made in form of puppets; psychologically they have been proven successful because they made the students more aware of themselves. If acting is included, such creative enterprise can contribute to a better feeling toward oneself. To make historic figures come to life again, puppets or marionettes can be used most effectively.

Fig. 67. Medieval sculpture. Painted wood. Group composition; part of an altar.

However, naturalistic means of interpretations would be entirely against the spirit of puppets and marionettes because both are designed for stage effects. In this connection, painting marionettes or puppets has not the meaning of making them more "natural." Color is used in this relationship only as a means of expression.* Stage design, therefore, should always be included to show the final effect of the puppet in its proper environment.

Graphics—The reproducing techniques

Not all graphic techniques fit different student personalities. We know from the history of art that some artists were masters in linear techniques, but that others preferred black and white in its three-dimensional effect. This different attitude toward the use of techniques should be known by all teachers. The line itself can have many different qualities, as has been pointed out previously. But from all these qualities two are outstanding: the line as an abstract interpretation of expressions, and the line as the

* For more information on puppets or marionettes see Kennard, Joseph S., *Masks and Marionettes.* New York: The Macmillan Co., 1935. Flexner, Marion W., *Hand Puppets, A Practical Manual for Teachers.* New York: French (S.) Inc., 1935. MacIsaac, Frederick J., *The Tony Sarg Marionette Book.* New York: The Viking Press, 1921.

Fig. 68. Toys made in the Home Economics Related Arts Classes under Professor Amy Gardner, Penn. State College.

interpreter of visual experiences. In the first, the line itself has the function of expressing feelings or emotions, whereas in the latter the line, as the boundary of forms, characterizes their three-dimensional quality. Both types of artistic expression lead to different techniques.

LINOLEUM CUT   The linoleum cut is the technique of cutting with differently shaped knives and gouges into linoleum. Depending upon the personality of the student, the cutting of lines or shapes might be more important than the effect of light and shadow, so often characterized as the aim in linoleum cut. From this it becomes evident that there are two techniques in a linoleum cut which are quite closely related to the creative types of students. For one the experience of cutting and its expressive quality, together with the relationship of shapes, is of main significance, whereas for the other, the visual interpretation of forms expressed in light and shadows (black and white) is the chief aim. Whereas the one student, who is inclined to express emotional qualities in his cuts, would feel frustrated when asked to translate his world into an experience of lights and shadows, the other student might find this technique precisely the one for which he was ready.

Fig. 69a. Linol cut with clear black-white appearance (twelve years), under the instruction of Miss Kathryn M. Royer, State College High School.

As is the case with other media, the technique of the linoleum cut must result from the experience of cutting into linoleum. Therefore, the students should not be required to first make a detailed drawing preliminary to cutting, but should try different things on scrap material with the knife without preliminary drawings. Later a brief drawing, which indicates the roughly outlined creative concept, should be sufficient for making a linoleum cut. Only when the student has experienced and digested the nature of the technique can he paint with brush and black ink his creative concept, because only then will he be able to use his brush and ink according to the functional lines made by the knife.*

If there are students who demand a more detailed structure than can be achieved with linoleum, woodcutting is the technique for them. In principle, however, woodcutting is the same in wood as linoleum cutting is in linoleum. For the secondary-school classroom, only in rare cases will the student want more detailed studies and structures than linoleum can offer (Fig. 69 *a, b,* and *c*).

* For more technical information on the linoleum cut see Frankenfield, Henry, *Block Printing with Linoleum, A Practical Manual.* Camden, N. J.: Howard Hunt (C). and Co., 1940. Dobson, Margaret Stirling, *Lino Prints.* New York, London: Pitman (Sir I.) and Sons, Ltd., 1931.

Fig. 69b. Linol cut showing repetition as a natural outcome of printing (twelve years old). Miss Kathryn M. Royer, Instructor.

ETCHING AND LITHOGRAPHY   The following discussion will not cover technical procedure of etching and lithography.* In this section, only the meaning of etching and lithography for personality development within the secondary-school classroom will be discussed.

Both techniques are far less popular than linoleum cutting because their use requires a greater variety of materials and tools and a greater technical knowledge by the teacher. These difficulties, frequently arising for no better reason than an unwillingness to try something new, should be overcome because etching and lithography are important means of creating self-confidence, especially during the period of adolescence. Drawings that

---

* For more information on etching and lithography read Pennell, Joseph, *The Graphic Arts.* Chicago: The University of Chicago Press, 1921. D'Amico, Victor, *Creative Teaching in Art.* Scranton: International Textbook Company, 1942.

Fig. 69c. Linol cut with organic lines of cutting (thirteen years).

often look "poor" or inexpertly done, can be greatly improved by converting them into an etching or lithograph. This is true not only because the etched line appears more permanent or "professional" but because the determination of the tone and shading of an etching is often influenced by accidental factors. Furthermore, those who have less creative talent should emphasize the skill factor of the technical procedure. Adolescent boys, especially, will find much pleasure in observing and going through the steps of etching and printing.

Roughly speaking, there are two techniques in etching: the dry-point process and the etching process. Technically the dry-point process is much simpler than the other. In fact no etching is involved in the dry-point process. The drawing is simply engraved into a copper, zinc, or plastic plate and then printed. The softer the plate, the easier it is to engrave with the dry-point needle. Although the dry-point process is less durable than the etching process, we do not need to produce works for eternity. The less durable plastic material has many advantages, especially of transparency, which permits the student to use any sketch he has spontaneously made. He simply puts the sketch under the transparent plate, uses it merely as a guide, and removes the plate soon after to go over it free-hand. It is important that etching, or better engraving, should not merely be a technical transferring of a creative concept. Again, the technique must grow out of the material, and sketches should be used only for rough guidance.

The other technique, genuine etching, although more complicated, offers a far greater variety of experiences than the dry-point technique. The zinc or copper plate is covered with a wax or asphaltum preparation to protect the metal from the acid, into which the plate is immersed after the drawing has been transferred to it. Since the drawing is made in wax, only the merest pressure is needed to incise it into the wax. The acid eats the metal where the slight incisions in the wax have exposed the plate. The depth of the engraved line depends on the time the plate is left in the acid solution, the longer the time, the deeper the lines. The depth of the engraving determines the boldness of the line on the print. Some lines can be covered again with asphaltum while the others stay open. If the process of etching is repeated, only those lines which were left open will be engraved deeper. This partial etching increases the interest, creatively and technically. Important elements of the design can be made more bold and outstanding, and unimportant elements can be made recessive.

After the plate is etched or engraved, preparation for printing should be made. First the asphaltum should be removed with turpentine and then the plate while yet warm, should be inked with etching ink by means of a leather roller or "inker." After that the ink should be wiped off, leaving filled only the engraved lines. The plate, still warm, is then covered with damp paper (ordinary drawing paper will do) and placed under layers of thin felt. The whole "bed" is then slowly pulled through the printing press under great pressure. The pressure forces the damp paper into the etched or engraved lines and draws out the ink onto the paper.*

All this can be made very exciting, adding interest to the creative part, particularly at an age level in which the desire for "professional" work and technical skill is great.

Whereas in etching the emphasis is on linear expression, in lithography, the form with light and dark shadings predominates. The simplest lithographic method that is suitable for the average secondary-school classroom consists of drawing with lithographic crayons directly on an aluminum plate having a prepared grained surface. This surface is treated with a special acid solution. When the ink is applied with a roller, it sticks to the

* For more information read West, Leon, *Making an Etching*. New York: The Studio Publications, Inc., 1932.

crayoned part only, but is repelled elsewhere. The print is made as in etching but with somewhat less pressure.* All other lithographic processes are too complicated for secondary schools. The process described above, however, is simple enough to be used successfully without special training, and at the same time gives the understanding of the principles of lithographic processes.

SILK-SCREEN AND STENCIL TECHNIQUES   As we have seen in the discussion of graphic techniques, the creative and emotional qualities find visible expression through the technique itself, but this is not the case in silk-screen or other stencil techniques. Here, emotional qualities are entirely subordinated to the decorative. This, too, naturally grows out of the technical procedure of cutting an accurate stencil. Whereas the creative concept can be given full freedom in engraving an etching plate or in drawing with a lithographic crayon, the cutting of a stencil, a design, or lettering on the film for later transfer to the screen is predominantly a technical procedure. In the silk-screen technique flat spaces are used. Since this is essentially two-dimensional, silk-screen work cannot be used realistically to compete with painting. Silk-screen techniques in their own realm can be used effectively for reproducing decorative designs. Unfortunately this technique has been overdone by those who do not understand its true characteristics. Naturalistic tendencies are entirely out of place in connection with the use of silk-screen printing.† Use of too many colors (and therefore also stencils) to produce realistic effects is inefficient and is indicative of a misapprehension of the nature of the medium. The simpler the technique used, the more effective it is in its own realm. The texture of the screen should be a contributing, not a distorting factor. Again, the decorative qualities of the silk-screen technique cannot compete with the emotional qualities of painting techniques.

The same holds true for the stencil techniques, which are more popular than the silk screen because stencils are merely·cut out of stencil paper and are therefore easier to handle. A stencil can be moved around at will, and unless this is done freely, the possibilities of the technique will not be understood. The use of one stencil in repetitions is another characteristic of the technique. Inasmuch as repetition is an attribute of design, a naturalistic concept cannot be adequately executed with the stencil. However,

* For more information write for *Multigraph Duplicators*. Cleveland, Ohio: Multigraph Corporation.
† For more information on silk-screen and stencil techniques read Biegeleisen, Jacob Israel, *The Silk Screen Printing Process*. New York: McGraw-Hill Book Co., Inc., 1941. Summer, Harry, *Handbook of Silk Screen Printing Process*. New York: Creative Crafts Press, 1939.

brushing along the outline of the stencil toward the inside often produces quite attractive shading, but only if it does not attempt to imitate nature. Also, the shading must remain in the realm of design. Decorative qualities are only weakened, not improved by naturalistic principles. To start out with two or three stencils of abstract shapes (namely, three circles of different sizes, one circle and a square, or a triangle) which are repeated in the same or different arrangements at equal intervals, is much better than using complicated flower patterns induced by naturalistic imitative urges. A textile is neither a place for a still life nor should it lose its characteristics by the emphasis of three-dimensional effects.

POSTER WORK—LETTERING   Since one of the essential elements of a good poster is its lettering, we shall discuss first the principles of good lettering.*

Pure lettering, defined as being concerned only with the formal representation of a word, is writing rather than drawing. In contrast to this formal representation, we shall see that lettering can also *express* the word's meaning, at least to a certain extent. In this connection lettering moves from pure representation to a form of expression.

That lettering should be *written* in itself indicates the technical approach—that is, use of a pen, letter brush, or wooden spatula. The letter then should organically grow out of the pen's shape, without twisting or unnatural motions or turns. The simpler the type of letters, the better it is for the beginning as well as for later stages of lettering. To begin with capital letters only has many advantages: a simplified alphabet, to mention only one. Simple letters are derived from the simplest lines—the straight line and the circle. Since the circle often occupies too much space, it can be replaced by an oval. However, as soon as the oval is introduced, the problems posed by irregularities multiply. Outlining the letters and later "filling them in" is contrary to the spirit of pure lettering. It can be done only when lettering serves other than formal representations of words.†

Also important for good lettering is its "spacing"—that is, the distribution of the single letters within a whole word or sentence. We distinguish between closed, half-open, and open letters. Closed letters have a perpendicular line on both sides, such as M, N, I, and H. Half-open letters have a perpendicular line only on one side, such as K, L, B, D, and so forth. Open letters have no perpendicular lines on either side, like C, A, G, O, S, and so forth. When two closed letters adjoin, the space between them is

---

* Chappell, Warren, *The Anatomy of Lettering*, New York: Loring and Mussey, 1935. Holme, Charles G., *Lettering of Today*. London: The Studio, Ltd., 1937.

† Friend, Leon and Hefter, Josephine, *Graphic Design*, New York: Whittlesey House, 1936.

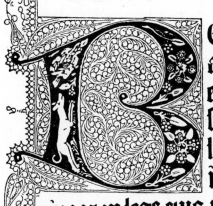

Eatus vir qui non
abijt in ⱺſilio impioꝝ:
et in via peccatoꝛū non
ſtetit: ⁊ in cathedra peſti-
lentie non ſedit, Sed
in lege ꝺꝺmini volutas
eius: ⁊ in lege eius meditabitur die ac no-
cte, Et erit tanꝗ lignū quod plātatū eſt

Anno dñi ⊙Millesiō·ccc·lvij·Jnvigilia Aſſūpcōis,

a

●Because of its story-telling character
the mural lends itself excellently for
the integration with other subject
matters.

b

Fig. 70. Pure lettering, a process of writing.
   a). Medieval lettering
   b). Modern lettering (twelfth grade)

much smaller than the space between two open letters. We conclude therefore, that only the optical space counts—that is, the space that actually
is between the two letters, like *M N* or *K L* or *O C*. These optical spaces
should be equal in good lettering.

    Good spacing in lettering consists, therefore, of a balance of the *optical*
spaces between letters in order to make the spaces appear equal. Most of
the irregularities of poor lettering derive from irregular letters and poor
spacing. Only after the student understands what good letters are and how
the letters should be spaced should variations of letters in different styles
and sizes be introduced. With regard to the lettering in different sizes,

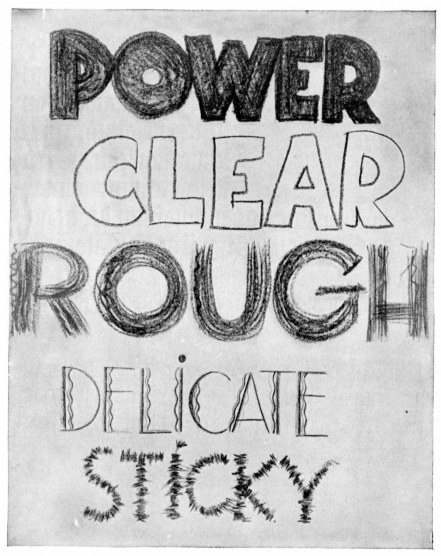

Fig. 71. Word illustrations.

writing "in block" introduces many possibilities in good spacing. Writing in block consists of lettering several lines in such a way that they finally form a rectangular or square block. One block can consist of lines of lettering of equal sizes as well as of lines which have different sized letters. A book title for instance, in which the title can be largest, the subtitle smaller, and the author and publishing firm again in different sizes, all written in block, would be an example of such lettering. This is not only of importance for the teaching of good lettering, but has also great educational value, since it compels the student to adjust one situation to another, the smaller lettering to the larger, and so forth. Title pages, letter heads for stationery, signs of different types would be practical examples in which the principles of spacing can be applied.

If, however, lettering is not used merely as a means of formal representation but as an *expressive symbol* in itself, no limitations with regard to technique should hamper the expressiveness of the letter. A very good approach to this type of *letter drawing* is *word illustrations*. The students are told to illustrate different meanings of words by adjusting the type of the letters to the word's meaning (Fig. 71). Contrasting words like "strong" and "weak," "bold" and "timid," "heavy" and "light," "night" and "day," "rough" and "smooth," "deep" and "shallow," "narrow" and "wide," "high" and "low," and "thin" and "thick," are very good suggestions for the beginning. Later on words can be introduced that stand for themselves, like "fire," "speed," "excitement," "storm," "fear," "shock," "drowning," "trembling," "suffocating," "heat," and so forth. Through illustrating such words the student will achieve an understanding of lettering as a living and expressive activity. With this in mind he will approach poster work in a different way. For the beginning of poster work it will be good to bring such word illustrations in contrast to the formal and written lettering. A poster for a movie "Storm over Asia," "Drowning in the Swamps," and the "Whispering Shadow" which not only contains these suggestive titles but also the name of the theatre, actors, admission price, and so forth, will give opportunities for such contrasts.

Spacing in designing a poster is of great importance. A poster that is equally covered with lines of lettering will be monotonous and not effective. Emphasizing and isolating important from less important parts is a means of directing attention to specific contents while breaking the monotony. A good poster should also contain contrasts between ordinary and meaningful spaces.

After practicing on posters of literary meaning, a poster of more general content should be chosen. Other techniques, such as work with air brush and silk screen, can be introduced.*

Techniques for design

EMOTIONAL FORMS OF DESIGN AND ITS ABSTRACT QUALITY   Any material will be suitable for emotional forms of design or abstractions which permits a free use of design forms, without restricting the individual

* For more information on poster techniques see Mangan, James T., *Design, The New Grammar of Advertising,* p. 73. Chicago: Dartnell Corp., 1940.

Fig. 72a. Emotional Design. Made by entirely inexperienced students under supervision of Professor Sybill Emerson, Penn. State College.

to rigid patterns. Especially in the beginning, much emphasis should be placed on techniques that facilitate a direct connection between kinesthetic experiences (the way the arm is moved while producing lines or shapes) and other body sensations (Fig. 72). Flat colored chalk that can be used for lines and shadings, therefore, is an excellent material since it records without difficulties body motions and the different pressure put on the material to receive different qualities of shades. Techniques, like tempera, which easily produce uneven surfaces and do not readily obey the flowing quality of an introduced rhythm should be saved for later experiences.

Finger painting is also an excellent introductory means for the stimulation of emotional qualities in abstract design, if this technique is not misused. All too often one can see finger painting used in competition with other forms of painting—that is, with naturalistic tendencies. Finger paint consists of the direct transference of motions into lines, shapes, and colors. Although it is an excellent means of stimulation when used in its own right, it can entirely miss its purpose when used to imitate nature.

The work with the airbrush, too, offers excellent possibilities if its special qualities are recognized. If the limitations of this technique are realized, no landscapes or portraits will become victims of a misunder-

Fig. 72b. Emotional Design. More controlled and organized. Made in the classes of Professor Sybill Emerson, Penn. State College.

stood technique. Sharp lines can be produced even with the best airbrush. If sharp outlines are wanted, stencils have to be introduced. Stencils, as we have seen, are entirely unsuitable for expressing realistic tendencies. The airbrush, therefore, can function best in the realm of design, particularly industrial design, since the technical procedure destroys most of the direct emotional qualities.

Since structure, too, is one of the important qualities of design, work with material of different texture will be very stimulating. Scraps of wood, metal, textiles, plastics, and paper can be arranged in such a way that they produce an excellent "symphony" of textures and shapes. Because texture is closely related to the sense of touch, students should go through the experience of finding different textures purely by the sense of touch. What a fine sensation it is to touch the softness of velvet after feeling the smoothness of a fine curved glass. Such experiences will greatly stimulate the visual experience associated with different types of textures, as different grains of wood, weaves of textiles, and so forth. Such designs will necessarily use the three dimensions as well as the plane. In its abstract quality it is a form of design in its own right, but it can also be used to

Fig. 73a. Functional design in wood.

create a better feeling for the use of different materials in interior decoration. But this leads to the next chapter, functional design.*

DESIGN AND ITS FUNCTION   Functional design must always be *in close interdependence with the material from which it is made and with the purpose for which it has to function.* Thus a design made for textiles should be made directly with the material, or designed in the spirit of the function of the textile for which it is intended. Since this relationship between design and material is of prime importance, it is best, particularly at the beginning, to design with the material in hand, without preliminary planning. Only when the nature of the material is thoroughly understood can plans on paper be introduced. A design for a vase, therefore, must be adjusted to the function of the potter's wheel and the nature of the material, "clay." In the same way a design for a piece of jewelry must grow out of the possibilities which different types of metal offer with regard to texture and flexibility.

The word "functional," therefore, refers to three different relationships that are equally important in any functional design: (1) the relationship between design and material, (2) the relationship of design to

* Perry, Evadna Kraus, *Art Adventures with Discarded Materials.* New York: Noble Publishers, Inc., 1933. Smith, Janet K., *Design, An Introduction.* Chicago, New York: Ziff-Davis Publishing Co., 1946.

Fig. 73b. Functional design in clay.

tools or machinery, and (3) the relationship between design and purpose.*

Let us discuss these qualities on one object of design. We may select for this purpose a piece of pottery made on the potter's wheel, glazed and fired in the kiln. The relationship between design and material seems to be clear as soon as we relate the plasticity of the clay to the working method on the potter's wheel. The process of turning is perfectly adjusted to the plasticity of clay. The relationship of design to the tool or machinery, in this case the potter's wheel, will be expressed only if we do not cover up what the potter's wheel has achieved. How often do we see the beautiful form created on the potter's wheel spoiled by denting some parts of the vase without any reason. Still more often do we find the surface quality, which the clay receives through the turning process, carefully removed and replaced by a smoothness which destroys the dynamic whirling effect which is a natural and functional outcome of the process of turning. The object will conform better with the true principles of functional design when this true relationship between design and potter's wheel is realized (Fig. 73). The more we hide the effects of the tool and its function, the more we move away from the truth of functional design. Finally, the design must have a relationship to the purpose for which it is made. The purpose of a vase may be purely decorative. The only thing then which we have to

* Kahn, Ely Jacques, *Design in Art and Industry.* New York: Scribner's (Charles) Sons, 1936; Holme, Geoffrey, *Industrial Design and the Future.* London: The Studio, Ltd., 1934.

Fig. 73c. Functional design in aluminum and glass.

consider is that the vase must not tip over easily: it must be able to stand safely. If it is to serve as a flower vase, however, its glaze must neither compete with the colors of flowers, nor can its shape be too wide on the top and narrow on the bottom. Such considerations must be applied to all pieces of design, each in its own realm with regard to material, tool, or purpose (Figs. 74 and 75).

The greater the variety of materials with which the student works, the wider will be his range of experiences. In general, materials are distinguished by whether they are inorganic or organic. Inorganic materials consist of various rocks and metals dug out of the earth and generally refined or in other ways made suitable for working. Such materials and products give rise to three principal divisions of industrial art: pottery, glass, and metalwork.

The logical French mind sometimes classifies these arts as "les arts du feu," the arts of fire, because firing is an essential process in their manufacture.

The organic materials are by-products of vegetable and animal growth, such as wood and cotton from trees and plants, and wool and skin from animals. These materials give rise to the following principal divisions of woodwork and textiles.

Other divisions, such as *leatherwork* and *paperwork,* are of minor importance, and the aesthetic principles applicable to them are easily deduced from the general principles that arise in connection with the other industrial arts.

In addition to the materials mentioned above one group, which cannot be placed in either of the foregoing groups because it is derived mainly from chemical processes, is becoming increasingly important. The principal materials which belong to this group are referred to most commonly as *plastics.*

"In addition to the arts which arise out of the working of these various materials, there is an art which consists in assembling and combining ready made units from the primary industrial arts. This art we may call the art of *construction,* and this art includes anything from combining metalwork and woodwork on a piece of furniture to the building of a house, a factory or a city." *

Functional design, therefore, refers to the relationship of this wide range of materials and their working methods to the purpose for which the design was created.

* Read, Herbert, *Art and Industry.* New York: Harcourt, Brace and Co., 1938, p. 43. Cheney, Sheldon and Cheney, Martha Candler, *Art and the Machine.* New York: Whittlesey House, 1936.

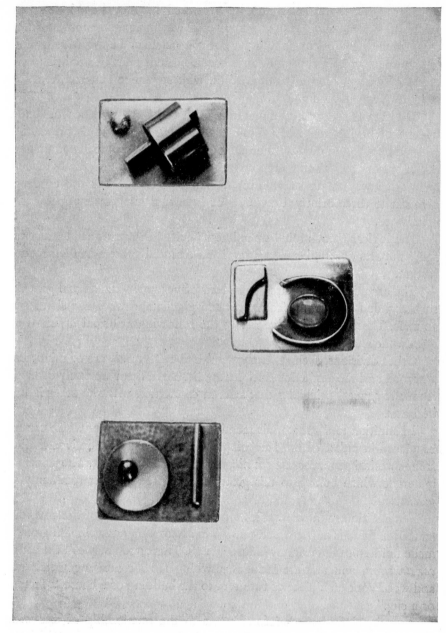

Fig. 74a. Modern design of jewelry by Karla Longrée.

Fig. 74b. Modern design of jewelry by Karla Longrée.

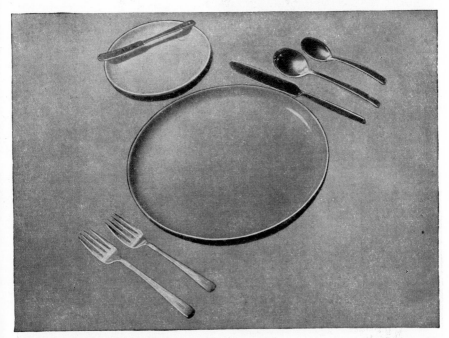

Fig. 75a. Modern table setting.

In the secondary-school classroom it is not only important to show this wide range of materials but also to introduce as many different working methods as possible and to relate them to the particular functional application of the specific material. It is important moreover, to direct the attention of our youth to man-made objects which show the effect of functional design in its relation to material and purpose.

Functional design in decoration   A piece of jewelry is not a necessity of life although it may make life more beautiful and enjoyable. Such pieces of design in which the decorative quality dominates shall be dis-

Fig. 75b. Cane-seat chair. Designed by Marcel Breuer. (Photo, courtesy Museum of Modern Art, N. Y.)

cussed in the framework of "functional design in decoration." How can a piece of jewelry have a functional design if its function is merely decorative? "Functional" here refers more to the functional relationship of material and design than to the purpose for which it is made. Quite often in decorative design, the purpose for which an object is made plays a major

Fig. 75c. Interior. Designed by Dan Cooper, N. Y. (Knickerbocker Photo Service.)

role. Let us take for example a lamp base and the shade. A lamp base must not tip over easily. Therefore, a well-designed lamp base must be designed to stand firmly. Beyond this function there is not much more to consider with the exception of the adjustment of the type of design to the material from which it is made and to the environment in which it will be placed. With regard to the shade, however, it is most important that it permits good lighting. Therefore, its design and material will not only have to serve aesthetic or decorative functions but also a definite purpose. That is why we can rarely speak of a merely decorative purpose in design because some functional purpose is always related to objects which deal with our daily living. The design of a piece of jewelry or a rug is not only dependent upon the material but also upon the purpose for which it is determined. A ring must be designed in some proportion to the finger or hand for which it is made; an earring is designed in relationship to the ear on which it hangs. Still, we can say that there is no necessity of wearing earrings, and therefore we can put earrings into the category of decorative design.

Functional design in industry   Every design in industry which has a definite relationship to the necessity of living is called "functional design."

That is why the design of a toothbrush with a functional handle and bristles that reach into all crevices between our teeth is as much an industrial design as the functional organization or planning of a city. Both are of equal significance as educational means.

But here also it is of importance to show the before-mentioned relationships. These can best be demonstrated by the designing of functional gadgets which are in our daily use, like a doorknob, different handles for different purposes (drawers, teapots, towel racks), electric switches, hinges of functional quality in design, keys, silver (spoons, forks, knives), clothespins, hangers for suits or coats, and so forth.

To direct attention to such details is most important because they often are overlooked in their significance for our daily living.*

Educators have an important mission to encourage the necessity of modern functional and well-designed furniture. Nowhere do we find such an adherence to the "old time" as in the average American home. Modern style in the American home has not penetrated beyond the kitchen and bathroom door. Kitchens, however, and bathrooms in general have functionally designed furniture and utensils. The average American is rather technically minded when it comes to the point of finding a better kind of transportation—the newest streamlined car cannot be new and modern enough—or a better kind of gas range, refrigerator, and so forth. In his living room, however, he wants to be surrounded by his ancestors. Although well-designed and functional modern furniture is far superior in comfort to any period-styled furniture, it has not yet found its way into the American home. It is no excuse to say that modern furniture is as yet too expensive for the average income. Period furniture is relatively less expensive because the great demand for it has justified the application of mass-production methods for its manufacture. A refrigerator, for example, is more expensive than an old-fashioned icebox. If there would be a great enough demand for modern furniture, the production would necessarily have to be increased and the prices would fall. The question is more one of introducing the correct type of modern furniture to a public which will gradually open its mind to the advantages of the new era. This can only be done by acquainting our youth with the spirit of functionally designed modern furniture.†

What are the characteristics of well-designed furniture? The main

---

* Faulkner, Ray; Ziegfeld, Edwin; and Hill, Gerald, *Art Today*. New York: Henry Holt and Co., 1941. Frankl, Paul T., *New Dimensions*, New York: Brewer and Warren, Inc., 1928.

† Mumford, Lewis, *Architecture*. Chicago: American Library Assn., 1926; *Sticks and Stones*. New York: Norton (W. W.) and Co., 1933. Frankl, Paul T., *New Dimensions*. New York: Brewer and Warren, Inc., 1928.

Fig. 76a. Functionally designed one-family house. Architect Raymond Hall. (Scott Residence, Woodsdale.)

Fig. 76b. Oslo. Business houses.

characteristics are the same as in all other forms of industrial design: a relationship between *design, material, tool,* and *purpose.* This means that meaningless ornaments are omitted since they do not contribute to the purpose of living with and in them. On the contrary, as dust collectors they would only be detrimental to living comfort. The design itself grows out

Fig. 76c. San Francisco. The Golden Gate. (Photo M. D. Ross, State College.)

of the beauty of the different materials used. The beautiful and natural qualities of wood are never covered, but are preserved as much as possible. They are contrasted with other materials, such as glass, textiles, and metal, each being used in its own right. Simplicity in line, therefore, is an important principle of modern functional furniture. Variety in decoration is not introduced by ornamentation but by the use of different materials. The purpose of the furniture determines its design qualities, and vice versa. Therefore, one of the main characteristics of modern furniture is that it serves a purpose in such a way that the material used is being shown in its best light. Functional lines are always beautiful. Workmanship naturally is necessary to bring out the above-mentioned qualities. Finally a fine

SUMMARY   CRISIS OF ADOLESCENCE—THIRTEEN TO SEVENTEEN YEARS

Stage	Characteristics	Human Figure	Space	Color	Design	Stimulation Topics	Techniques
The Stage of Decision Crisis of Adolescence	Critical awareness toward environment and representational outcome. Clearer identification of visual and haptic types or "in-betweens." *Visual Type* Intermediaries: eyes. *Haptic Type* Intermediary: body. Main creative concern: subjective experiences, emotional expressions in which creator feels involved.	*Visual Type* Emphasis on exterior proportion, surface appearance, visual interpretation of light and shadow. Depiction of a moment's impression. Sketchy techniques or realistic interpretations of objective validity. *Haptic Type* Emphasis on inside feelings as contrasted to outside appearance. Depiction of character and expression, often of symbolic qualities. Proportions of value. Individual interpretations.	*Visual Type* Perspective space representation. Apparent diminution of distant objects. Changing intensity with distance. Meaning of horizon. Emphasis on three-dimensional qualities. *Haptic Type* Retrogression to base-line expressions. Perspective of value in relationship to the self. Value relationship of objects to one another.	*Visual Type* Changing qualities of color with regard to environment. Color reflections. Analytic attitude toward color with regard to distance, mood, and so forth. *Haptic Type* Expressive meaning of color. Subjective color expressions. Emphasis on local color. Psychological and emotional significance of color.	*Visual Type* Aesthetic interpretations of form, balance, and rhythm. Decorative quality of design. *Haptic Type* Emotional interpretation of abstract quality of design. Functional design. Industrial design.	Visual and haptical stimulations. Environment and figure. Posing model with interpretations. Sculpture. Graphics. Design. Poster work.	Sketching in crayon. Oil paint. Tempera. Water color. Sculpture in: clay, wood, plaster castings. Graphics: Linoleum cutting, etching, lithography, lettering, poster work. Silk screen. Airbrush. Stencil. Design: decorative functional in: stone, metal, glass, textiles, wood, paper, leather.

piece of furniture depends on both the quality of the materials used and above all on the creative power of the designer.*

EXERCISES

(1) Compare drawings of a fifth grade and eighth grade by pointing at characteristics which show the critical awareness toward the creative work of the eighth-grade student.
(2) Collect the drawings of a junior-grade high school and classify them according to their creative types.
(3) Study the characteristics of haptic drawings with regard to:
    (a) Preference of topics.
    (b) Proportion.
    (c) Subject matter and its presentation.
    (d) Meaning of color.
(4) Study the characteristics of visual drawings with regard to the same characteristics.
(5) Make a study of the meaning of the line throughout the history of art, by selecting one example of each category:
    (a) Line in its kinesthetic function in primitive drawings.
    (b) The line as base line in Egyptian or Assyrian drawings.
    (c) The line in its expressive quality in early Byzantine murals.
    (d) The line used as boundary to separate forms.
    (e) The line expressing three-dimensional qualities as seen in perspective.
(6) Make a similar study of lights and darks by selecting one example:
    (a) Lights and darks in their decorative qualities.
    (b) Lights and darks expressing three-dimensional form.
    (c) Lights and darks expressing dramatic effects of illumination.
    (d) Lights and darks expressing mystic effects as illumination.
    (e) Lights and darks in their expressive qualities.
    (f) Lights and darks to express atmosphere.
(7) Make a similar study of the meaning of color by selecting one example of each type:
    (a) Color in its decorative quality.
    (b) Color in its dynamic, dramatic qualities.
    (c) Color in its expressive quality.
    (d) Color to express atmosphere.
    (e) Color bound up with form.
    (f) Color used abstractly.

* Moholy-Nagy, L., *The New Vision*. New York: Norton (W. W.) and Co., 1938. Read, Herbert, *Art and Industry*. New York: Harcourt, Brace and Co., 1938. Agan, Tessie, *The House*. Philadelphia: Lippincott (J. B.) and Co., 1939.

(8) Show sample of time-space representation in art:
    (a) Different time sequences used in one representation (mainly in murals).
    (b) Space-time representations in motion pictures.
    (c) Mixtures of plan and front views (especially in Egyptian art).
    (d) Outside and inside representations.
(9) Relate one picture of each art period to the time it was created with regard to:
    (a) Subject matter.
    (b) Technique.
    (c) Mode of representation
10) Show the functional use of stone, metal, clay, and wood in sculpturing. Select one sculpture of each material and describe it.
11) Collect pictures of industrial products with functional use of the material.
12) Make a study of the use of different building materials in modern architecture.

LABORATORY WORK

Drawing

Media: Crayon, charcoal, Conté crayon, pencil, pen and ink, brush.
Subject matter:
    (1) Draw actions from your own experiences like:
        (a) Carrying a heavy load on the shoulder.
        (b) Picking up a coin which you have lost.
        (c) Lifting a heavy stone (bag).
        (d) Pushing a card.
        (e) Pulling on a rope.
        (f) Swinging an ax.
        (g) Reaching for something.
        (h) Climbing a ladder.
        (i) Going upstairs.
        (j) Coming downstairs.
        (k) Two persons carrying a log.
        (l) Two persons digging a hole.
        (m) Two persons sawing lumber.
        (n) A group of workers on the highway.
    (2) Draw actions from the posing model with suggestive topics:
        (a) A beggar.
        (b) A scrub woman.
        (c) A woman (man) carrying a basket.
        (d) A person reading a book.
        (e) A farmer raking.
        (f) A tired person.

(3) Drawing from life model without suggested actions, including portrait
(4) Drawing of scenes in open air:
   (a) Landscapes.
   (b) Industrial sections.
   (c) City life.
   (d) Farm life.
(5) Animals.
(6) Combine figures and animals in compositions.
(7) Cartooning and Caricature.

Painting

Media: Tempera, water color, oil, gouache, and combinations of these.
(1) Easel paintings:
   (a) Personal experiences of 1. the self; 2. the immediate environment.
   (b) How people live.
   (c) How people make their living under the circumstances adjusted to the environment of the student (farming, mining, industrial occupations, trades, and so forth).
   (d) Different social atmospheres.
   (e) Different moods in landscapes.
   (f) Home life, adjusted to the different home situations of the students (farm home, city home, country house, mountain home, and so forth).
   (g) People and their characteristics.
   (h) Recreations:
      1. In the theater.
      2. In the movie.
      3. Listening to a concert.
      4. In the library.
      5. Athletics and sport.
   (i) Religion and its relationship to life.
   (j) Historical events.
(2) Mural paintings
   (a) Emotional or temporary murals:
      1. For a special dance occasion.
      2. For a music festival.
      3. For the school cafeteria.
      4. For a bakery.
      5. On current events.
      6. A circus or a fair.
   (b) Planned or permanent murals:
      1. Industrial processes:
         From the wheat to the bread.

From the cotton to the textile or garment.
From the lumber yard to the bungalow.

2. Traveling and transportation murals for:
An airport.
A bus station.
A railway terminal.
A boat.

3. Historical murals for:
The city hall with a local event.
The court room with a national event.

4. Sociology:
The life of the people of the different classes.
In different epochs and cultures.
A mural for a church, Sunday school.

Sculpturing

(1) Model a clay mask of a definite expression referring to the self (without model):
(a) Yawning.
(b) Laughing.
(c) Thinking hard.
(d) Whistling.
(e) Crying.
(f) Singing.
(g) Smiling.
(h) Sleeping.
(i) Being frightened.
(j) Being angry.

(2) Cast a mask in plaster, using a one-piece mold.

(3) Model a full head in which the position of the head contributes to the expressions:
(a) Tiredness.
(b) Singing.
(c) Excitedness.
(d) Looking out.
(e) Listening.
(f) Being sad.
(g) Turning around, searching for something.
(h) Praying.

(4) Cast a head in plaster:
(a) In a waste mold.
(b) In a piece mold.

(5) Model a figure:
(a) Actions as suggested in drawing.
(b) Movements of emotional significance.

    (6) Cast a figure in plaster of Paris:
        (a) In a waste mold.
        (b) In a piece mold.
    (7) Model a group composition of:
        (a) Mother and child.
        (b) Two friends.
        (c) Workers.
        (d) Family.
    (8) Model animals.
    (9) Carving in wood (see (1) and (7)).
   (10) Cutting in plaster of Paris.
   (11) Cutting in soft stone.
   (12) Experimenting with synthetic materials.
   (13) Model puppets in papier mâché.
   (14) Model animals in papier mâché.

Design

    (1) Pure design:
        (a) Emotional abstractions.
        (b) Planned nonobjective painting.
        (c) Design in different materials: two and three dimensions.

    (2) Industrial design in material:
        (a) Pottery:
            1. Coil method.
            2. Work on the potter's wheel.
            3. Firing methods.
            4. Glazing.
            5. Decorating.
        (b) Textile design:
            1. Textile printing:
                a. Block printing.
                b. Stencil printing.
                c. Airbrush.
                d. Silk screen.
                e. Batik.
                f. Tie and dye.
            2. Weaving techniques:
                a. Hooking.
                b. Needle point.
        (c) Design in wood emphasizing its character:
            1. Design and execute a doorknob or handle.
            2. Design and execute a bowl on a lathe.
            3. Design and execute a simple lamp base.
            4. Design and execute a simple, functional piece of furniture.

    (d) Design in metal:
        1. Functional use of wire and sheet metal.
        2. Jewelry.

(3) Costume design appropriate of the occasion and the individual:
    (a) Sports clothes:
        1. Romantic type girl or boy.
        2. Athletic type girl or boy.
    (b) Street wear:
        1. Stout persons.
        2. Slender persons.
        3. Tall persons.
        4. Slim or average.
    (c.) Evening clothes fit to:
        1. Personality.
        2. Build.
        3. Complexion and coloring.
        4. Fitness.
    (d) Design costumes that will enable a tall person to look shorter.
    (e) Design costumes that will be becoming to a short person.
    (f) Design a wardrobe for yourself including hat, bag, gloves, tie, socks, handkerchiefs, belt, and buttons.
    (g) Design a costume for a special purpose:
        1. Sunday.
        2. Easter.
        3. Christmas.
        4. Traveling.
    (h) Design a lounging costume for yourself consisting of dressing robe and pajamas.
    (i) Show how design affects appearance:
        1. Predominance of straight vertical lines.
        2. Predominance of straight horizontal lines.
        3. Predominance of vertical and horizontal lines.
        4. Irregularly curved lines.
        5. Rhythmically curved lines.
    (j) Combine different textures of fabrics and furs.

(4) Interior Design.
    (a) Make a drawing to scale of the living room of your family. Cut out the furniture and move it on your drawing to scale until it serves best the function and provides most space for moving about.
    (b) Redecorate your own room or any other room with which you are well acquainted.
    (c) Redecorate the college cafeteria library, or office room.
    (d) Design a combination living-bedroom-workroom for yourself.

(e) Design a functional kitchen.

(f) Design an apartment for your family.

(g) Make a scale model of a summer cottage consisting of four rooms and bath.

(h) Select textiles and colors for:
1. Office room.
2. Classroom.
3. Kitchen.
4. Cafeteria.
5. Living room.
6. Bedroom.

(i) Redecorate an old piece of furniture by:
1. Removing all unnecessary parts.
2. Reconsidering shape.
3. Renewing worn-out material.

(5) Poster design and advertising:

(a) Study various types of print.

(b) Distinguish between letters that are written and those that are drawn.

(c) Use different lettering pens.

(d) Learn to letter with the lettering brush.

(e) Make word illustrations of:
Heavy.
Light.
Bold.
Strong.
Delicate.
Hurry.
Rough.
Smooth.
Fun.
Serious.
Help.
Dangerous.

(f) Make road signs:
Stop.
Curve.
Steep Hill.
Slippery.
Crossroad.

(g) Design table cards.

(h) Design posters of:
1. Humanitarian purpose:
   "Give to the Red Cross."

"Think of the Blind."
"Give to the Poor."
"Contribute your Share to the Community Chest."
2. For traffic purpose:
"Prevent Accidents."
"Watch the Red Light."
"Don't Play in the Street."
"Drive Slowly."
3. For the community:
"Keep Your Streets Clean."
"Don't Step on the Flowers."
"Papers Belong in the Waste Basket."
"Don't Spit on the Floor."
"Don't Spread Colds."
4. For a special occasion:
A football game; for a race.
A dance.
A church service.
A lecture.
A festival.
A concert.
5. For commercial purposes:
Use different articles for advertising purposes as:
Soap.
A bottle of perfume.
A dress; a suit.
Foods.
Cars.
Tires.
Gasoline, and so forth.
(6) Window display
(a) Make a display that stresses uniqueness and quality.
(b) Make a display that stresses uniformity of quality.
(c) Make a good arrangement of a dress.
(d) Make a display for a "sale."
(e) Make a good arrangement of a whole outfit.
(f) Arrange one window of a:
1. Grocery.
2. Women's store.
3. Men's store.
4. Drug store.
5. Shoe store.
6. Jewelry store.
7. Department store.

(g) Arrange one window for a special occasion:
    1. Easter.
    2. St. Valentine's Day.
    3. Christmas.
(7) Theater and Stage Design:
    (a) Formal aspects:
        1. Study the effect of horizontal and vertical lines.
        2. Study the effect of different levels.
        3. Study the effect of lighting in relationship to cast shadows.
        4. Study the effect of lighting with regard to the importance of the illuminated part.
        5. Study the meaning of big spaces versus small spaces.
        6. The meaning of foreground and background.
        7. The center of interest.
        8. The emotional content.
        9. The social atmosphere.
       10. Period and style.
    (b) Design stage sets and characters for puppet shows.
    (c) Design stage sets and characters for marionette shows.
    (d) Design a stage set and lighting for a dramatic scene:
        1. A graveyard.
        2. A prison.
        3. A wilderness.
    (e) Design a stage set and lighting for a mass scene
        1. A fair.
        2. A riot.
        3. A festival.
    (f) Design a stage set and lighting for a small village square.
    (g) Design a stage set and lighting for a scene in an industrial section or factory court.
    (h) Design a stage set and lighting for a drawing-room comedy.
    (i) Study the characters of one play and design the costumes and make-up.

History of Art

Starting from our present-day relationships of form and content best seen in modern architecture, similar relationships should be discovered in works of art throughout the history of mankind.

(1) It is best to start with a good piece of modern architecture in your home town:
    (a) Gather all available information concerning the factors that determined the style and execution of the architecture.
    (b) Do the same for an older building.
    (c) Try to apply the same criteria to a Gothic cathedral.

(2) Find (in a functionally designed chair) what was important to the architect and what determined his design:

(a) Material.
(b) Function.
(c) Design.

Do the same with a poor imitation of a "style" furniture, such as you usually find in mail-order catalogues.

Analyze what determined a colonial carpenter to give his chair its shape.

(3) Show three different types of modern pictures and discuss them according to their different attitudes toward art expression:

(a) Abstract art:
> Calder (constructivism).
> Kandinsky (emotional approach).
> Mondrian (planned design).

(b) Expressive art:
> Picasso (haptic emotional).
> Leger (decorative).
> Rouault (purely expressive).
> Lawrence (urge for primitivity).

(c) Mural Painting:
> Rivera (planned mural with story-telling content).
> Orozco (emotional tendencies).

(4) Show the relationships between art and life in the different epochs and cultures in fine arts and applied arts:

(a) A spoon in:
> Early primitive cultures.
> Egyptian art.
> African art.
> Greek art.
> Roman art.
> Medieval art.
> Renaissance.
> American Indian.
> Colonial.
> Modern.

(b) Show the same for a house.
(c) Show the same for a picture and its connection with life.

(5) Show the connection between technique and content of a picture of the different epochs and cultures:

(a) Paintings in caves of the most primitive cultures (why in caves? material?).
(b) Frescos in basilicas (why on the walls?).

(c) Stained windows of a Gothic cathedral (why the window for pictures?).

(d) Miniatures in books of the medieval age (why the books?).

(e) Tempera on wood with gold background of medieval art (why wood and why a golden background?).

(f) Tempera with sharp outlines on canvas of early renaissance (why sharp outlines?).

(g) Mixed technique of oil and tempera of the later part of renaissance with "softer" character: Tintoretto, late Titian (why applied in many coats, and why the "softer character"?).

(h) Impressionist paintings in oil of the former century.

(i) Modern use of various materials.

(6) Show the connection between the form of a utensil and its function, and point out dominance of either one in the different epochs and cultures.

(7) Find out the relationships of characteristics of styles with their epochs and cultures. Start with the functional straight lines of modern architecture.

CHAPTER VIII

Abnormal Trends
as Seen
in Creative Activity

E<small>VERY HANDICAP IS CONNECTED WITH A GREATER OR LESSER DETACH-</small>ment from the environment depending on the degree and kind of handi-cap.* This is true for emotional and mental, as well as physical or even social handicaps. Whether we can—in the individual case—speak of a handicap depends not only on the handicap itself but even more on the individual and his ability to adjust. Weak-sightedness, to give an example of a physical handicap, can mean quite a serious handicap for one individ-ual, but another might find adequate ways of overcoming it. Whereas the one might still depend on the rudiments of his sight, the other never depended much on his visual experiences and could, therefore, quite easily adjust to his impaired sight. Still, even the slightest handicap needs some kind of adjustment, which deals mainly with the problem of finding ways of overcoming a detachment from environment imposed by the handicap. Whether one is simply shy, having emotional barriers that do not permit him to communicate easily with the outside world, or whether one is com-

* See Lowenfeld, B., "Psychological Aspects of Blindness," *Encyclopedia of Psychology.* New York: Philosophical Library, 1946. The author wants to express his gratitude to his brother, Dr. Berthold Lowenfeld, Director of Educational Research of The American Founda-tion for the Blind, for his many helpful suggestions in this chapter.

pletely emotionally blocked and is entirely cut off from environment, the problem differs only in degree.

The weak-sighted or the blind individual is restricted in contacting environment by the physical impairment of his sight; the person who is hard of hearing or deaf is restricted in his communications by his inability to hear; the crippled or lame individual is hampered in his contacts by the restrictions in his movability. The mentally or emotionally handicapped is in extreme cases, unable to conceive environment. The socially handicapped person, however, is isolated from environment by the restrictions which society imposes upon him. In general, the greater the physical handicap, the greater the feeling of isolation. The greater the mental or emotional handicap, the smaller the degree of consciousness of isolation. The totally insane person is completely shut off, unable to conceive his isolation from environment.

Any conscious experience of isolation from the environment, when forced upon an individual through mental or physical disturbances, naturally creates in addition a lack of self-confidence. Being placed in a normal environment, the handicapped person has to compete with it. Since he is usually unable to do so, he feels inferior and withdraws if he has no possibility of compensating for his handicap.

If creative activity is used as a means of adjustment, it must counteract this feeling of isolation. Before we can counteract such feelings we must know them in their single trends. An analysis of the type of isolation which results from the different types of handicaps will, therefore, lead to a better understanding of the nature and kind of stimulation best suitable for the different groups of handicaps.

There is, however, one problem that all handicapped people have in common—namely, to find a way of compensation for their feelings of isolation. The methods of approach for the various groups will be different as the causes that basically created the feeling of isolation are different. Before we enter into a discussion on methods, we should distinguish clearly between simple *retardation* and mental or emotional *disturbances* on the one hand, and physical handicaps that *can* be *corrected* and those which *cannot* be *corrected,* on the other hand.

MENTAL RETARDATION AS EXPRESSED IN CREATIVE ACTIVITY

A retarded individual usually is one who has not attained the mental capacity of normal individuals of the same age level, and involves no other abnormal condition. Mental retardation indicates only a discrepancy between mental and chronological age. In creative activity we might find an eight-year-old child still scribbling and therefore still concerned with his motor activity. Instead, he should already relate his drawings to environment. He might, however, have undergone a perfectly normal development of his scribbling, only he started at a later age and remained in each single stage for a longer period. He might, then, perhaps at nine years, reach his preschematic stage and at twelve years, schematic representations, still using geometric lines. The sequence of his development might be perfectly normal but the age level at which he reaches the various stages of development does not correspond with the normal average as presented in previous chapters. Retardation, therefore, can be detected by comparing the characteristics found in productions of normal individuals with the creative work of the retarded individual. A discrepancy can be found either in the representation of the human figure, in the concept and representation of space, or in both.

The progress of the development of a human being is very flexible, and rigid criteria of what is normal are not valid. Furthermore, diagnoses ought not to be made merely for their own sake. If we find that there is a distinct discrepancy between what we may expect at the different age levels and what actually exists, we have to do something to find a more forceful stimulation. That only means that we have to increase our efforts or even suggestive power in order to create in the child the desire to increase his active knowledge. The normal child's receptivity for stimulation will be reached much more easily, but the retarded child needs a much greater suggestive power in order to become stimulated. There is, however, no basic difference in the work of the retarded individual and the work of a normal one. Because the retarded child has fewer possibilities of expression, creative activity will also have the effect of releasing emotional tensions.

Abnormal Retardation in the Mongoloid Type

The following presentation of an extreme case of retardation, the case of an imbecile, only receives its significance when seen from the broader aspect of the effect of creative activity on human development. But even if we would neglect the general significance that such a case has for normal psychology, the fact still remains that the individual herself was released from a more or less static status of passive mental and emotional existence. Furthermore, her adaptibility to institutional life grew remarkably. Although having to be attended to first, she afterwards even took care of her own little apartment which, for therapeutic reasons, was put at her disposal.*

A. L. was 27 years old. Her behaviour patterns were childish. She loved to play with dolls, loved repetitions, and laughed at the slightest stimulus. Her mental age was that of a five-year-old child. When she was asked to draw, she would draw "head-feet" representations only, which is a characteristic representation of a five-year-old child, only that she was repeating them again and again in a stereotyped way. In Fig. 77a she expresses herself going downstairs. Environment was added upon stimulation by the author. At the right she is picking flowers.

Knowing that the next stage should include the "body," all stimulation was directed toward the goal of consciously experiencing the body. Since food meant very much to her, she was given plenty of it that morning, to the extent that she even complained about a stomach-ache. This opportunity was used to ask her to draw herself with her stomach-ache, holding her stomach as she did. Fig. 77b shows that although she first introduced a symbol for the body which she was holding with her arms, she later forgot its meaning and returned to her inflexible "head-feet" representation by drawing the "features" into the symbol first designated as "body."

To the right of this drawing is A. L. wearing her orange Sunday dress (orange line between "legs"). But neither did this experience divert her from her inflexibility, or better, fixation to a definite schema. Since nothing could stimulate her to arrive at a different concept, I gave her clay to work with. Fig. 77c shows A. L. sitting on a stone as she loved to do. Working with another medium such as clay, which she never had used before, obviously diverted her from her inflexible "head-feet" concept. After she was given paper and crayons, she applied the experience gained in her clay work to a new topic. She depicted the body for the first time (Fig 77d). The significance, however, lies in the fact that she became released from her static inflexibility. The person to the right was spontaneously added by her and represents the author holding his arm around her shoulder. Also, she added the environment spontaneously.

This change from modeling to drawing was continued from now on, since it contributed greatly to making her more flexible in her thinking and concept. Fig. 77e shows a clay work of herself with her "child," as she used to call her doll. Remarkable is the quite complicated way of putting the "baby's" arm around her shoulder. It was suggested that she put on her dress and go out for a walk with her doll. Fig. 77f shows her enjoying her

* Experiments made at Lochland School, Geneva, New York, an institute for mentally deficient children. The author would like to use this opportunity to acknowledge gratefully the help and cooperation he received from Miss Florence H. Steward, director of the institute.

Fig. 77. Drawings by an imbecile (twenty-seven-year-old individual).

a). "Going Downstairs." Five-year-old level of head-feet representation.

b). Stimulation on body creates no deviation of inflexible schema. "Stomach-Aches."

c). "Sitting on a Stone." First diversion from "head-feet" representation. (From the modeling drawn by the author.)

d). "Sitting on a Stone." Drawing showing introduction of body.

e). "*A* and Her Child." Modeling (drawn by the author).

f). "*A* and Her Child." Drawing showing greater awareness of the self.

g). "Riding Horseback." Emotional freedom is clearly seen when compared with *Fig. a.*

"child." Most significant in this drawing is the increased desire to express body actions and also, for the first time, emotions. Whereas in former drawings only an indication of "hand" is given by means of one line, in this drawing the five fingers were represented. She even counted them with great pride. The meaningfulness of the arms, represented by a double line, reminds us of the discussion on emotionally emphasized parts during the schematic stage (seven to nine years of age) of the normal child (see pages 40 and 54).

Approximately one year after making this drawing, she drew Fig. 77g, "Riding Horse Back," which she loved to do, probably because of the kinesthetic sensations which, as in rocking or swinging, contribute greatly to her pleasure. This drawing is self-explanatory. Besides the change of the single features, she developed a remarkable freedom in expressing her emotions. She now draws herself laughing loudly, showing her tongue and teeth. She adds her two ears, even the openings in them, and the nose is drawn sideward. The saddle, her suit, even the stirrup into which she puts her feet, are indicated. The galloping horse is represented by the "bent" legs. Environment has become a part of her and her way of drawing.

Compared with her first drawing, this last drawing not only shows the great emotional change and freedom she now enjoys but also a more advanced possibility of mental activity which clearly showed itself in the change of her personality. It further demonstrates how creative activity has actively contributed to bringing her out of the emotional and mental isolation that prevented her from becoming an active member of her group.

Although Mongoloid types (as glandular defective types) cannot be made normal, the great improvement of this case should clearly point out *the general significance of creative activity with regard to releasing emotional tension and rigidity, opening the way to a freer mental development.*

CREATIVE ACTIVITY AND THE HANDICAPPED

As so often before, the study of extreme cases has resulted in the clarification of our ideas about the normal individual. It is, therefore, with a definite purpose that this chapter is placed at the end of this book. It should again show the close interdependence between emotional and mental growth and creative expression. More than that, it should demonstrate the influence of creative activity on the minds and emotions of those who are not privileged in having normal physical or mental attributes.

The educational problems presented by children with different handicaps shall now be discussed in case histories which are significant not only for the handicapped as such but for education in general.

Modeling as a Means of Self-Expression for the Blind

It is the aim of good methods of teaching to set free all the abilities in an individual and direct them into the most productive channels. This is true for teaching at all grade levels. It is valid for the normal and the abnormal, for the handicapped as well as for the physically fit. "Setting free" means removing all the inhibitions that stand in the way of the individual's healthy and normal development. An essential part of education consists of removing such inhibitions so that the enrichment of knowledge and experience can be achieved with the least possible effort. This is true for educational methods applied to the normal but it is of even greater importance in teaching those who cannot make full use of their senses and become inhibited mainly though improper contact with those not handicapped. No doubt the blind person feels his inferiority much more when he works with seeing persons who make him aware of his dependency than when working alone. However, this is true only when the activities with seeing persons are mainly designed for the latter. The obvious discrepancy in quality and speed and often the inability of perceiving his own work as a whole have a discouraging effect on the blind.

As we know, the blind individul can perceive objects that are larger than his hand only by moving his hand over the object. Thus, he can only receive partial impressions which he has to unify into a simultaneous whole. The integration of these partial impressions into an impression of the whole object is often achieved only with considerable difficulties. This is one of the peculiar handicaps caused by blindness, which is partly responsible for the blind individual's isolation. It is not only his physical inability to get around, but also his mental incapacity to imagine the world which surrounds him. The space in which the blind individual lives is mainly controlled by his sense of touch. In his world distant objects do not seem to be smaller, as they do for the normally sighted. For the sense of touch, distant objects do not change in size. It has been discussed previously (see Chapter VII, p. 151) how a blind person who made himself acquainted with a room and became very much interested in a desk lamp, modeled it afterward as the outstanding part of the room. In other words, different objects in space receive their proportion by the value the objects have for the blind individual. *The perspective of space is in this world a perspective of value.* When blind children after a ride on a steamship were asked to model the boat, they started with the inside, especially with the place that had made the greatest impression upon them. The captain had showed them around, making a special effort to get them acquainted with the important parts of his boat. So some of the children started with cabins, others with the dining room, and even with the engine room. Some children were able to make a quite detailed model of the inside by adding one part to the other. The outside hull, however, as the imperceivable part, was in many cases left out entirely. Others covered the boat because they knew that it must have a hull, though their main interest remained centered on the inside representation of the boat.

In a Utopia where the blind would only live with the blind it would be possible that the blind with their peculiar space concepts would not feel their handicap at all, just as we do not feel any disadvantage in our inability to see ultraviolet rays. It would, however, be entirely wrong if we should draw from this the conclusion that the blind should avoid any contact with their natural environment. On the contrary, it means we must search for ways that will help them to overcome their isolation by achieving an adjustment to the given environment, which will not make them too conscious of their handicap. That means that educators of the blind should avoid as much as possible any technique that adds other inhibitions, not necessarily connected with sightlessness, to the restrictions directly resulting from the handicap. This leads us to the realization, that before one can remove inhibitions, it is necessary to recognize them as such. Self-evident as this statement may appear, it is necessary to emphasize it in a discussion about the meaning of modeling in schools for the blind.

It should be observed, for example, that it would be completely wrong to attempt to set free the creative power of a blind individual by trying to remove the inhibitions caused by his lack of sight through an attempt to familiarize him with visual impressions. His haptic experiences are different from visual ones and cannot be "optified." For an instance of this we have only to turn to the many teaching situations where imitative visual likeness is praised as the highest achievement. *Optical characteristics which are our common measurements are by no means applicable to the work of the blind.* One would in fact achieve the exact opposite, just as one would inhibit creative ability by forcing a visually minded, normally sighted person to pay special attention to tactile, or touch impressions, or kinesthetic experiences.

Being unable to see is not always an inhibitory factor. On the contrary, as has been shown in other discussions of this book, it has been proven that blindness may become the basis of a specific and unique creativeness.* In it there is not only a distinct difference from visual art expression but also (Fig. 39) a specific approach to creative art. This specific approach results from the need of building up a whole image from partial perceptions.

* *The Nature of Creative Activity.*

What the blind individual cannot always, or can only seldom, achieve in life, he can do in art: out of the many partial impressions he builds up a "whole" and arrives thus at a synthesis of his image. What a release of tension when he can contact environment—his sculpture—without interference in his own mode. Through his continuous contact and establishment of relationships between his thinking and his sculpture he increases his ability to integrate his partial impressions, which are touch impressions, into a "whole." This ability surely is not confined only to the field of modeling but reflects upon the whole emotional and mental growth, as I shall later demonstrate.

Since we are aware of this distinct difference in the approach of the blind toward creative activity, why should we not attempt to realize the blind person's Utopia, at least in this single field by leaving him his own realm of creativity? We should use any opportunity to give him back his shaken self-confidence, thereby influencing other fields of work where he often does not dare to assert himself because of the feeling of inferiority resulting from the natural restrictions on his personal and individual freedom.

Attempts have already been made to recognize modeling as a subject in the curricula of a few of the institutes for the blind. But there remains the sad and depressing experience that the "seeing taste" of physically normal "educators" is determining the way of expression and production of the blind. It is time to realize that the most primitive creative work born in the mind of a blind person and produced with his own hands is of greater value than the most effective imitation.

Modeling with the Deaf-Blind—Case History

Because of the lack of another important sense, hearing, the deaf-blind individual is far more dependent than the blind upon bodily experiences, upon contacts of the self with the outer world. Bodily experiences are the connecting medium between the ego and its surroundings. If they are disturbed or disordered, conscious contact with the outside world is lessened or entirely destroyed. It is therefore most important, in the education of the deaf-blind, to emphasize and stimulate bodily sensations as much as possible. Thus, although the deaf-blind person learns to speak by means of the vibration method, language remains an abstract, sounds without meaning, unless the teacher brings it into relation with reality. This is possible, of course only through the sense of touch, through bodily feelings which are in close relation to the kinesthetic sensations. But mere acquaintance with various objects does not constitute the whole experience, because the circumstances under which the acquaintance is made determine the nature of the experience.

Experiments have shown that modeling in clay is an excellent means of giving force to these subjective expressions, because it not only allows the teacher to control the circumstances through which experience is attained but permits a plastic representation of touch sensations and bodily feelings. Details that are important in the child's experience are over-emphasized in the plastic representation, but meaningless parts are neg-lected or even omitted. During my investigations it was apparent that these proportions of value as sensed by the deaf-blind and other nonvisual persons, clearly demonstrated the subjective attitude of such individuals toward their surroundings. For a teacher, this development opens new possibilities for understanding and influencing the world of imagery of blind and deaf-blind pupils. An analysis of the results of plastic modeling will not only reveal the lacks and limitations of both the imagination and the bodily feelings, but will serve as a gauge of mental development as the instruction proceeds.

Our purpose here is to show the pedagogical results obtained from employing this method in the very difficult case of a deaf-blind girl at Perkins Institution. This eleven-year-old girl had been totally blind and deaf since birth, and had been exceptionally shut in and restricted in her experiences. She was extremely limited in her expressions, and had much more difficulty than the average deaf-blind person in learning language through vibration. She spoke only when she was forced to do so, and then very poorly. Recognizing that creative activity stimulated by bodily feelings would serve as an excellent medium in the development of lan-guage, I encouraged this pupil to begin at once certain experiments in plastic modeling. It is easy to understand the adjusting effect of this kind of work on the mentality of the deaf-blind, because being able to express themselves in any medium not only enlarges their mental scope, but also gives them self-confidence. Through experiencing the self, the handicapped person establishes contact with his surroundings, loses his feeling of isola-tion, and becomes an integrated member of society. A very important result in this closer association with environment is the stimulation of language development through association of the word and its meaning.

When I began to work with the deaf-blind pupil at Perkins Institution, I let her sit down at the modeling table and, touching her body and placing her finger on my mouth when speaking, I told her, "You are sitting." Again touching her body in order to make her conscious of her position, I said, "You are a sitting girl—a sitting girl." She began to work with the clay, and Fig. 78a, illustrated here, was her first plastic. First she made

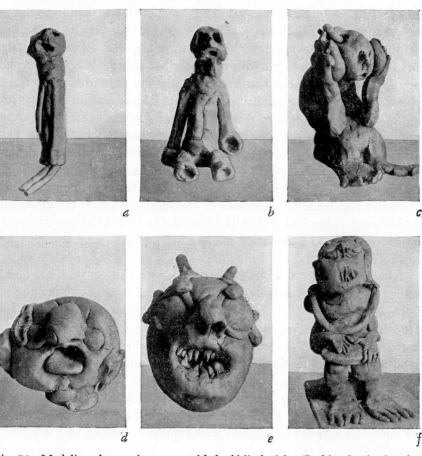

Fig. 78. Modelings by an eleven-year-old deaf-blind girl. (Perkins Institution for the Blind, Watertown, Mass.)

a). "Sitting."
b). "I put an apple in your hands."
c). "I am very tired, sleepy."

d). "I am yawning."
e). "I am eating candy."
f). "I am reading."

the body, then the legs, which she placed at the correct angle with the body, showing at once that she wished to indicate the "sitting girl." Then she made the arms, but these, as the illustration shows, were without differentiation, and she was also unaware of their importance in connection with the body. She then made the neck and the head; on the head she fashioned a nose but it was drawn out from the clay rather than added; then she made holes to represent the eyes, and one hole as a mouth.

For the next lesson I brought her an apple in order to make her conscious of the feeling of her hands. Putting it into her hand, I said to her, "I put an apple in your hand." Then I took the apple away again, and repeated the performance several times, always closing her fingers over the apple while saying the words. Finally she took up the clay, and made the plastic (Fig. 78c). In this the arms have acquired definite meaning, not only the arm connected with the apple but also the other arm which she modeled associatively. Closer observation will show that the feet are represented in the same manner as the hands. This is obviously an expression of the relation between them which probably comes from the sameness of their use in feeling vibrations. This mental progress on the part of the pupil marked her first step in finding her own method of expression: for the first time she indicated in the differentiation of the hands her realization of the close connection between action and representation. This experience also made her conscious of the starting point of the arms, and suddenly she recognized their relation to the body. Step by step we made use of modeling as a means of interpreting in plastic representation her own bodily sensations.

After two weeks she made Fig. 78c representing a very tired girl. Placing her fingers upon my face while speaking, I had said, "You are very tired—sleepy—very tired." She grasped the meaning of my words and leaned forward, relaxing and assuming the position which she later represented in the plastic. Touching her arms, I continued speaking to her. "You are holding your head," I said, "you are holding your head in your hands." Then, suddenly, came my greatest reward, for she repeated spontaneously, "holding m-y head in m-y hands." The emphatic use of the word *my* indicated that she did more than repeat a sentence, for through her sense of touch she had in one brief experience pushed back the limits of her little world of knowledge.

I cannot convey the sense of gratitude I felt while watching my pupil form this plastic figure. Holding her head in her hands—this heavy, tired head—she became conscious for the first time that she had ears; she grasped them, then added ears to the clay model, overemphasizing them because of their importance to her by exaggerating their size. On this occasion she also found that she had a pin in her hair and this, too, she added to the plastic, as is seen on the left side of the figure. It is obvious, too, that she began at this time to realize the function of fingers in the grasping of objects. The number of fingers is incorrect and they are drawn out from the clay, not modeled as single parts. This indicates that she had become conscious only of their function and her modeling shows only a representative symbol for "hand" and not single fingers. She used a similar technique in forming toes on the feet in this third figure. It is important to note the fact that she drew out fingers and toes. By adding them separately she would have shown her consciousness of them as individual parts a step not yet achieved in this modeling. But the great step in the development of her imagination and space perception was achieved when she was able to give her model the intended position; she had become aware of the relationship between movement and representation, as well as the differentiation between upper arm, forearm, hand, and fingers. This latter is shown by the position of the elbows resting on the thighs, and the hands holding the head.

I never saw this child more excited than after having finished this plastic. Spontaneously she began to speak to me and to her tutor, who was present. She eagerly started another figure. While she had made rapid progress in her plastic interpretations of the body, there had been very little change in the representation of the face. Therefore, I called her attention to the yawning of a tired girl. "You are yawning—very tired—yawning," I said. I imitated yawning to demonstrate the idea; then she yawned too, and set about forming Fig. 78d. First of all, she abandoned her former technique of drawing features out from the clay; instead, she made the entire head by adding parts to represent ears, eyes, nose and mouth, indicating that she had become conscious of each individual part. Moreover, she modeled a tongue and placed it in the proper position in the open, yawning mouth. This act of adding indicates an analytical process of thinking such as this: "I have a tongue, and form it, and place it in the right place in the mouth." It should be understood that this is a very complicated mental act. Putting on the nose presupposes holding and forming the nose consciously, and placing it properly. The further differentiation of the nostrils shows very clearly the advance from the representative symbol to an actual form of the object. As a single symbol the chin is added and it is significant to note that the ears are no longer exaggerated, indicating that they have now assumed normal importance.

Guiding her attention more and more toward individual experiences, I asked her whether or not she liked candy. "Yes," she answered. I had a piece of candy in my pocket and gave it to her. Then I asked her, "Is this candy hard?" She did not understand until I had given the words meaning by biting something hard myself. Then I asked once more, "Is the candy hard?" "Yes," she replied. "But show me, how hard?" I said, and she bit the candy into pieces.

At this point I gave her some clay as the traditional signal for starting to interpret the new experience, resulting in Fig. 78e. It can be seen at once how important the representation of the teeth is to her which she has now formed for the first time. But one can also recognize the emphasis of the two eyelids, the action of which accompanies the experience of pressing the teeth together. You can feel this muscular movement on your own face if you reproduce this situation. On this day she had two hairpins of which she was very proud; this may account for their exaggeration and again shows the importance of personal experiences.

After four weeks of work I gave her a braille book. She understood how to read a little. I asked her to read for a while, then I said to her, "Girl reading." She answered by saying, "I *am* reading." I again repeated "reading," handing her the clay. She immediately started to work, modeling the representation of a reading girl (Fig. 78f). Only the day before she had received a necklace as a birthday gift and, as you can imagine, it was of great importance to her. In studying this plastic, one should not be misled by the large ring around the neck of the figure. This is supposed to represent her necklace.

If one looks closely at this plastic one can find that in it each single part has been added. Therefore we may assume that her consciousness of her own body has undergone a decisive change. Instead of a symbolical lump of clay for a hand, she has made a hand with five single fingers cast in a definite position—that taken when reading a braille book. "One, two, three, four fingers—five, thumb," she said while she worked, and she placed the thumb separately in its proper position as seen on the right side of the picture. She became conscious not only of the fingers but also of their kinesthetic functions in reading. Now every part of the body is emphasized; shoulders, elbows, knees, and so forth. During the last week, while working on Fig. 78f, she talked spontaneously, naming all the details and actions that have occupied her attention: "Eyes, lids, finger, reading, book, legs," and so forth. A remarkable improvement in her general attitude took place. She was feeling much happier and freer and started to communicate spontaneously with other children. Her ability to speak developed rapidly, since it was carried by a released desire for contact with the environment.

Not only has creative activity relieved the tension which did not permit the individual to communicate freely but it has also contributed to her general growth. The consciousness of body feelings, actions, and kinesthetic experiences brought her in closer contact with the surroundings. But no words can better show the adjusting effect than can the comparison of the first with the last piece of modeling.

The Weak-Sighted and the Partially Blind

Between those who can see and those who are blind there are cases whose sight is not adequate for visual perception yet whose "blindness" is disturbed because they are not entirely without light. These are the weak-sighted and the partially blind and they are psychologically the most difficult to deal with. The remaining sight may for the one individual be an asset if he has the aptitude to use it, but for the other it can be an irritation, a disturbance in his orientation if he is depending in his aptitude on the mode of perception of the blind. In other words, *a visually minded weak-sighted individual will be blessed by the remnants of sight left to him, but the haptically minded individual will be disturbed by it.*

Whereas the visually minded partially blind individual, in his work, brings the outside world closer to himself by choosing *environment* as the main subject for his pictorial representation, the haptically minded concentrates on the self. He chooses almost exclusively the expression of the human figure as his subject matter.

The mere physiological question might arise as to whether or not it is harmful to the impaired eyes to put the strain of drawing and painting on them. This is a problem the physician has to solve. For the purely functional possibility of drawing for those cases where there is no medical objection to use the eyes the following points are of importance: (1) The nature of the eye defect and degree of visual acuity must be such that it allows accurate fixation of a point. (2) The training of the eye and the nature of its vision must be such that it is possible to follow the direction and goal of a line.*

Among the first visual perceptions are those of color. The visual impressions of the partially blind are at first mostly vague, but unless the organic defect is too severe they can be trained to achieve very fine distinctions.

As has been mentioned before, the blind build up their concepts out of individual elements each of which has been apprehended through the sense of touch. Out of these elements they construct a synthesis of appearances. In the same way, according to the kind of degree of their partial sight, the weak-sighted build their conceptions out of visual or tactual part impressions. This is true, however, only for the reproduction of the form as a whole. Those partially blind subjects whose orientation is visual are helped in achieving their concept of the "whole" by visual impressions, however shadowy and uncertain they may be, whereas those whose orientation is haptic make no use of such impressions. In both cases the similarity of their creative processes to those of the blind is clear because neither group is able to achieve directly an impression of the whole. In all cases it is constructed out of separate partial impressions. The partially blind who is a visual type assimilates these partial impressions to his visual concept, however indefinite this may be, and in this way gradually develops a struc-

* *The Nature of Creative Activity.*

Fig. 79. "Branch with Blossoms." Several steps in the painting of a partially blind youth, done from nature. This shows clearly the restricting effect of a too-close dependency on nature. Compare with *Fig. 80.*

turally more complete image. The partially blind who is a haptic type, on the other hand, will approximate more closely the haptic blind both in regard to his conceptions as a whole and in his creative output. The two following cases may clarify these statements of general principles.

S. G., a sixteen-year-old boy, has been partially blind since birth (congenital cataract of both eyes). When he draws, his eyes are approximately 1⅛ inches from his work. His field of vision is restricted to 4½ inches. He had the desire to draw a branch with blossoms. Fig. 79a shows several steps of this drawing. First he inspected the blossoms closely with his eye in order to get the *optical* impression demanded by his type (visual). Naturally, since he is mostly concerned with depicting his visual experiences he relates his subject matter almost exclusively to environment. Having given the blossoms a superficial visual inspection he proceeded to draw Fig. 79a. The one-sided view that his eye acquired had probably led him to believe that there were several petals. He then drew Fig. 79b, but perceived neither the number nor the arrangement of the individual

Fig. 80. "Branch with Blossoms." Painted by the same partially blind fourteen-year-old youth from imagination.

petals. He once again brought the blossom closely to his eye and convinced himself that—because of his high visual defect, which for all practical purposes is equivalent to blindness—he was unable to achieve an impression of the blossom as a whole. He therefore turned the flower and studied the arrangement of the petals. Fig. 79c proves that the act of turning—that is, letting the individual petals pass his eye—resulted in his placing them next to one another in the drawing. This arrangement did not satisfy him, since it did not express the "roundness," an impression of which he had got while turning the blossom. He therefore drew Fig. 79d, in which we can see the influence of the act of turning. Finally, after he had further investigated the flower tactually and by tearing the petals off satisfied himself that there were a number of them, he drew them in the correct circular order in Fig. 79e. After that he studied closely the arrangement of the different blossoms and leaves on the branch. With more certainty and self-confidence he then painted Fig. 79f. After a further visual examination he found that his tactual impression completely corresponded with the optical impression and thereby all further restrictions on his painting were removed. I then took the little branch away from him and he produced Fig. 80, which is, as it were, a mental synthesis of his visual and tactual experiences. It is incomparably more forceful, less concerned with considerations of reality, and altogether a far freer creation.

We see, then, that the optical experience has been constructed out of numerous partial impressions which by a mental act have been fused into a single image. *

This is also true to a certain degree for normal-sighted individuals when sketching from nature, only that their partial impressions are much larger. From these observations the following conclusions can be drawn: *For creative production the mental picture is of far greater importance than any realistic representation.*

The partially blind individual has by the process of drawing clarified his vague impression of nature. Through creative expression he has brought environment closer to himself, an act which contributed greatly to help him overcome the feeling of isolation imposed upon him by his impaired sight.

While adding more and more experiences to his imaginative activity, S. G. painted trees and houses in very different settings—in sunshine, at night, and in various moods. Fig. 81, one of his later paintings, is one in which he seems to have overcome the greatest obstacles. Through his own experiences and power he arrived at the concept of perspective space. We stand before a miracle when we see S. G. at work. His eyes are extremely close to the paper and he follows bodily even the smallest stroke of his brush because he is not able to see two things next to each other. Nevertheless, he achieves a unified picture. We cannot explain this in any other way than by realizing that the picture as a whole is present in his mind. Only thus can he achieve the astonishing unity of the numerous partial impressions whose synthesis produces the picture he has in mind. The boy in whom the physical ability to see has been restricted to the barest minimum, who is practically blind, achieves this miraculous effect

* *The Nature of Creative Activity.*

Fig. 81. "Street Scene." Painted by a fourteen-year-old partially blind youth, visually minded.

of "natural vision." It is a triumph of the spirit, which has transcended the physical defect and enabled the creator to express without hindrance a sensory experience which nature has denied him. Through the power of his work, he has entered into his birthright.

There is, however, as we said before, another type who experiences his remaining sight rather as a disturbing factor than as an asset. He is neither anxious to use his sight nor does he desire to familiarize himself visually with the outside world. He depends far more on his sense of touch and his body experiences.

"The Cry for Help" (Fig. 82) is the product of such a type. H. A., who made the painting has been partially blind since birth (congenital ambly-opia). He is sixteen years old and has far better sight than S. G. In spite of this he does not use his sight either for orientation or for observation. He uses it only when forced to do so. Drawing certainly created in him the desire to use it.

He started his drawing of the head with a simple elliptic outline to which other parts were added in the order of their importance for effecting the intended expression of "The Cry for Help." Thus he begins and con-

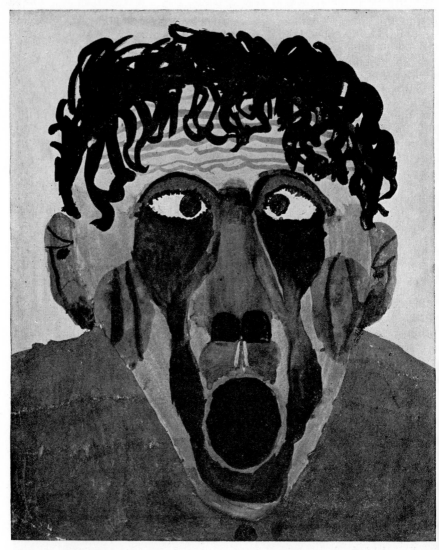

Fig. 82. "The Cry for Help." Painted by a sixteen-year-old partially blind youth, haptically minded.

tinues to work in an entirely *synthetic* way. The drawn-up eyebrows and the widely opened mouth were put in first, for in them the greatest tension is felt. The strong tension between eyes and mouth is probably the most important bodily experience in the act of screaming. This tension, as the drawing clearly shows, starts at the cheekbone just below the eyes and can be felt as a strong pull downward from the nose. This has been depicted with clarity and certainty by the two symbols of expression running from the nose and eyes downward toward the jaw and around the mouth. It is a reasonable analogy to compare the sensation of stretching with that of an elastic band, which in the drawing narrows towards the middle of the cheeks. This forceful experience dominates the whole head. "Tension" in the truest sense of the word is brought into the gesture, and its expressive content is heightened by the eyes squinting with horror. The hollowness of the cheeks is indicated by a dark color as though the artist wished to take something away from the cheeks. This darker shade must not be interpreted as a shadow. It is purely a symbol for "taking away," the symbol for a hollow. The black, wide-open nostrils which have been especially emphasized below the nose, are also important as symbols of expression. The nose has been only partially circumscribed and therefore stands out mainly by contrast with the surrounding shapes, although in accordance with the synthetic mode of procedure it, too, has been "added" as an independent part by means of a darker tone. The wrinkles of the forehead have not been differentiated much and have been treated more as a whole because they do not give rise to clear separate sensations. The ears, which have also been added to the head, clearly show lines that are a result of touch observation. The two ridges are parallel as they would appear to the fingers following the shape of the ear. Again corresponding to the sense of touch, the opening has been placed in the center of the ear. The head is finished by adding the wildly disordered hair. Also of importance are the shoulders, which have been drawn up as in fear. In this painting, quite different from the other, only body feelings and kinesthetic experiences were expressed. During such processes of realizations of the self the individual's thinking constantly goes back and forth, from a conscious awareness of his feelings to the realization of his representation. *This kind of experience is of great educational significance because only through the self and the realization of it will the individual find real contact with the outside world.*

In this kind of creative work the visually minded, partially blind individual pulls his environment closer to himself, whereas the haptically minded individual realizes environment through a more intense awareness of his own ego.

Emotional Maladjustment and Creative Development

Emotionally maladjusted individuals either react emotionally different from normal persons or have great difficulties in adjusting to little changes with regard to themselves or their environment. The causes for such reaction and disturbances are widely different and are not subject to a

Fig. 83. Drawings of an emotionally maladjusted eleven-year-old girl.

a). Inflexible schematic repetitions.
b). "Sitting Under a Tree." No spatial correlations.
c). "Picking Strawberries." First correlation with environment.
d). "Picking Strawberries." Second phase of direct connection of arm to berry.
e). "Swinging on Rings." Greater awareness of body action.
f). "Picnic Out of Doors." Profile is introduced.

Fig. 83—Continued)

g). "Family." Freedom of action and spatial correlation show adjustive effect.

h). "Dancing Around a Flagpole." Notice spatial conflict between group and pole.

i). "Our House Burns." Spontaneous expression of oppressed past experience with the effect of final release.

j). "My Best Sunday Dress."

k). "Dancing Around a Tree." Correct spatial correlations of the completely adjusted child.

discussion within the framework of this book. It shall only be attempted here to show the influence of creative activity on the abnormal for the purpose of establishing in a more convincing way the interdependence between creative and mental growth.

A. B. was a very nice eleven-year-old girl who frequently showed queer reactions. When unexpectedly asked to do something, she seemed to be blocked entirely. For instance, when somebody asked her, "Anne, bring me a glass of water," or "Blow your nose" she might stiffen her hands, spreading them in a cramp-like position while crying, "Why should I bring a glass of water? Why doesn't John have to bring it? Why . . . ," and so forth. In other words, she could not unexpectedly be brought out of her present state. She could not face a new situation without being blocked. In drawings she could fill pages with the same figures, that of a girl (Fig. 83a), repeating them again and again, an indication that she did not want to be diverted. She felt quite well by assuring herself that she can draw a given pattern. *This repetition of inflexible schemata is characteristic for such emotional inflexibilities.* In the garden of Lochland School, an institute for mentally deficient children where I made these experiments, was a bench on which Anne loved to sit. The bench was in the shade of a tree. When I met Anne there, I asked her to draw herself sitting on the bench under the tree. Of course, I did this only after establishing friendly contact with her. Fig. 83b represents Anne sitting on the bench under the tree. If we examine this drawing closely, we see that the child made merely a schematic representation of a girl. No experience or movement is indicated, although she had the experience of sitting on the bench under a tree. Whenever we asked the child to draw "a girl" she would always draw the same representation, regardless of any suggested bodily activity or environment. The abnormal child is bound up with its schematic representation, repeating it again and again. We can also see from this drawing that no contact with, or relation to, the environment is expressed. Neither is the child sitting on the bench as was suggested, nor is the bench under the tree. The child shows a complete failure to comprehend relations to the environment, and also a trend to draw schematic representations without any consciousness of bodily feelings. A profound change in the emotional response of the child was produced by the stimulation of such bodily feelings. It was easy to arouse her interest in picking strawberries, since eating them was a very pleasurable experience to her.* Then she was asked to draw "picking strawberries" (Fig. 83c). She drew the usual schematic representation. When she had finished her

---

* While she picked the strawberries she was repeatedly encouraged to pay attention to her bodily movements.

drawing I asked her, "Look, did you really pick the berries?" The child, a little confused, connected the line for the arm down to the berry. Having got this reaction, I made her repeat the actual picking movements and also the drawing with the result that this time she drew a direct line from the shoulder to the strawberry (Fig. 83d). This was the first great improvement, consisting, of course, not in the fact that she was able to draw this connection, but that she abadoned her schematic representation. After one month's work with repeated stimulations of her bodily feelings she began to experience connections to things outside of her body, as can be seen in Fig. 83e depicting "swinging on rings," which she loved to do. Gradually she became aware of her muscular sensations, using the joints in her representations, as Fig. 83f shows very clearly. Until this time she had drawn only front views; now we see for the very first time the change to profile representation, which as an original contribution on the part of the child shows her closer connection to her creative work. After two months she finally reached a stage expressed in the drawing of Fig. 83g, where she experienced not only her own bodily movements but also such difficult connections with outside figures as carrying the baby. If her first drawing is compared with this one, it will be clear that her greater consciousness of the self indicated in this drawing represents not only a very great improvement in her creative work but also an expression of her improved general condition.* Her emotional reactions were much more normal, although she still withdrew into her "stiffness" now and then.

Once the children were dancing around a flagpole (Fig. 83h). Most interesting is the conflict in her subjective spatial experience of dancing around the pole in a circle which she represents by the children holding one another, and the placing of the pole on the edge (the base line) of the paper. A few weeks afterward Anne came excitedly into my room asking whether she couldn't make a drawing of "a family and their burning house and how mother saved her best dress" (Fig. 83i). "This am I," she said, pointing at the girl with the dress just catching fire. "My dress just starts burning and mother saved only hers." On the bottom of the drawing are two girls carrying their injured sister. But most significant is the enormously exaggerated representation of mother's dress. Such pathological exaggerations are always indicative of the special significance of an experience.

Regardless of the truth which lies behind this story, the drawing reveals clearly the relationship between Anne and her mother. It also made her face an important incident which was brought into her conscious mind

* Lowenfeld, V., "Self-Adjustment Through Creative Activity." *American Journal of Mental Deficiency*, Vol. XLV, 1941.

by the freedom she acquired in her creative work. Similar to psychoanalysis a connection with the subconscious past had been established. This is one of the most important therapeutic steps for an emotional recovery. Since the dress (psychologically, the dress might be a substitute for something else) played such an important part, I asked her to put on her best Sunday dress. Then she drew Fig. 83j. The suggested larger size of the drawing stimulated her not only to draw a "beautiful dress with a rich design" but made her also draw more details of the self. Her consciousness of the self has rapidly changed. She now draws a neck, lips, eyelids, brows, and so forth, indicating her greater active knowledge of the self.

After the children had been dancing around a tree, a few weeks later, she drew Fig. 83k. At that time she had completely lost her "queer" reactions. She acted entirely normal and could enter public school. If we compare the last drawing with the first one, or even with the drawing "Dancing around the Flagpole" we will understand the relationship between Anne's emotional growth and her creative work. More than that, we can easily realize the adjustive effect it had on Anne.

Mental Disturbance in the Creative Work of Two Cases

The more the child is mentally disturbed, the more he becomes bound up with the self, losing contact with his environment. In the more advanced mental disturbances, however, there is not only a lack of connection with the environment but also an entire loss of correlation in bodily actions.

There are many intermediate steps. As has been pointed out, we have introduced methods of art education for the abnormal group only for the purpose of giving a better understanding of normal trends. Often in the past a clearer knowledge of the normal individual has been gained by investigating extreme cases. Therefore, we cannot present all types of creative abnormalities and their psychiatric implications.

Vera was thirteen years old and considered as a borderline case of schizophrenia. She talked much to herself and to "someone else," going in circles around the same ideas. She neither wanted to be touched bodily, nor did she like any interference with her present state. She loved to draw. In certain periods she always drew the same types of figures, often influenced by picture-book illustrations, although she never did any direct copying. While being in such a state of constant repetition, the following experiment was made. It should be mentioned that Vera was at that time rigidly drawing repetitions of a schematic figure in profile, seemingly strongly influenced by a picture-book illustration (Fig. 84a).

Fig. 84. Drawings by a thirteen-year-old, mentally disturbed child.

    a). Inflexible fixation on imitative schema.

    b). "Holding One Another" made her express the "arms" first. No correlation could be perceived.

    c). Enlarged drawing with partial correlation.

    d). Established correlation and change of inflexible fixation on schema.

Vera was asked to participate in a game with other children. A play "Pulling One Another" was arranged purposely. Vera was put in the middle between two other children who tried hard to find out "who is the strongest one" by pulling both arms of Vera. This whole game only was introduced for the purpose of making Vera aware that she has *two* sides which are equally important. These could be drawn only in front view, whereas all her drawings were stiff profile representations. After Fig. 84a was drawn, in which neither pulling nor any other indication of pulling was represented, the game was repeated. This time *holding* one another while pulling was emphasized, not the pulling as such. Fig. 84b shows the attempt to represent this experience. After she had drawn the two hands holding each other, she continued again in the usual way with her profile representation. Impatient that she could not attach the "hands" to her rigid profile representation, she got up and complained that the paper was not large enough. After a larger sheet of paper was provided, Vera drew Fig. 84c. In this drawing she achieved some relation between the two figures to the right by turning them toward each other, but the third figure is still isolated. Although she could not change her profile concept, she was able to turn two profiles toward each other, which indicated at least the *desire* to establish contact between the figures. Needless to say, no criticism was voiced while Vera was drawing. She was asked to point at herself on the drawing and to show how she feels when she is being pulled. She became excited and asked for another sheet on which she made the final drawing, Fig. 84d. Here, as it can clearly be seen, she comprehended the connection between the three figures. Through a close stimulation of body feelings she experienced the significance of both sides of her body. This experience diverted her from her stereotyped profile representations. This ability to change concepts is an important element in the process of learning and adjusting to new situations.

A much more difficult case was that of a thirteen-year-old boy, also of Lochland School, who was completely incapable of recognizing any connection between the line on the paper and his arm movements. He might have been looking out of the window, while making lines on the paper, without recognizing the fact that he had drawn them. Since no control of his motions was established, his drawings looked like disordered scribbling. Movement was not only greatly enjoyed by him, but also relieved him considerably from tensions. Therefore we started a game in which he tried to follow my suggestions for motions. In the beginning I started by moving his hands while saying, "Go up and down." Later I put a crayon into his hand saying, "Go up and down on the paper," which he did (Fig. 85a), recognizing for the very first time the connection between the lines on the paper and his motions. In these attempts we find the corresponding steps to the development of scribbling as previously dis-cussed. With close relations between kinesthetic experiences and drawing on the paper established, he became visually interested in the lines, too. After one month I could lead him around on the paper exactly as I wanted to by saying, "Go up, down, left, right, down," and so forth, making the type of broken line shown in Fig. 85b. I also introduced circular movements and their representation. Later he was stimulated to draw first stages of representations related to objects, such as stairs, table, chair, house, ball, and so forth. For example, I said, "Go first up, then right, then up, then right," finally asking him, "What is that?" He answered, "Steps" (Fig. 85c); or I said, "Go up, right and down; this is supposed to be a house. Put in the windows and draw the roof on it" (Fig. 85d). The method in these experiments was to start with kinesthetic experiences and finish with a visual concept. Fig. 85e is one of his later drawings, "A Boy Throw-ing Stones," which he loved to do. This was the first drawing that he did on his own account. With it he had discovered a clear relationship between his actions and his representations, and from now on he came often spon-taneously to my room, made quickly a few drawings, and left with all signs of relief. Although it cannot be claimed that the boy became normal, a mental improvement could clearly be seen. The director and psychiatrist of the School recognized the great change in the condition of this boy.

SUMMARY

In this chapter we have shown that in many instances art education can clarify its problems by means of analyzing extreme cases. The phe-nomenon of visual and nonvisual or haptic experiences of shape and form, for instance, can best be studied and demonstrated at the borderline of seeing and blindness, where extreme cases of both types reveal themselves fully. The influence and broadening effect of art expression on the develop-ment of speech could be impressively demonstrated in the case of a deaf-blind subject who from the very beginning had to struggle for the mean-ing of every word. The relieving effect of creative activity upon our emo-tions has been shown by the study of those who suffer from emotional tension or maladjustment. The influence on our mental growth, finally, has been demonstrated by mentally defective subjects, whose rigid patterns were most difficult to change.

We have seen that the common approach to creative work with all handicapped was based upon the recognition of their *isolation from the environment* and that the means of overcoming it depended upon the

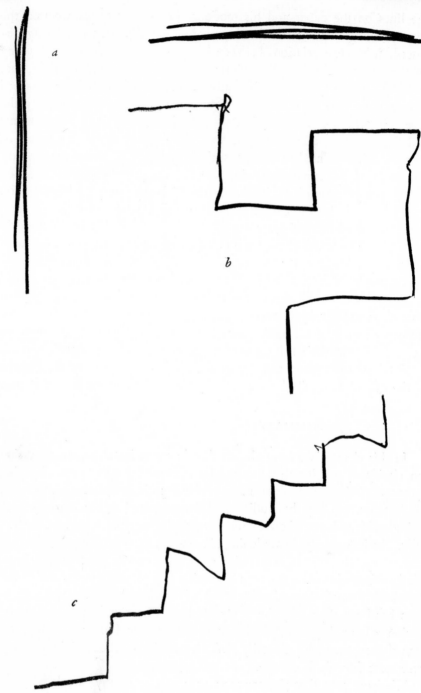

Fig. 85. Drawings of a mentally disturbed fifteen-year-old youth. (Courtesy Lochland School, Geneva, N. Y.)

a). Go "up-down"; "left-right."
b). Go "right-down-right-up-right-down-left-down."
c). Go "up-right-up-right-up-right"; "what is it?" Starting with kinesthetic experiences, ending with a visual concept.
d). Go "up-right-down"; "this is supposed to be a house."
e). "I am throwing stones."

kind of handicap. In physical handicaps the isolation is mainly caused by the physical defect and the resulting feelings of inferiority. Creative activity can become a means of overcoming this isolation—physically and mentally—through improving those sensory experiences which deal with the establishment of communications, and emotionally by relieving tensions and inhibitions that stand in the way of a sound development. In mental defectives, however, isolation from the environment is an effect of their inability to comprehend environmental factors together with a lack of bodily feeling. The one is indicated by a total absence of spatial correlations in their drawings; the other by a fixation on an inflexible schematic representation. Through stimulating the bodily feelings a closer and more conscious relation with the environment is achieved and rigid patterns are given up and flexibility is acquired. Through experience of the self the individual gains contact and connection with the environment, which can bring him out of his isolation and make him a more useful member of society.

CHAPTER IX Summary
of All Stages

IN THE INTRODUCTION TO THIS BOOK THE SUBJECT MATTER OF ART
was discussed and clarified as our subjective relationship to man and
environment. It is this subjective relationship which changes with the age
levels. Therefore, it was our task to analyze, investigate, and study these
changes. Only when these changes in our relationships to man and environment are comprehended do we have an approximate assurance that we
understand the changing quality of our imaginative activity during the
different age periods. It is the knowledge of this changing imaginative
activity and its expression which is one of the most important prerequisites
for successful art stimulation.

*The following chart has been compiled only for the purpose of sur-
veying these changing conditions with regard to our relationship to man
and environment.* It would be a great misunderstanding if this chart would
be used as an abbreviated prescription for suggested art activities. The
chart has only a dynamic meaning: to show at one glance *horizontally* the
development of the experiences of shape, space, and color, and the
adequate stimulation for each age period. *Vertically,* the chart shows the
growth from one stage of development to another again in the different
realms of shape, space, color, and design. Thus the chart shows simultaneously what cannot be summarized in text form. However, the chart
will be understood only if it is used after the content of the book has been
thoroughly understood.

Stage	Characteristics	Representation of Human Figure	Representation of Space	Representation of Color	Design	Stimulation Topics	Technique
Scribbling (two to four years)	Disordered: no motor control. Longitudinal: motor coordination. Circular: variation of control. Naming: *change of thinking* from kinesthetic to imaginative.	None. Only imaginatively.	None. Only imaginatively.	No conscious use. Color used to distinguish between scribblings.	None.	Through encouragement. In the direction of the child's thinking.	Large black crayon. Smooth paper. Finger paint for maladjusted children. Colored crayons. Clay.
Pre-Schematic (four to seven years)	Discovery of *relationship* between representation and thing represented.	Search for concept. Constant change of symbol.	No "order" in space. Relationships according to *emotional* significance.	Emotional use according to appeal. No relationship to reality.	No conscious approach.	Activating of passive knowledge mainly related to the self. "I" stage.	Crayons. Clay. Poster paint. Large bristle Brush. Large sheets of paper.
Schematic Stage (seven to nine years)	Discovery of *concept* through repetition becomes *schema*.	*Definite* concept depending on active knowledge and personality characteristics. Human schemata expressed by means of geometric lines.	First *definite* space concept: base line. Discovery of being a part of environment. Subjective space representation. Space-time concept.	*Definite* relationship between color and object. Through repetition: color, schema.	No conscious approach. Design characteristics received through urge for repetitions.	"We," "Action," "Where," topics in time sequences (stories). Inside and outside.	Colored crayons. Chalks. Poster paint (tempera). Large paper. Bristle brush. Clay.

Stage	Characteristics	Representation of Human Figure	Representation of Space	Representation of Color	Design	Stimulation Topics	Technique
Dawning Realism Pre-Adolescent Crisis (nine to eleven years), Gang Age	Greater awareness of the self. Removal from schema. *Removal* from geometric lines. Lack of cooperation. Stage of transition.	Greater stiffness. Emphasis on clothes. Difference between boys and girls. Tendency toward realistic lines. *Removal* from schematic representation.	*Removal* from base-line concept. Overlapping. Discovery of plain. Difficulties in spatial correlation due to egocentric attitude.	*Removal* from objective stage of color. Subjective color experiences with emotional significant objects.	First conscious approach toward decoration. Use of materials and their function for design.	Cooperation through: (1) Group-work. (2) Working method. (3) Topic. Different professions. Suits, dresses. Overlapping.	*No* crayons because of removal from linear expressions. Poster paint. Clay. Chalk. Linoleum cut. Textiles. Wood. Metal.
Pseudo-Realistic Stage Stage of Reasoning (eleven to thirteen years)	Developed intelligence, yet unawareness. Realistic approach (unconscious). Tendency toward visual or nonvisual mindedness. Love for dramatization.	Joints. Visual observation of body actions. Proportions. Emphasis on expression of nonvisually minded.	Urge for three-dimensional expression. Diminishing sizes of distant objects. Horizontal line (visually minded).	Changes of color in nature (visually minded). Emotional reaction to color (nonvisually minded).	First conscious approach to stylizing. Symbols for professions. Function of different materials.	Dramatic actions in environment. Actions from imagination and posing (with meaning, like "Scrubbing"). Proportions through emphasis on content. Color moods. Murals: "from-to." Design in material. Modeling.	Water-color. Gouche (water color and tempera). Poster paint. Bristle brush. Hair brush. Clay. Linoleum. Materials for design: textiles, wood, metal, papier mâché.

Stage	Characteristics	Representation of Human Figure	Representation of Space	Representation of Color	Design	Stimulation Topics	Technique
The Stage of Decision

Crisis of Adolescence (thirteen to seventeen years) | *Critical awareness* toward environment. Three groups: (1) *Visual type* (50 per cent): Intermediaries: eyes Creative concern: environment, appearance. (2) *Haptic type* (25 per cent): Intermediary: body Creative concern: self-expression, emotional approach of subjective experiences. (3) In-betweens (25 per cent): Reactions are not definite in either direction. Creative concern: abstract. | *Visual Type:* Emphasis on appearance. Light and shadow. Depiction of momentary impressions. Realistic interpretations of objective validity.

Haptic Type: Emphasis on inward expressions. Emotional qualities. Proportion of value. Individual interpretations. | *Visual Type:* Perspective representations. Apparent diminution of distant objects. Atmosphere. Appearance. Mood. Three-dimensional qualities. Light and shadow.

Haptic Type: Perspective of value with relationship to the self. Value relationship of objects. Base-line expressions. | *Visual Type:* Appearance of color in nature. Color reflections. Changing qualities of color environment, with regard to distance and mood. Analytic attitude. Impressionistic.

Haptic Type: Expressive, subjective meaning of color. Local color when insignificant. Color changes with regard to emotional significance. Psychological meaning of color. | *Visual Type:* Aesthetic interpretation of form, balance, and rhythm. Decorative design. Emphasis on harmony.

Haptic Type: Emotional design of abstract quality. Functional design. Industrial design. | Visual *and* haptical stimulations. Environment *and* figure. Appearance and content. Posing with interpretations. Sketching. Sculpture. Graphics. Design. Painting. Mural. | Sketching in: crayon, oil paint, tempera, water color. *Easel painting. Mural Sculpture* in: Plastic media. Casting. Wood. Stone. *Graphics:* Linoleum cut. Etching. Lithography. Silk screen. Stencil. Air-brush. Poster work. Lettering. Design: decorative, functional, industrial. |

References

BASIC PHILOSOPHY

Bartlett, Francis Grant, and Crawford, Claude C., *Art for All*. New York: Harper and Bros., 1942.

Bayley, Nancy, "Mental and Emotional Growth and Personality Development," *Mental Hygiene in Modern Education,* Chapter II. New York: Farrar and Rinehart, 1939.

Bowley, Agatha H., *Guiding the Normal Child*. New York: Philosophical Library, 1943.

Commission on Secondary School Curriculum, *The Visual Arts in General Education*. New York: Appleton-Century Co. (D.), Inc., 1940.

D'Amico, Victor, *Creative Teaching in Art*. Scranton, Pa.: International Textbook Co., 1942.

Dewey, John, *Art as Experience*. New York: Minton, Balch, 1934.

Faulkner, Ray; Ziegfeld, Edwin; and Hill, Gerald, *Art Today*. New York: Henry Holt and Co., 1941.

Gibbs, Evelyn, *The Teaching of Arts in Schools*. New York: Greenberg, Inc., Publisher, 1936.

Gregg, Harold, *Art for the Schools of America*. Scranton, Pa.: International Textbook Co., 1941.

Hartman, B. and Shumaker, A., ed., *Creative Expression: The Development of Children in Art, Music, Literature, and Dramatics*. New York: John Day, 1932.

Hurlock, E. B. and Thomson, J. L., "Children's Drawings: An Experimental Study of Perception," *Child Development,* 5, 1934, 127–138.

Kellett, K. R., *A Gestalt Study of the Function of Unity in Aesthetic Perception*. Psychological Monograph, 51, No. 5, 1939.

Koffka, K., "Problems in the Psychology of Art." In *Art: A Bryn-Mawr Symposium*. New York: Bryn Mawr, 1940.

——— *Principles of Gestalt Psychology*. New York: Harcourt, Brace and Co., 1935.

MacDonald, Rosabell, *Art in Education.* New York: Henry Holt and Co., 1941.

Mitchell, E. L., *Curriculum Experiences for Elementary Schools.* Delaware Curriculum No. 1, 1940.

Rannells, E. W., *Art Education in the Junior High School.* Lexington, Kentucky: University of Kentucky, 1946.

Read, Herbert, *Education Through Art.* London: Faber and Faber, 1943.

Skinner, Charles E. and Harriman, Philip Lawrence. *Child Psychology.* New York: The Macmillan Company, 1941.

Strickler, Fred, *An Art Approach to Education.* New York: Seiler (A. G.), 1943.

Winslow, Leon Loyal, *The Integrated School Art Program.* New York: McGraw-Hill Book Co., 1939.

FIRST STAGES OF SELF-EXPRESSION (TWO TO SEVEN YEARS)

Bayley, Nancy, *The Development of Motor Abilities during the First Three Years.* Society for Research in Child Development, Monograph 1, 1935.

Eng, Helga K., *The Psychology of Children's Drawings from the First Stroke to the Coloured Drawing.* London: Trench, Trubner, and Co., 1931.

Gesell, Arnold, *How a Baby Grows.* New York: Harper and Brothers, 1945.

Goodenough, F. L., "Studies in the Psychology of Children's Drawings." *Psychol. Bull.,* 25, 1928.

——— "Children's Drawings." In *A Handbook of Child Psychology.* Worcester: Clark University Press, 1931.

Line, W., "The Growth of Visual Perception in Children." *Brit. Journal of Psych.,* XV, 1931.

Lowenfeld, Viktor, *The Nature of Creative Activity.* New York: Harcourt, Brace and Co., 1939.

McCloy, W., *Passive Creative Imagination.* Psychological Monographs, LI, No. 5, 1939.

Mott, S. M., "The Development of Concepts, A Study of Children's Drawings." *Child Development,* 7, 1936.

Read, Herbert, *Education through Art.* London: Faber and Faber, 1943.

——— "The Art of Children." In *Education through Art.* London: Faber and Faber, 1943.

Wellman, Beth L., "Motor Development from Two Years to Maturity." *Review of Educational Research,* No. 6, 1936.

THE UNAWARE STAGES OF CREATIVE EXPRESSION
(SEVEN TO TWELVE YEARS)

Browne, Sibyl; Tyrrell, Ethel; and Abbihl, Gertrude, and Evans, Clarice. *Art and Materials for the Schools.* New York: Progressive Education Assn., 1943.

Cizek, Franz, *Children's Coloured Paper Work.* New York: G. E. Stechert and Co., 1927.

Cole, Natalie Robinson, *The Arts in the Classroom*. New York: The John D. Day Co., 1940.

D'Amico, Victor. *Creative Teaching in Art*. Scranton, Pa.: International Textbook Co., 1942.

Downey, June E., *Creative Imagination*. New York: Harcourt, Brace and Co., 1929.

Mathias, Margaret E., *Art in the Elementary School*. New York: Charles Scribner's Sons, 1929.

———— *The Teaching of Art*. New York: Scribner's (Charles) Sons, 1932.

Mitchell, Edith L. and Tannahil, Sallie B., "Art in the Elementary School." In *Art in American Life and Education*. Bloomington, Ill.: Public School Publishing Co., 1941.

Munro, T., "Franz Cizek and the Free Expression Method" and "A Constructive Program for Teaching Art." In *Art and Education*. Marion, Pa.: Barnes Foundation Press, 1929.

Payant, Felix, *Our Changing Art Education*. Columbus, Ohio: Keramic Studio Publishing Co., 1935.

Pearson, Ralph, *The New Art Education*. New York: Harper and Bros., 1941.

Sobotka, Grace, *Art Instruction in the First Six Grades*. Ann Arbor, Mich.: Edwards Brothers, 1935.

Tomlinson, R. R., *Picture Making by Children*. London: Studio Publications, 1934.

———— *Crafts for Children*. New York: Studio Publications, Inc., 1935.

Viola, Wilhelm, *Child Art and Franz Cizek*. New York: Reynal and Hitchcock, Inc., 1936.

Winslow, L. L., *The Integrated School Art Program*. New York: McGraw-Hill Book Co., 1939.

THE CONSCIOUS CREATIVE APPROACHES

General Aspects

Cole, Luella, *Psychology of Adolescence*. New York: Rinehart and Company, Inc., 1942.

D'Amico, V. E. and others, *The Visual Arts in Secondary Education*. New York: Appleton-Century Co. (D.), Inc., 1940.

Faulkner, Ray; Ziegfeld, Edwin; and Hill, Gerald, *Art Today*. New York: Henry Holt and Co., 1941.

Giles, Mary A., *Working Creatively in the Visual Arts with High School Students*. New York: Progressive Assn., 1931.

Hambidge, Jay, *Dynamic Symmetry*. New Haven: Yale University Press, 1936.

Lowenfeld, Viktor, *The Nature of Creative Activity*. New York: Harcourt, Brace and Co., 1939.

———— "Tests for Visual and Haptical Aptitude." *American Journal of Psychol.*, Vol. 58, 1945.

Meier, N. C., "The Graphic and Allied Arts." In *Child Development and the Curriculum*. Bloomington, Ill.: Public School Publishing Co., 1939.

Munro, T., "Adolescence and Art Education." In *Methods of Teaching the Fine Arts*. Chapel Hill: University of North Carolina Press, 1935.

———— "Creative Ability in Art, and its Educational Fostering." In *Art in American Life and Education*. Bloomington, Ill.: Public School Publishing Co., 1941.

Mursell, J. L., "*The Application of Psychology to the Arts*." New York: *Teachers College Record*, 37, 1936.

Payant, Felix, *Create Something*. Columbus, Ohio: Design Publishing Co., 1943.

Pearson, Ralph, *The New Art Education*. New York: Harper and Bros., 1941.

Poore, H. R., *Art's Place in Education*. New York: Putnam's (G. P.) Sons, 1937.

Smith, Janet K., *Design: An Introduction*. Chicago: Ziff-Davis Publishing Co., 1946.

Whittford, W. G. *An Introduction to Art Education*. New York: Appleton-Century (D.) Co., Inc., 1939.

Appreciation of Arts

Buswell, G. T., *How People Look at Pictures, A Study of the Psychology and Perception of Art*. Chicago: University of Chicago Press, 1935.

Chandler, A. R., *Beauty and Human Nature, Elements of Physchological Aesthetics*. New York: Appleton-Century (D.) Co., Inc., 1934.

Evans, Joan, *Taste and Temperament*. New York: The Macmillan Co., 1939.

McMahon, A. Philip, *The Art of Enjoying Art*. New York: McGraw-Hill Book Co., 1938.

Munro, T., "Powers of Art Appreciation and Evaluation." In *Art in American Life*. Bloomington: Public School Publishing Company, 1942.

Opdyke, George H., *Art and Nature Appreciation*. New York: The Macmillan Co., 1933.

Reid, Louis A., *A Study in Aesthetics*. New York: The Macmillan Co., 1931.

Schoen, M., *Art and Beauty*. New York: The Macmillan Co., 1932.

Design

Cheney, Sheldon and Cheney, Martha Candler, *Art and the Machine*. New York: Whittlesey House, 1936.

Franke, Paul T., *New Dimensions*. New York: Brewer and Warren, Inc., 1928.

Graves, Maitland, *The Art of Color and Design*. New York: McGraw-Hill Book Co., Inc., 1941.

Holme, Geoffrey, *Industrial Design and the Future*. London: The Studio, Ltd., 1934.

Kahn, Ely Jacques, *Design in Art and Industry*. New York: Scribner's (Charles) Sons, 1936.

Maholy-Nagy, *The New Vision*, New York: W. W. Norton and Co., 1938.

Mangan, James T., *Design, The New Grammar of Advertising*. Chicago: Dartnell Company, 1940.

Read, Herbert, *Art and Industry*. New York: Harcourt, Brace and Co., 1938.
Smith, Janet. *Design, An Introduction*. Chicago, New York: Ziff-Davis Publishing Co., 1946.

Graphic Arts

Biegeleisen, Jacob Israel, *The Silk Screen Printing Process*. New York: McGraw-Hill Book Co., 1941.
Binder, Joseph, *Color in Advertising*. London: The Studio, Ltd., 1934.
Chappell, Warren, *The Anatomy of Lettering*. New York: Loring and Mussey, 1935.
Cooper, Austin, *Making a Poster*. New York: Studio Publishing Co., 1938.
Frankenfield, Henry, *Block Printing with Linoleum*. Camden, N. J.: Hunt (C. Howard) and Co., 1940.
Friend, Leon and Hefter, Josephine, *Graphic Design*. New York: Whittlesey House, 1936.
Holme, Charles G., ed., *Lettering of Today*. London: The Studio, Ltd., 1937.
Pennell, Joseph, *The Graphic Arts*. Chicago: University of Chicago Press, 1921.
Summer, Harry, *Handbook of Silk Screen Printing Process*. New York: Creative Crafts Press, 1939.
West, Leon, *Making an Etching*. New York: The Studio Publications, Inc., 1932.

Sculpturing and Modeling

Glass, Frederick James, *Modeling and Sculpture*. New York: Charles Scribner's Sons, 1929.
Jackson, James, *The Handicraft of Woodcarving*. New York: Pitman Publishing Corp., 1921.
Loland, Charles G., *Woodcarving*. New York: Pitman Publishing Corp., 1931.
Putnam, Brenda, *The Sculpture Way*. New York: Frederick A. Stokes Co., 1939.
Sowers, J. T., *Woodcarving Made Easy*. New York: Bruce Publishing Co., 1936.
Toft, Albert, *Modeling and Sculpturing*. Philadelphia: J. B. Lippincott Co., 1936.
Wilenski, R. H., *The Meaning of Modern Sculpture*. New York: Frederick A. Stokes Co., 1933.

Architecture and Furniture

Agan, Tessie, *The House*. Philadelphia: Lippincott (J. B.) Co., 1939.

Goldstein, H. and V., *Art in Everyday Life*. New York: The Macmillan Co., 1940.
Hitchcock, H. R. and Johnson, Philip, *The International Style, Architecture since 1922*. New York: W. W. Norton and Co., 1932.
Mumford, Lewis, *Architecture*. American Library Association, 1926.
—— *Sticks and Stones*. New York: W. W. Norton and Co., 1933.

Rogers, Tyler S., *Plan Your House to Suit Yourself*. New York: Charles Scribner's Sons, 1938.
Wright, Frank Lloyd, *Autobiography*. New York: Longmans, Green and Co., 1932.

Crafts

Bayer, Herbert; Gropius, Walter and Ise, *Bauhaus*. New York: Museum of Modern Art, 1938.
Butler, J. B., *Problems in Metal Work*. New York: Manual Arts Press, 1929.
Flexner, Marion W., *Hand Puppets, A Practical Manual for Teachers*. New York: French (S.), Inc., 1935.
Kennard, Joseph S., *Masks and Marionettes*. New York: The Macmillan Co., 1935.
MacIsaac, Frederick J., *The Tony Sarg Marionette Book*. New York: The Viking Press, 1921.
Mansberger, Dale E. and Pepper, C. W., *Plastics, Problems and Processes*. Scranton: International Textbook Co., 1938.
Perry, Evadna Kraus, *Art Adventures with Discarded Material*. New York: Noble and Noble, Publishers, Inc., 1933.
——— *Crafts for Fun*. New York: William Morrow and Company, Inc., 1940.
Read, Herbert, *Art and Industry*. New York: Harcourt, Brace and Company, 1935.

Art Materials

Clannon, Edward, *Making Your Own Materials*. New York: Museum of Modern Art, Committee on Art in American Education, 1943.
Doerner, Max, *The Materials of the Artist*. New York: Harcourt, Brace and Co., 1934.
Mayer, Ralph, *The Artist's Handbook*. New York: Viking Press, 1940.

ABNORMAL TRENDS IN CREATIVE ACTIVITY

Baker, H. J. and Traphagen, V., *The Diagnosis and Treatment of Behavior Problem Children*. New York: The Macmillan Co., 1935.
Bender, Lauretta, and Wolfson, W. Q., "The Nautical Theme in the Art and Fantasy of Children." *American Journal of Orthopsychiatry*, 13, 1943.
Burt, C., *The Young Delinquent*. New York: Appleton-Century Co. (D.), Inc., 1925.
Harms, Ernest, "The Arts as Applied to Psychotherapy." *Design*, Vol. 46, No. 6, 1945.
Liss, Edward, "The Graphic Arts." *The American Journal of Orthopsychiatry*, Vol. VIII, No. 1, 1938.
Lowenfeld, Berthold, "Psychological Aspects of Blindness." In *Encyclopedia of Psychology*, Philosophical Library, 1946.

—————— "The Blind Child and His World." In *What of the Blind?* New York: American Foundation for the Blind, 1942.

—————— "Book Illustrations for Blind Children." *Journal of Exceptional Children,* Vol. 10, No. 3, 1943.

Lowenfeld, Viktor, "Self-Adjustment through Creative Activity." *American Journal of Mental Deficiency,* Vol. XLV, 1941.

—————— "Modeling as a Means of Self-Expression in the Schools for the Blind." *The Harvard Educational Review,* Vol. XII, No. 1, 1942.

—————— *The Nature of Creative Activity.* New York: Harcourt, Brace and Co., 1939.

—————— "The Meaning of Creative Activity for the Deaf-Blind." *The Teachers Forum,* American Foundation for the Blind, Vol. XII, 1940.

Mosse, Eric P., "Painting Analysis in the Therapy of Neuroses." *Psycho-Analytical Review,* 1940.

—————— "Color Therapy." *Occupational Therapy,* Feb. 1942.

Schaefer-Simmern, H., and Sarason, S. B., "Therapeutic Implications of Artistic Activity." *American Journal of Mental Deficiency,* Vol. 49, 1944.

Waehner, T. S., "Interpretation of Spontaneous Drawings and Paintings." *Genet. Psychological Monograph,* Vol. 33, 1946.

—————— "Formal Criteria for the Analysis of Children's Drawings." *American Journal of Orthopsychiatry,* Vol. 12, 1942.

Index